MAKING UP THE DIFFERENCE

BOOK TWENTY-FIVE
LOUANN ATKINS TEMPLE WOMEN & CULTURE SERIES
BOOKS ABOUT WOMEN AND FAMILIES, AND
THEIR CHANGING ROLE IN SOCIETY

MAKING UP THE DIFFERENCE

Women, Beauty, and Direct Selling in Ecuador

ERYNN MASI DE CASANOVA

UNIVERSITY OF TEXAS PRESS ◆ *Austin*

The Louann Atkins Temple Women & Culture Series is supported by Allison, Doug, Taylor, and Andy Bacon; Margaret, Lawrence, Will, John, and Annie Temple; Larry Temple; the Temple-Inland Foundation; and the National Endowment for the Humanities.

Requests for permission to reproduce material from this work should be sent to:
  Permissions
  University of Texas Press
  P.O. Box 7819
  Austin, TX 78713-7819
  www.utexas.edu/utpress/about/bpermission.html

♾ The paper used in this book meets the minimum requirements of ANSI/NISO Z39.48-1992 (R1997) (Permanence of Paper).

LIBRARY OF CONGRESS CATALOGING-IN-PUBLICATION DATA

Casanova, Erynn Masi de, 1977–
  Making up the difference : women, beauty, and direct selling in Ecuador / Erynn Masi de Casanova. — 1st ed.
      p. cm. — (Louann Atkins temple women & culture series ; bk. 25)
  Includes bibliographical references and index.
  ISBN 978-0-292-74391-5
  1. Direct selling—Ecuador.   2. Women—Employment—Ecuador.
3. Women—Ecuador—Economic conditions.   4. Cosmetics industry—
Ecuador.   I. Title.
  HF5438.25.C3646   2011
  381′.456685509866—dc22
                                                                    2011000794

ISBN 978-0-292-73483-8 (E-book)

FOR HENRY
&
FOR MARILYN AND "BIG FRANK"

CONTENTS

"I AM FROM EL GUASMO, and I'm not embarrassed to say so," began María Bustamante, as she stood in front of a gathering of women direct sellers in Guayaquil, Ecuador, to make an announcement. El Guasmo is Guayaquil's most well-known poor neighborhood, located at the extreme southern end of the city. Although the infrastructure of El Guasmo has improved greatly since my first visit to the area in 1999, with many newly paved streets and small palms planted in the median, and fewer open sewage ditches, the neighborhood still lags behind other areas of the city. María, who sells products for a direct sales company called Yanbal,[1] lives on one of El Guasmo's many unpaved streets; her home, like countless others, does not have running water in the kitchen. She lives on the same block as a few other sellers from her group, and very near her grown son and daughter-in-law and their two young children. Before joining Yanbal, María was a housewife, though she had completed a few years of college before her children were born. Getting together enough food to feed the family is a challenge for many families in María's neighborhood. About one-third of Guasmo residents earn below the monthly minimum wage, which was $200 per month in 2008. Although unemployment is high (12 percent for those aged eighteen through twenty-nine), more than a third of women (36.6 percent) are employed. This high rate of female participation in the paid labor force, relative to that of other neighborhoods, may be correlated with the high proportion of female-headed households: more than 30 percent of homes in El Guasmo are led by women. Many women are active in informal selling, making up part of the 55 percent of neighborhood residents involved in informal employment.[2] (Informal employment is understood here as that which is generally not regulated by the state, includes no legal protections, and is not based on a formal contract between employer and employee.)

AFTER THE DUSTY, UPHILL WALK to Narcisa Pazmiño Beltrán's cement-block house from the pharmacy where the taxi had dropped me off, Narcisa showed me the box cutter she was carrying for protection, hidden between the pages of the glossy, four-color catalog she used to sell cosmetics. This shouldn't have surprised me, given the worried look on the taxi driver's face as he drove away. When I had asked him to drive me to Bastión Popular, a neighborhood at the northern fringe of Guayaquil, he was surprised,

saying I didn't look like I was from that area. When I explained I was meeting a friend, he warned me to be careful as there were "bad people" in the
neighborhood. Poverty is common in Bastión, with more than one-third
of residents earning less than minimum wage. One of the ways that Narcisa generates income is through her work with Yanbal, selling perfume,
makeup, jewelry, and other personal care products. Because Bastión Popular is relatively isolated in terms of public transportation, Narcisa has to
take two buses and travel two hours to get from her home to visit clients
in the downtown area. Because of this geographic marginality, formal employment is scarce for Bastión residents; yet unemployment levels are com-
parable to those in more prosperous parts of the city, due to the whop-
ping 55 percent of people working in the informal sector. As in other parts
of Latin America, informal employment has been on the rise in Ecuador,
largely because of the work of women like Narcisa.

RELATIVE TO "MARGINAL" NEIGHBORHOODS such as El Guasmo and
Bastión Popular,[3] the Barrio del Seguro, where Marjorie González lives
with her husband and two young sons, is much more comfortable, with
paved streets and some large finished houses. Marjorie's home is a high-
ceilinged, ground-floor apartment next door to a school. When I visited her for the first time on a sunny afternoon in late 2007, many of the
school's uniformed female students were milling about in the street, which
was closed to traffic; their giggling and socializing could be heard from a
block away. El Barrio del Seguro belongs to a category of neighborhoods
that the INEC calls "consolidated areas," meaning that basic infrastructure
and services (telephone lines, garbage pickup, running water, and electricity) are reliable. The consolidated areas of the city include several of the established neighborhoods, or *ciudadelas*, in the northern part of Guayaquil,
most of downtown, and a few other regions. When statistics are consulted,
the portrait that emerges of the wide swath of the city considered "consolidated" is one of relatively high levels of education, employment (including
among women), and informal sector employment. Marjorie began her work
life in the formal sector, as an office employee, and now earns an income
by selling for a handful of direct sales companies, including Yanbal, as evidenced by the array of products displayed prominently in a glass-fronted
cabinet in her dining room.

THE RESEARCH PRESENTED IN THIS BOOK represents a foray into
what sociologist Mitchell Duneier (1999) has called the "extended place
method" of ethnographic fieldwork. Rather than being a traditional eth-

nography based in one research site, this study reflects the working conditions of women selling cosmetics and other products for a transnational corporation, as well as my preference for following direct sellers through the city as they went about their daily life. I learned a great deal about the study's participants when we attended meetings or spent time in sales directors' offices together. In addition, I was able to get a deeper understanding of the social and physical spaces they occupied by accompanying them on walks through their neighborhoods, on visits to clients (which sometimes took place during such walks), or to social gatherings.

Although I felt I knew the city of Guayaquil, having spent time and conducted research there on and off since 1999, the Yanbalistas (Yanbal sellers and sales directors) opened my eyes to the tremendous geographic—as well as social and economic—distances that *guayaquileños* (residents of Guayaquil) cross in order to make a life for themselves and their families. These Yanbalistas include women like Narcisa Pazmiño, who, in the course of a typical day's work, travels from her home in the marginal northern neighborhood of Bastión Popular (the poetically named "People's Fortress") to visit clients downtown and in the south of the city, and then back to northern Guayaquil to place an order at her director's home office. When my feet were tired, Narcisa found the energy to keep going; this crisscrossing of the city is what puts food on many tables. Thus it is not place as such that interests me, but rather the places that people hold within webs of social connection that span and sometimes overrun the space of the city. My approach to ethnography also put all of my interactions in the field (in Ecuador and especially Guayaquil) under a sociological microscope, so that any time Yanbal came up in conversation, the discussion became data that fed my knowledge of this social world. I found out that nearly everyone I met, from a professor of economics at a local university to the woman who ran the stationery store on the block where I lived for several months, had a family member involved in direct selling or had been involved as either a client or a seller. By always keeping my eyes open for where Yanbal might appear, I was able to go beyond the social networks where my research began and discover other points of view.

DURING APPROXIMATELY FIVE MONTHS in the field between September 2007 and June 2008, I was a daily or near-daily presence in the office of Yanbal group #105 and at this group's events in Guayaquil, led by Ligia García de Proaño, my husband's aunt. The office was located on the second floor of a six-story upscale professional office building in northern Guayaquil, across the street from a major mall. In the air-conditioned office and conference rooms, I acted as a sometime office assistant: answering phones; proofreading letters and e-mail messages; entering orders into the online system; helping prepare meetings, presentations, and prizes; setting up and running laptop computers and projectors during meetings; and assisting during meetings in various ways. When not in the office, I attended meetings at other directors' offices or at Yanbal's corporate offices in Guayaquil, spent time with "beauty consultants" (distributors, or low-level sellers) and sales directors in their homes, or accompanied them while they worked.

Over time, I moved deeper into the social world of the direct selling organization, going beyond the duties of researcher and ad hoc assistant. New activities included singing and dancing to the Yanbal anthems played at events, which I came to know by heart. Along with Ligia's daughter, Johanna, I choreographed and led a dance routine at the annual Christmas party for consultants in group #105. At another Christmas party, for the directors in Ligia's "family" network, I was asked to give a brief talk, speaking about micro-sociology and gendered communication styles to the nearly one hundred women in attendance. Some women from other groups who did not know me well simply assumed that I was a consultant or director or a part of Yanbal's corporate staff.

The event during which I felt most like a participant and least like a researcher was the national convention for the company's top directors, held in Guayaquil in the spring of 2008. Invited to attend the convention by the company's general manager in Ecuador, I was the only nonstaff attendee who had not earned the right to attend through a year of hard work. A somewhat uncomfortable feeling, of intruding on something that others had won, hung over me during the first day of the three-day event. By the end of the convention, however, that feeling had dissipated somewhat. I learned dance routines and the convention song along with the women; pushed my way to the front of lines just as the veteran convention-goers did; enjoyed some of the training/motivational sessions so much that I simply forgot to take notes; overate; and danced until my feet were swollen.

Direct selling organizations (DSOs) like Yanbal are often described as "feminine" organizations, a characterization that made sense to me after attending the convention. That I was six months pregnant at the time made making new acquaintances, especially among the dozen or so pregnant directors, much easier than it would have been otherwise. In two pregnancies, I had never before been so aware of my visibly pregnant body in interpersonal interaction. Although it may seem counterintuitive, being pregnant among five hundred women, most of whom have children, made me a minor celebrity. Combined with my being a foreigner and a student researching Yanbal's sales force, my round belly drew women to me; some launched into stories about their trajectory with the direct selling organization or their groups, and some wanted their photos taken with me. While I had found that being a mother had helped me create rapport with the women I met during my research,[4] I did not usually have my son physically with me when I was in the field,[5] so that my motherhood was more symbolic or abstract. Being pregnant brought my identity as a mother to a concrete, physical level, which heightened women's response to me; everyone wanted to touch my belly, share a childbirth story, or give a piece of advice.

I do not wish to make too much of my inclusion in the social world of Yanbal and its sales force. Several obstacles and power imbalances set me apart from the women I was studying, distancing me from them and making rapport more difficult to achieve. The first of these challenges was the double-edged sword of my connection to sales director Ligia García. Without this key informant and expert in all things Yanbal, and her generosity and openness, it would have been impossible for me to conduct this research. However, she is a highly visible and prominent person within this direct selling world. In many situations, my association with this successful and influential sales director and my identity as her "niece" outweighed my foreignness and my status as a student or researcher.

This personal connection had a diverse range of perceptible effects. Many people praised Ligia when speaking with me, calling her a role model or a leader, whom they viewed with respect, admiration, and deference. Some consultants and directors revealed things to me that they thought Ligia might disapprove of, quickly following these revelations with comments such as "Ligia doesn't know this" or "Don't tell *la señora* Ligia." Although she has no direct or enforceable authority over consultants or other directors, Ligia's opinion carries weight with these women. Based on her previous behavior or comments, sellers and directors felt that they could predict her reactions to their claims or activities. In a few cases, consultants who knew of my closeness to Ligia asked me to try to influence her on some small matter.

In addition to this high-profile connection with one of the country's most successful Yanbal directors, my identity as a North American, a *gringa*, distanced me from the research subjects. In this role, I was sometimes viewed and treated as a source of information and possibly money. Being from the United States takes on additional meanings in the context of Ecuadorian migration to my country, which is a long-standing pattern that has accelerated in recent years. One direct seller asked me if I could help her find her brothers, who had migrated to the United States and gotten "lost," disconnected from the family in Guayaquil. Another asked my advice as she struggled with the decision of whether to send her four-year-old granddaughter, whom she was raising, to live with her paternal grand-parents in New York.

Another woman joked that she wanted to move to the United States and become my domestic employee, a joke that felt hollow, as if an invitation from me could instantly make this far-fetched idea a reality. This made me feel uncomfortable and shattered for me any illusion of rapport that could reach across socioeconomic or national differences in this particular interaction. This woman was also the most excited about the modest honorarium I gave to interviewees, recommending no fewer than three of her "daughter" consultants to be interviewed, in what I perceived as an effort to spread the *gringa*'s money around within her social network. In fact, my decision to give sellers money to compensate them for the time they spent with me in interviews was generated by my consciousness of the economic chasm between us, a situation in which what represented a manageable expense to me was a significant amount of money to them. Ironically, I am not sure whether this monetary gift did not, in some cases, simply call attention to our differences in resources and status.

EACH OF THE THREE PARTS of this work examines direct selling in Ecuador from a slightly different angle. Taken together, these sections represent an in-depth exploration of a social world that is unique, yet can illuminate our understandings of work and gender in Ecuador and other developing countries.

The first part presents a gender relations perspective on direct selling. Chapter 1 uses the experiences of women to critique the image, promoted both by direct sales organizations and by the academics who study them, of direct selling as the ideal work for women seeking to balance paid employment with domestic responsibilities. Chapter 2 focuses on the role of men, whose direct and indirect involvement in this economic activity, on their own or in relation to female partners, shapes the work of direct selling in Ecuador.

Part II discusses the emphasis on image within this cosmetics DSO. Chapter 3 uses qualitative content analysis to examine the messages of beauty, gender, race, and class conveyed through the visual and textual language of Yanbal's sales catalogs. The cultural valuation of whiteness and upper-class status is juxtaposed with the phenotypic and financial realities of most Ecuadorians. Chapter 4 looks at how the idealized image of the Yanbalista is constructed through both official training materials and interpersonal interactions among women affiliated with the DSO. This chapter considers how cultural norms of feminine appearance are related to the material conditions in which women live and work. Chapter 5 uses ethnographic data to show the importance of images of success and status within the DSO, which is structured around prizes, contests, and effusive recognition of top performers.

Part III places the experiences of women direct sellers in the context of labor and consumption in contemporary Ecuador. Chapter 6 attempts to answer the question of what women would be doing if they were not working in direct sales. This hypothetical question leads to a discussion of work histories, multiple income-earning strategies, and future career plans of direct sellers. These experiences are considered in the context of expanding informal employment, the lack of part-time work in the formal sector, and employment discrimination. Chapter 7 attends to the consumption piece of the direct sales picture, since every act of selling is also an act of buying. The ways that direct sellers manage customers and determine payment structures are explored here, and the perspectives of clients are included. The background for these informal exchanges is the expansion of consumption in urban Ecuador and Guayaquil in particular, which I have witnessed in a decade of conducting research there.

The conclusion relates the study's findings to the social scientific literature on gender, work, and globalization and reiterates the ways in which cultural norms and material conditions interact to shape the world of direct sales in Ecuador and women's experience of it.

EDITORIAL CONVENTIONS USED IN THIS BOOK

All the names used in this book are real, except where noted (one change was made to protect the individual from the possible negative consequences of sharing his story). Given the choice between using their real names and using pseudonyms, the participants in this study elected to be identified. I concur with Linda Seligmann, who wrote regarding her decision not to use pseudonyms: "These are real people; others can talk to them, and they can talk back. We live in the same world" (2004, 11). In Ecuador, people have two legal surnames: one from their father, followed by one from their mother. For example, if a woman's mother was named Alexandra González Martínez and her father was Alonso Herrera Comín, she would be María Herrera González. Thus, maternal surnames usually drop out of use after a generation. Married women generally continue to use the same last name(s) all their lives, although some keep their paternal surname and add the preposition "de" and their husband's paternal surname. To give an example of this, if María Herrera González married Juan Santos García, she could refer to herself as María Herrera de Santos. She would most likely keep the surnames she was born with in legal documents, however. To make matters a bit clearer, I tend to use both surnames the first time I introduce a study participant in these pages, and only the first surname thereafter. For women who use the married form of their name, I refer to them by that entire name or simply use first and last (maiden) name. When interviewees gave me only one last name, I present their name as they initially reported it to me, respecting their self-representation, even if I had access to records listing both of their last names.

In terms of the written representation of language in this book, all translations are mine, and I have included the original Spanish text in brackets in places where I felt it was important to show the colloquial expression or maintain the flavor of the person's speech—places in which I would, as a bilingual reader, be wondering about which words the subject used, exactly.

Regarding quotations of participants' statements, in instances where I am certain about the exact wording of participants' speech (from transcription of recorded interviews or verbatim quotes written down immediately), I have either formatted their words as block quotations or enclosed them in standard quotation marks. In cases in which I wrote up participants' verbal expressions at the end of the day in field notes and cannot be certain of the exact wording, I have enclosed their words in single quotation marks. In these instances, I am confident that the meaning of the utterances remains more or less unchanged, although I cannot claim that the exact wording is consistent with what was said.

NOTES

1. The term "direct sales" is defined as a means of distributing branded products that uses person-to-person sales as opposed to fixed retail locations. Common examples of direct sales organizations include Avon, Tupperware, and Amway.

2. All the statistics cited in the preface are drawn from the *ESIS* (*Encuesta del Sistema de Información Social*) survey published on CD-ROM by the National Institute of Statistics and the Census (INEC) in 2007.

3. The term "marginal," which is taken from the colloquial Spanish *marginal*, refers to neighborhoods that are both far from the center of the city and lacking in attention from local, regional, and national governments.

4. See Mose Brown and Casanova (2009) for an in-depth discussion of the role of motherhood in fieldwork interactions. For other qualitative researchers' recent reflections on the role of pregnancy and children in the field, see Candelario (2007), Friedemann-Sánchez (2006), and Reich (2003).

5. My four-year-old son, Joaquín, accompanied me to Guayaquil during the months of research. Although the unique experiences of having a child in the field were often challenging in the moment, we are now able to laugh at his shocked reaction to a strong tremor that shook the city in October 2007, and our awful battle with head lice, which dragged on for a month and a half.

ACKNOWLEDGMENTS

IT MAY BE CLICHÉ TO SAY that this book would not exist without the input of many, many people, but I will say it anyway. Unlike my often-hapless New York Knicks, I have been fortunate to be associated with a winning team in this endeavor. Typing their names here is one small step toward beginning to thank them for their kindness and support.

First, my thanks go to the people who mentored me and contributed to the development of this research project at the Graduate Center of the City University of New York. Mitch Duneier, the chair of my dissertation committee, encouraged me during my first forays into ethnographic research and taught me a great deal about how to do fieldwork and write ethnography. His consistently high standards have challenged me to think about ethnography in terms of ethics, responsibility, and rigor and have shaped how I approach qualitative research as a reader and a humble practitioner. He says that you can't be afraid of people if you want to be an ethnographer, yet I find that ethnography is a way to overcome my fear of people; every time I carry my little notepad or my voice recorder into the field, the fear has to be conquered anew (if only for the day). Hester Eisenstein pushed me to think about the material conditions of women's everyday lives and helped me home in on feminist research and theories that were connected to my work. Her genuine excitement about the project helped me to believe that what I was doing was doable after all. Charles Green could always be counted on to remind me of how corporate capitalism plays a role in the spread of direct selling, and to keep an eye on how local and global ideas about race influence identity construction and cultural representations. Our leisurely chats in his office, with its spectacular views of Manhattan, often extended beyond my research topics into sports, parenthood, and travel. Other supporters at CUNY have included Jack Hammond and Victoria Pitts-Taylor. Julia Wrigley read a complete early draft of the manuscript at a crucial moment and urged me to clarify my argument and develop the concepts necessary to support it; throughout the dissertation process she served as an ad hoc committee member, working in the shadows and helping provide me with the big-picture perspective. Fellow graduate students and alumni from the Graduate Center must be tired of hearing about this project, but they have listened, read, and helped me keep things in perspective; Carlene Buchanan Turner, Joanna Dreby, Patrick Inglis, Soniya Munshi, and Andrea Siegel must be thanked by name here.

Outside of CUNY, Linda Seligmann, Florence Babb, Greta Friedemann-Sánchez, Marina Prieto-Carrón, and Leila Rodríguez Soto provided useful feedback on parts of the project. Adela de la Torre has always been ready with letters of recommendation and professional advice. Thanks also go to Littisha A. Bates and Amy Lind, who read the nearly final draft and gave me helpful comments. Amanda Staight, who worked as my research assistant in 2009–2010, was a great help with organizing the manuscript, index, and bibliography. I am grateful to my editor Theresa J. May and the team at University of Texas Press, who have been wonderful collaborators in the production of this book.

The second group that I must thank is composed of all the people who helped me conduct my research in Ecuador. *A mis queridas Yanbalistas (y ex-Yanbalistas): les doy un millón de gracias por su generosidad, humor, y sinceridad*: Martha Bermeo Bermeo, Betty Brigss Mantilla, Ana María Briones, María Bustamante, Nelly Cabrera, Carmen Carrillo, Carolina Cevallos Plaza, Elizabeth Contreras, Érica de la A, Ramona Delgado, Carmen Díaz Baldeón, Fanny Flores, Cecilia García Torres, Marjorie González, Diana Hurel Molina, Mariuxi Hurel Molina, Gioconda Ibarra Ruiz, María Litardo Santos, Marjorie López, Mercedes Mantilla Aguirre, Érika Martínez García, Jacinta Menoscal, Sara Murillo Balladares, Maryuri Palma Pico, Vanessa Paredes Márquez, Narcisa Pazmiño Beltrán, (Carmen) Patricia Pérez Álava, Mary Sánchez, Daniela Solís Nevárez, Nancy Torres Zambrano, Sandra Vásconez Silva, (Mary) Belén Vera Marín, Micaela Vera Muñoz, Jackeline Vivanco, "Carlos Zambrano," Tania Zambrano Burgos, y Narcisa Zambrano Valdez. In Yanbal's corporate offices, my thanks go to Robert Watson, Priscilla Molina, and Paulina Bueno, among others. My *hada madrina* (fairy godmother) always gives of her time and activates her social networks to help me with whatever project I am working on: thank you, Psc. Irma Guzmán de Torres! At the Universidad Espíritu Santo (UEES) in Guayaquil, I must thank Dr. Albert Eyde and Econ. Jorge Calderón Salazar, as well as Mónica Rambay. Thanks to Soc. Roberto Sáenz of the National Institute of Statistics and the Census (INEC) for sharing important city- and neighborhood-level data on Guayaquil. Oscar García helped me understand the employment context in the city and on the coast. Thanks to BONIL, who allowed me to reproduce one of his works. And to think of the dozens of hours that my wonderful transcription team saved me: Giannina Jaramillo, Jorge Mosquera, Anita Pereira, Catalina Plúa, Ing. Byron Ruiz Barroso, and the MVP of that team, Gabriela Salgado Coronel.

Third, I must thank my family, extended family, and adopted family, here in the United States and in Ecuador. This group includes my parents, who have encouraged my intellectual curiosity to the point of allowing me to read encyclopedias at the dinner table as a child and write a research paper on hallucinogenic drugs in eighth grade (what must they have thought of that topic choice?). Marilyn and Frank Masi, my grandparents, have been a steady source of love, support, laughter, and music. My husband's parents have helped smooth the way for my work in Ecuador from the beginning. The Lorca-Valdés family in New York graciously adopted us and treated us to enough *parrilladas* to last a lifetime. Thank you to the "other mothers" whose dedication to my children throughout the project and beyond has allowed me the quiet time necessary to write, read, think, work, and sometimes just take a nap: *gracias*, Sra. Pilar, Sra. Gladys, Sra. María, and especially, Tía Lola. Thanks to all of my *familia política* in Guayaquil and Manabí and throughout Ecuador: Prima Johanna Proaño García, Tía Fátima Casanova Bravo, *tías, tíos, primos, primas,* and Tía Azucena Casanova Bravo, who will be missed. *Gracias a los primos Merizalde Proaño por compartir su mamá y su casa con nosotros.*

Tamara Mose Brown has accompanied me every step of this journey, reading every word of the manuscript many times over. She has been an irreplaceable, and sometimes irrepressible, role model, critic, collaborator, and friend, and I hope that she will continue to be. Thanks to Trevor Jason Brown and Marisa A. Zapata for help with the images that illustrate the book. I also must thank Alisa Garni: *comadre*, sounding board, friend, partner in anxiety and celebration. I am grateful to Sodany Son and Mónica Árciga for their loyal friendship through the years. Thanks to Henry for listening to crazy brainstorms and methodological minutiae at all times of day and night, for cheering me on, for keeping me sane, and for loving me even when my mind was somewhere else. I owe you more than I can repay. Joaquín and Soledad accompanied me to the field, amaze me each day with their beautiful minds and spirits, and—every now and then—test my patience ever so slightly.

There are two women without whom this study, and this book, would have been impossible. *A la Sra. Ligia García de Proaño, gracias por invitarme a conocer su mundo y por ponerme el ejemplo de cómo conseguir el éxito e inspirar el respeto. A la Sra. Lola Proaño Yela, gracias por abrir su casa y su corazón y por cuidarnos con tanta ternura. Las quiero mucho.*

MAKING UP THE DIFFERENCE

AVON LADIES IN THE AMAZON?

PERFUME BECOMES POLITICAL

When the distributors and sales directors of Ecuador's largest direct selling corporation, Yanbal, returned to work in early January 2008 after their Christmas and New Year's holidays, they encountered an unpleasant surprise. The administration of Ecuador's president, Rafael Correa Delgado, had passed a wide-ranging tax reform law. One provision of the new law was the Impuesto a los Consumos Especiales (ICE), a tax on "special" purchases. Taxes were raised on goods and services that were perceived as unnecessary for meeting basic daily needs, such as cigarettes, liquor, and cable television. But the tax that directly affected Yanbal—and its more than 100,000 distributors—was the one on perfumes. The original proposed tax on perfumes had been 35 percent, but intense lobbying by Yanbal and other affected parties brought the rate down to 20 percent, which was effective immediately upon passage of the law in the final week of December 2007. The first two weeks of 2008 were chaotic, as Yanbal distributors learned of the tax and had to pass the bad news on to customers. A tax of 20 percent increased the cost of some already costly perfumes by $12 to $15, and the company's online ordering system had to be reprogrammed to automatically add in the tax, along with the existing sales tax of 12 percent.

The tax law was part of President Correa's campaign to make the country's traditional elites contribute more tax revenue, in an effort to redistribute wealth in Ecuador, which is ranked sixteenth in the world in terms of income inequality (UNDP 2008).[1] But Yanbal distributors and sales directors strongly objected to the portrayal of their products as luxuries for the rich. In an emotional letter to directors and salespeople, Yanbal Ecuador reiterated its Ecuadorianness, saying that the company was committed to the

Just after the passage of the ICE, which shocked direct sellers around the country, a massive march was held in Guayaquil to celebrate the first anniversary of the president's administration. In the magnified portion of this cartoon depicting the march, the association the ICE made between perfume consumption and elite status is lampooned through the following dialogue: Marcher #1: "I think there is a *pelucón* [a slang term coined by President Correa to denote wealthy Ecuadorians] infiltrator." Marcher #2: "Why?" Marcher #1: "I smelled perfume." This cartoon appeared in *El Universo* on January 8, 2008. (Courtesy of BONIL, Ecuadorian graphic humorist)

development of the country and created jobs for Ecuadorians, not just as distributors (sellers), but also as workers in the plants that produced some of the products sold. After meetings in Quito between government officials, Yanbal's corporate executives, and high-ranking sales directors, some directors took matters into their own hands, pushing for collective political action. The issue came to a head on January 25, when women direct sellers took to the streets in Guayaquil (Ecuador's largest city and the primary site for this research) and Montecristi (the site of the Constitutional Assembly) to protest the tax. These sellers insisted that the fragrances they sold were not special consumables but were for average Joes and Janes, not the super-rich. One sign at the Montecristi protest read: "The elites buy Coco Chanel, but the majority buy national [Ecuadorian-produced] perfumes from us" (*El Universo* 2008c). A cartoon in *El Universo*, the leading daily newspaper in Guayaquil, poked fun at the new tax law, and specifically the idea that only wealthy people use perfume (BONIL 2008).

For many Ecuadorians, perfume is viewed not as a luxury or optional item but as a key element of everyday personal hygiene and acceptable self-presentation. Ecuadorians spend $13 million each month on perfumes, much more than the $6.7 million they spend on cosmetics and the $5 million on soap (Escobar 2006a). As the most recognized purveyor of perfumes in the country, Yanbal stood to lose millions with the introduction of the ICE.

Yanbal and the people associated with the company found themselves at the center of a political storm because of their dominant share of the perfume market. They defended their right to be exempt from the tax by highlighting the humble origins of many distributors and consumers and interpreting perfume as a need rather than a luxury. Ligia García de Proaño, my husband's aunt and a high-ranking Yanbal director, was so livid about the new tax that she called a person who used to sell in her group, a military man who was then working as President Correa's bodyguard. The bodyguard agreed to let Ligia know where the president could be found next time he was in Guayaquil. And one afternoon in late January, the supreme strategist Ligia (along with her "mother" director[2]) made sure she was eating chicken alongside the president in a small restaurant in northern Guayaquil. When the ladies sidled up to Correa after his meal, they complained about the tax. He told them that he was familiar with their plight and that the new tax on perfumes was a mistake that he intended to fix.

The president repeated this sentiment on his national radio show on February 2, 2008, saying he had been meeting with representatives of Yanbal in order to find a way to keep perfume prices from changing, thereby ensuring that the distributors' "commissions weren't hurt and that they continue selling and earning their little bit of money [*su platita*]" (*El Universo* 2008b). It is possible that the president downplayed the economic gain of the women to make it seem like his modification of the new tax policy was of no great consequence. By validating the assumption that sellers were not earning much, however, Correa reinforced stereotypes that trivialize this type of women's work. The idea implicit in his statement is that these women are not supporting their families but just contributing a little something, making up the difference between the family's income and expenditures, or earning pocket money for themselves. In the end, Yanbal's staff and sales force succeeded in lowering the ICE on many items and eliminating it on others; the tax was also added to the manufacturing price rather than the sale price of each item, lowering the amount paid and meaning that less of the tax was passed on to customers. Because the strong demand for perfumes continued unabated as prices stabilized, sales were up to record numbers by the middle of 2008, although they later dropped.[3]

THE PRESENT STUDY

This book examines how cultural norms and material conditions shape Ecuadorian women's direct selling work. Cultural norms include socially accepted ideas about gender (femininity and masculinity), work, and family. The material conditions of women's lives are an amalgam of socioeconomic status/social class, income, social networks, and education. In her groundbreaking work *The Second Shift*, Arlie Hochschild introduced the concept of "gender strategy," defined as "a plan of action through which a person tries to solve problems at hand, given the cultural notions of gender at play" (2003 [1989], 15). In analyzing the experiences of urban Ecuadorians involved in direct selling, I argue that women's (and men's) *gendered economic strategies* represent the reconciling of cultural norms with material conditions. That is, gender strategies pertaining to income-generating activities take into account not only the dominant cultural narratives of gender but also the concrete socioeconomic situations in which individuals, couples, and families find themselves. In some cases, as will be shown throughout this book, cultural ideals are adapted, reshaped, or challenged by individuals' gendered economic strategies due to the exigencies of survival within a given set of material conditions and limitations. Although the word "strategy" implies a certain amount of choice (Benería 1992), choices are always constrained, especially for the poorest members of society.

The primary concern of this study, then, is to shine a spotlight on the interplay and connections between cultural norms and material conditions and how these cultural, social, and economic "givens" frame women's economic activities, including direct selling. Taking seriously the suggestions for feminist research laid out by Mohanty—to explore "women's own ideas of their work and daily life" and begin to "take apart the idea of 'women's work' as a naturalized category" (2003, 74)—I examine the conditions of women's work in the sales force of a transnational corporation and relate these conditions to ideas about gender roles.

While I am primarily interested in showing women's lives, work, and perspectives, I also use their stories to shed light on the paradox of Yanbal's success in Ecuador's unpredictable and sometimes downright chaotic economy. I asked executives in Yanbal Ecuador's corporate headquarters to explain why, out of the eight countries in which the company operates, Ecuador consistently has had the highest sales volume.[4] They responded that, because of the country's small size and high rates of poverty, multinational corporations have not seen expansion into Ecuador as profitable.

With fewer cosmetics, fragrances, and personal care products coming in from outside the country, Yanbal had an open field in which to manufacture, import, and distribute its products.

Although I don't dispute this claim, I argue that the flexible nature of this type of selling also allows people to access what are perceived as high-quality products and leads to higher sales volume of Yanbal products than many retail-based brands. Simply put, clients can pay for their Yanbal products a few dollars at a time rather than having to come up with the entire $50 cost of a perfume, an option that they do not have in many formal retail settings. Because the items sold by Yanbal are costly and valued elements of an attractive self-presentation, they are seen as desirable; because they can be paid for over time, they become affordable. This direct selling organization (DSO) has managed to weather serious economic crises and retain its sales force through the selling power of the brand, the company's ability to take advantage of social and cultural valuation of appearance and hygiene, and flexible payment arrangements between sellers and buyers (discussed in detail in chapter 7). Yanbal benefits from the fact that many Ecuadorians, as the protesters correctly claimed, see items like perfume as necessary for daily life, not as a luxury for the elite.

WOMEN AND DIRECT SELLING IN THE ECUADORIAN ECONOMY

Ecuador is located in the northwestern corner of South America, between the Pacific Ocean and the Amazon rain forest, and is bordered by two other Andean countries, Colombia and Peru. The population is currently 13.9 million, with more than 1.5 million (possibly as many as 2 million) Ecuadorians reportedly living abroad; popular migration destinations include the United States, Spain, and Italy (Jokisch 2007; Jokisch and Kyle 2008). It is estimated that approximately two-thirds of the population are of mixed ancestry (primarily European and indigenous); these Ecuadorians are referred to as mestizo by demographers and other social scientists. Another quarter of the population is said to be indigenous, although these percentages are hotly debated in political and academic circles. Approximately 5 to 10 percent of Ecuadorians are black, or Afro-Ecuadorian; the national census, which most likely undercounts blacks, gave a figure of 4.9 percent in 2001 (Halpern and Twine 2000; INEC n.d.). The country is divided into four distinct geographical or ecological zones: the Pacific coast, the Andean region, the Amazon, and the Galápagos Islands. The capital city is Quito, but the most populous is Guayaquil, with just about

3 million residents in the metropolitan area. A full 38 percent of Ecuadorians lived in poverty in 2006 (*World Factbook* 2008); and in Guayaquil, 87 percent were poor (Floro and Messier 2006, 235).

Ecuador has primarily been an agricultural society since its independence from Spain in 1822, and although import substitution industrialization was attempted more than once (Weiss 1997), the country never industrialized to the extent that some of the larger South American nations did. The focus on agricultural exports that essentially began with the cacao boom of the late nineteenth to the early twentieth century has reappeared again in more recent periods, with export-oriented banana and flower cultivation. The discovery of oil in the Amazon region in the 1960s and 1970s shaped economic development policies, funding development programs that extended the life expectancy of Ecuadorian citizens, increased school attendance, and reduced infant mortality, leading to the assertion that "much of the oil income was well spent" (Moser 1993, 177). Oil, along with bananas, is now one of the country's largest export sectors (Weiss 1997). Because of this orientation toward exports as the primary path to economic development, it can be argued that the Ecuadorian state has evolved through "a transnational lens," and this is especially true of Guayaquil, historically and currently the country's largest international port (Goetschel 1999).

Guayaquil has historically been a magnet for migrants from other parts of the country, in an urbanizing trend similar to that of other Latin American nations. The population of Guayaquil more than doubled between 1960 and 1982 (from 500,000 to 1.2 million) and then nearly doubled again between 1982 and 1988, rising to 2 million (Moser 1993, 179). Today about three-fifths of Ecuador's population lives in cities (Radcliffe 2008, 285). Much of Moser's description of the city, written in the 1990s, still holds true:

> Guayaquil's commercial activity is focused around the forty grid-iron blocks of the original Spanish city, which in the 1970s were encircled by inner city rental tenements. To the north on higher ground are the predominantly middle- and upper-income areas, while to the west and south are tidal swamplands which provide the predominant area for low-income expansion. Settlement of this peripheral zone, known as the *suburbios* (literally suburbs) occurred between 1940 and 1980 when the low-income population excluded from the conventional housing market invaded this municipal-owned swampland (1993, 179).

Thus, the increase in population has been accompanied by the city's "spatial expansion" (Moser 1993, 182). Since the geography of the area has made expansion southward less feasible in recent years, a new ring of lower-income settlements has risen outside of the well-to-do neighborhoods at the city's northern edges.

Structural adjustment policies—changes in national economic strategies and budget allocations—that were implemented in order to obtain International Monetary Fund loans in the early 1980s resulted in increased unemployment, high inflation rates, and a reduced social safety net, consequences also seen in other parts of the world.[5] These changes affected women differently from men, adding to their unpaid work in the home and making the household's daily maintenance more difficult (Lind 2005; Moser 1997; Pitkin and Bedoya 1997; Rodríguez 1994). Moser (1993) identified three groups of low-income women affected by structural adjustment in Guayaquil in the 1980s: those who were "coping," those who were "burnt out," and those who were just "hanging on." Structural adjustment also contributed to a rise in income inequality, and at one point in the early 1990s, Ecuador had the most skewed income distribution in Latin America (Weiss 1997, 17). Ecuador's debt represented a higher proportion of its gross domestic product than that in other indebted nations such as Brazil and Mexico (ibid., 9).

In response to a crisis of foreign debt and radical fluctuations in the national currency, the sucre, Ecuador adopted the dollar as its currency in 2000 (Beckerman and Solimano 2002). Although there are debates about the effects of dollarization, Ecuadorians generally agree that goods and services became more expensive after the switch to the dollar. This benefited some independent businesspeople, such as taxi drivers, who could now charge a minimum of one dollar per trip. Consumers saw their money disappearing at quicker rates, however. As a family member put it to me, "We were talking calmly about thousands and millions [of sucres]," and all of a sudden, something costing just one dollar seemed cheap. People tell me that they are still sometimes shocked when they translate dollar amounts back into sucres and realize how much more everyday items cost relative to pre-dollarization average prices.[6] Most Ecuadorians did not benefit from dollarization, and it did not reduce inflation as aggressively as it was intended to do (Lind 2005, 137).

Since the 1999–2000 economic crisis that led to the adoption of the U.S. dollar as Ecuador's official currency, the economy has experienced growth, with significant interruptions and a great deal of political instability (Beckerman and Solimano 2002). Current president Rafael Correa Delgado was elected in 2006 on a platform of social programs funded in large part by oil revenue, and a more defiant stance toward international financial institutions such as the International Monetary Fund. Correa also promised to rewrite the country's constitution, a process undertaken by the elected Constitutional Assembly; the final document was approved by the voters in 2008. (The Constitution had previously been rewritten in 1998.) Much has been made of Latin America's "turn to the left" in recent years, and scholars debate the extent and consequences of the changes made by leaders such as Hugo Chávez in Venezuela, Evo Morales in Bolivia, and Rafael Correa in Ecuador. It is unclear what effects new policy stances (such as defaulting on debt and the nationalization of the petroleum industry) will have for citizens.

Although Ecuador was the first country in Latin America to extend the vote to women, the country was a bit late (in comparison with its neighbors) in developing a feminist movement (Rodríguez 1994). Women's movements have tended to focus on local and community issues, and the lack of a powerful national movement means that smaller movements "create diverse relationships with political parties, NGOs [nongovernmental organizations], churches, and local governments" (Radcliffe 2008, 287). Laws establishing sex-based quotas for candidates for elected office have been passed but not enforced, despite the inclusion of women's rights provisions in successive versions of the Constitution (ibid., 293). Recent scholarship has examined women's social movements—some of which identify themselves as feminist and some of which avoid that label—at both the local and national levels (Lind 2005; Prieto 2005; Radcliffe and Westwood 1996; Rodríguez 1994). Most of the women in my study fit Radcliffe's description of Guayaquilean women who, disenchanted by political corruption and clientelism, "have disengaged from collective actions, being forced to 'hang on' to a precarious set of survival strategies" (2008, 287).

GLOBALIZATION, INFORMAL SECTOR GROWTH, AND DIRECT SALES

As in other Latin American countries, employment in the formal sector in Ecuador has declined rapidly in the past few decades, and employment in the informal sector has risen. Informal work is "unprotected," "neither 'on the books' of employers nor regulated by the state" (Poster and Salime 2002, 191). Examples of informal sector jobs include domestic service and small-scale selling. In Latin America around the year 2000, informal employment currently made up 51 percent of all nonagricultural employment, and nearly 60 percent of working women in the region were engaged in informal employment (ILO 2002). Although some new employment opportunities have emerged, as in the flower export sector, 6.1 percent of Ecuadorians were unemployed in November 2007 (the rate had dropped from 9.9 percent in January 2007), and 46 percent were underemployed (*Gestión* 2007, 82). By March 2009, with the spreading effects of the U.S. economic crisis, 14 percent of Guayaquil's residents were unemployed, and nearly 51 percent underemployed (*El Universo* 2009). It is estimated that one million Ecuadorians have emigrated just since 1999 in search of work in countries such as the United States, Italy, and Spain (Jokisch 2007). These conditions are caused by internal economic dynamics and decisions made by Ecuadorian politicians and businesses, by global economic processes, and by international bodies and multinational corporations.

Some scholars of globalization focus on the expansion of multinational corporations from their bases in the "First World" into the "Third World" (Salzinger 2003; Sklair 2000; Tabb 2001). Such growth is led by a transnational group of managers, chief executive officers, and financial advisers that Sklair (2000) has called the "transnational capitalist class." Multinational corporations are often seen as pushing out domestic competitors and taking advantage of lower labor and production costs in developing countries to produce goods cheaply and export them to other countries, thereby increasing profit margins for owners and shareholders. As production facilities move across borders, so do the products of multinational corporations, expanding the range of options for consumers in both poor and rich countries. Studies on global capitalist expansion that do not depart from a feminist perspective often overlook the people involved, focusing on the corporation or the domestic or global economy. Feminist researchers have assembled a growing body of micro-level studies of women participating in global processes, which have as yet had little impact on macro-level theories of globalization (Freeman 2000).

When individual people (especially women) are the unit of analysis in studies of economic globalization, the purpose is often to expose exploitation or the mechanisms by which these workers are incorporated into transnational corporations. Research has often examined the position of "Third World" women workers vis-à-vis corporations headquartered in the United States and Europe (Fernández-Kelly 1983; Freeman 2000; Salzinger 2003). Such studies illuminate the ways in which ideas about women workers that originate outside the countries in which they work interact with home-grown ideologies about women's place in society. These insights are useful; however, they are limited in that they generally take into account only women working in fixed workplaces (e.g., factories, data processing centers) that are part of the formal economy.[7]

While international financial institutions and multinational corporations that fit the traditional labor-capital model are major engines of economic globalization, direct selling companies are increasingly crossing geographic borders and tapping into a mostly female labor force using radically different methods from those of, say, the maquiladoras in export-processing zones.[8] Direct sales organizations, including Avon, Tupperware, and Amway, have been expanding into new markets in Asia and Latin America, a strategy that has proved successful and profitable for these companies (Cahn 2006; Hopkins 2007; Vincent 2003; A. Wilson 1999). It is the work of the millions of women in the sales forces of these companies that generates this profit. In the context of narrowing opportunities in the formal economy, and the low status of many types of informal work, selling for a transnational direct sales organization is often an appealing option.

BACKGROUND ON DIRECT SALES

Direct selling is the marketing of consumer goods by representatives (known as distributors) of the producers of the goods to customers, bypassing the typical system of fixed retail locations.[9] It is characterized as a "low cost, low entry-barrier, business opportunity that allows individuals, mostly women, to work a flexible range of hours selling branded goods for commission" (Brodie, Stanworth, and Wotruba 2002, 70). The elimination of the overhead costs of retail stores allows direct selling organizations to return some of the profit made on the products to distributors as commission and can potentially increase the company's profits over those of a traditional retail operation. In addition, since distributors are nominally self-employed, direct sales companies do not deal with payroll administration or offer benefits such as health insurance for the workers in their sales force.

When DSOs rely on current distributors and sales directors (distributors with advanced standing) to recruit new sellers, they are referred to as "network direct selling organizations" or "multi-level marketing organizations" (Brodie and Stanworth 1998; Cahn 2006). According to Nicole Biggart, whose 1989 book *Charismatic Capitalism: Direct Selling Organizations in America* is probably the most well-known study of direct sales in the United States, network DSOs are characterized by the creation of "sponsorship lines that create financial ties between distributors" and a "formal status hierarchy" based on recognition, prizes, and titles. The network form of organization is now the most prevalent in direct sales. Avon and Yanbal are two such organizations, in which distributors who reach a certain level gain a percentage of their recruits' sales. The distributors who oversee these lower-level sellers are the "upline," and the people they have recruited form their "downline" (Biggart 1989, 16). Within this type of organization, notes Pei-Chia Lan, distributors act as consumers, retailers, and recruiters (2002, 169). In Yanbal, as in the U.S.-based Mary Kay and other DSOs, the relationships between distributors are analogized to family roles, so that a distributor is a "daughter" (*hija*) to her "mother consultant" and "mother director" (*madre directora*), who recruited her into the organization and continue to supervise and mentor her. Subgroups of distributors (people connected by the same sponsor) are sometimes referred to in industry parlance as "genealogies" and are depicted by family tree–type diagrams in both the academic literature and administrative materials produced by the corporations (Biggart 1989, 17; Lan 2002, 176). In many cases, people who are family members in real life are also connected in the DSO world, which is a unique feature of direct sales: "by distributing their goods . . . through vast networks of ordinary people, companies extend their reach into intimate spheres and personal relationships" (A. Wilson 2004, 164).

Direct sales is a $113 billion business employing nearly 63 million people worldwide, 80 percent of whom are women.[10] In Ecuador in 2008, direct selling brought in $400 million, with a sales force of 380,000.[11] Despite these impressive figures, it is generally agreed that the direct sales sector experiences an annual turnover rate of 100 percent among distributors (Biggart 1989, 156; Cahn 2006, 129). High turnover can be explained in part by the self-driven nature of the work and the lack of penalties for dropping out. Some turnover is seasonal; for example, some Ecuadorian women join to earn enough money for Christmas gifts for their families, and then stop selling once the holidays are over. For network DSOs and dedicated distributors, this means that constant recruitment is required. Most direct sales companies offer distributors some type of training, ongoing assistance, and support, often delivered by sales directors at support centers such as the one Peter Cahn (2006) studied in Mexico and those that served as some of my research sites for this book. Events (meetings, seminars, parties) rely on materials produced by the company to both sell products and recruit distributors. As Ara Wilson notes, "the direct sales mode is comprised of discourse: of messages conveyed in catalogues, sales techniques, inspirational meetings, promotional materials, and advertisements" (1999, 78). These texts draw on and create desire for products while also constructing desirable identities for consumers and sellers. (Yanbal's catalogs are analyzed in detail in chapter 3.)

The academic literature on direct sales has significant lacunae and limitations. There is a lack of ethnographic data, which means that we do not often see the everyday lives and perspectives of distributors. Three important aspects of direct selling merit further examination. First, as feminist scholarship has shown, socially constructed ideals of femininity in male-dominated societies give rise to intricate rules regulating feminine behavior and physical appearance. Women transmit their class (and/or ethnic) identities and aspirations through dress and appearance. There has yet to be an in-depth study of a single cosmetics DSO, which is an ideal avenue for analyzing the construction of femininity and the commodification of beauty in everyday life.

Second, studies of women distributors have sometimes tended to look at them as the prototypical actors of economic theory: as isolated, autonomous, rational individuals. However, women are embedded in households in which they have domestic responsibilities and must contend with the demands of caring for husbands or partners and/or children. Women's decision to begin selling cannot be viewed outside of this context, especially in societies with relatively rigid gender roles. The perceptions of family members and the negotiations that take place between them must be brought more fully into the picture. Since direct selling involves women from many different social class backgrounds, by studying this type of work we can also compare how work-family conflicts are dealt with in households of different socioeconomic statuses.[12]

Finally, with all the talk of selling in the literature on direct sales, consumption tends to get lost in the shuffle. Each act of selling is also an act of buying, so why do scholars often talk only to sellers and not consumers? The burgeoning social science literature on consumption—which largely neglects direct sales—presents the opposite problem: a focus on consumers to the exclusion of sellers. Each act of consumption is also an act of selling. A study that draws on the insights of each approach can illuminate the links between buying and selling in this personalized sales sector; to do this, research must be conducted with consumers, and sales interactions must be observed, documented, and analyzed. Of course, the argument can be made (as in Cahn 2006) that most sellers begin as consumers, but this is not a sufficient exploration of the topic. Why do some consumers become sellers while others do not? How does the consumption of these products fit in with other consumption practices? How do social class, social networks, and gender come into play in buying and selling? Although this study primarily focuses on sellers, it fills a gap in the literature on direct selling by also conducting research with buyers in order to better understand the dynamic selling relationship.

YANBAL'S TRAJECTORY

It is worth looking at how Yanbal came to operate in Ecuador and how it became the leader in its field. Founded in Peru in 1967, the company recently celebrated thirty years of doing business in Ecuador. Like many DSOs such as U.S.-based Mary Kay, the image of Yanbal is closely linked to that of its founder, Fernando Belmont. According to Yanbal's general manager in Ecuador, Belmont learned about direct sales during his college education in the United States, thought that the model could be successful in Latin America, and returned to Peru to found Yanbal. Belmont later emigrated to Argentina, launching Yanbal subsidiaries in Chile, Ecuador, Colombia, and Mexico. When he returned to Peru, he founded a company he called Unique, due to conflicts over rights to the name Yanbal between Belmont and his brothers (who had taken over Yanbal when he left the country). Belmont's company has grown in terms of revenue and the number of official distributors and has expanded geographically. Today Yanbal operates in seven Latin American countries: Bolivia, Colombia, Ecuador, Guatemala, Mexico, Peru, and Venezuela. There are more than 500,000 Yanbal consultants in these countries (Yanbal n.d.). In 2006, Yanbal decided to follow the waves of Ecuadorians migrating to Spain, and currently 3,000 women are working as Yanbal beauty consultants in that country (Correa and Velasco 2007, 126). There is talk of expanding to the United States, with its large populations of immigrants from Latin America, many of whom already know Yanbal/Unique products from their home countries.[13]

Yanbal was named number forty-six on a recent list of Ecuador's five hundred largest companies, compiled by the national news magazine *Vistazo* (Correa and Velasco 2007). The company's sales increased 24 percent from 2005 to 2006, with reported revenues of $125 million. In the personal care and beauty sector, Yanbal is the second-highest seller, just behind the multinational corporation Unilever and beating out not only Avon and other DSOs but also Colgate Palmolive, Procter & Gamble, and Johnson & Johnson (ibid.). The company was one of the fifteen named "most respected" in Ecuador by the business magazine *Líderes* in 2007. Yanbal Ecuador is the second-best company to work for in Ecuador, according to a new survey of employees (not distributors) by the organization Great Place to Work (*Vistazo* 2008, 33). It is the most recognizable brand name in cosmetics and has the largest market share of fragrances (Escobar 2006b, 27; *Hoy* 2005). In the realm of direct selling, Yanbal's major competitors in Ecuador are Avon (a U.S.-based multinational), L'Bel (formerly called Ebel, a Peruvian company owned by Fernando Belmont's brother), and Oriflame (a Swedish company).

DIRECT SALES AS INFORMAL "WOMEN'S WORK"

Women's work must be examined in relation to their economic alternatives in a given setting. What would they be doing if they weren't selling? Is direct selling seen as more gender-appropriate than other types of work? Is direct selling the only income-generating activity distributors are engaged in, or is it one piece of a multipronged economic strategy on the part of the woman and/or the household? These questions are drawn from the literature on women and work in developing countries, and they go beyond the tendency to categorize women's work as formal or informal, part-time or full-time.

The informal economy in Latin America, as elsewhere in the developing world, has exploded in the last few decades (Benería 2003; Benería and Feldman 1992; Portes, Castells, and Benton 2004). Women in the paid labor force are disproportionately engaged in informal work, which accounts for 51 percent of all employment in Latin America (Benería 2003; ILO 2002). Women's "multiple income strategies" (Rothstein 1995) often include participation in both formal and informal employment either simultaneously (as in Freeman 2000) or at different times, as well as multiple forms of informal employment (Weiss 1997, 21) and combinations of "wage labor and self-employment as well as temporary migration" (Benería 2003, 112). In some households, the informal economy is the primary source of income, with formal employment complementing or supplementing informal earnings (Pérez-Alemán 1992). Such a combination of strategies, and the appeal of informal sector work, can be explained in part by women's primary responsibility for caring for the home and family, which "continues to have an impact on their choices and ability to participate in paid production" (Benería 2003, 119). In addition, neoliberal economic policies have made the daily tasks of what some scholars would call "social reproduction" more difficult by reducing government support and social programs (Benería 2003; Lind 2005; Moser 1989). Feminist economists including Lourdes Benería and Nancy Folbre have examined the economic and social value of women's unpaid domestic work and "care work"[14] as part of a growing body of feminist research that Benería (2003) has called the "accounting for women's work project." This unpaid work affects women's participation in informal as well as formal labor markets (a topic further explored in chapter 1).

Is direct selling an informal economic activity? It is not highly regulated by commercial laws, and distributors are nominally self-employed rather than being official employees of DSOs, meaning that they are not guaranteed job security and do not receive health insurance or other benefits (Elson 1999, 616). In addition to the distributors who are officially registered with the companies, there are also legions of people who informally "help" these official distributors in various ways. Thus, there are degrees of informality in the business of direct selling.[15] Yet informal and formal economic activities and actors are often connected. As Linda Seligmann puts it in her description of the informal sector in Peru, "the chain of intermediaries within the informal market economy is closely intertwined with the production and sales processes of formal economy businesses, and the chain itself facilitates the circulation of products in an inefficient economy" (2004, 87).

Despite the informal aspects of their sales forces, DSOs do have legally employed staff, from janitors and factory workers in manufacturing plants to accountants and experts in marketing and psychology. In addition, direct sales differs in important ways from other activities commonly called informal, such as market selling or illicit activities like prostitution. Direct selling organizations, and the activity of direct selling itself, seem to have a foot in both the informal and formal economy, an increasingly common situation as the "neat dichotomies between 'formal' and 'informal' work are breaking down" (Elson 1999, 617). In terms of the actual daily activities and the lack of a fixed workplace, direct selling looks most like informal work. In the case of direct sales and similar types of work, artificial conceptual boundaries between work done in the "public" sphere and work done in "private" become less relevant.

In some developing countries, direct selling is an increasingly attractive income-earning strategy, especially for women, due to its ease of entry and self-directed work process. Direct sales organizations benefit from cultural norms and structural forces that steer women away from full-time jobs in the formal economy, and they also benefit from the material conditions that lead to women's need to earn an income. The findings of this study underline the importance of examining direct sales as a rapidly expanding type of work, a formal-informal hybrid that appeals mainly to women and helps promote the expansion of consumer capitalism around the world. The women whose experiences are presented here are part of the "feminization of labor" (Standing 1999) occurring in developing countries, yet their work takes place largely outside the formal economy and outside the prototypical globalized workplace of the export processing factory.[16] As in-depth studies of formal sector employment have shown, women's work must be considered not only in terms of the needs and discourses of transnational corporations but also in relation to locally produced ideals of gender and locally specific social and economic conditions (Bank Muñoz 2008; Freeman 2000; Friedemann-Sánchez 2006; Salzinger 2003).

DSOS AS GENDERED ORGANIZATIONS

According to sociologist Pei-Chia Lan, DSOs are "often portrayed as homelike settings characterized by horizontal cooperation and affective bonds, in contrast to other workplaces governed by the principles of bureaucracy and competition" (2002, 165). Indeed, social scientists studying these companies often insist on their differences from more "typical" capitalist firms.[17] Biggart argues that the mixing of family and work and the assigning of familial terms to work relationships leads to a "'feminine' form of organization qualitatively distinct from 'masculine' forms" (1989, 71). This familial aspect is clearly seen in Yanbal, with its "mother" directors and their "daughters" and "granddaughters." Hierarchies are based on recognition of achievement rather than authority or control over subordinates, and the emphasis is on creating a supportive and noncompetitive environment in which all distributors can succeed, according to Biggart's model.

Around the time of the publication of Biggart's *Charismatic Capitalism* (1989), feminist thinkers were beginning to elaborate theories about the masculine character of organizations in U.S. society. Rather than viewing bureaucratic and administrative structures as gender-neutral and rational, and seeing the human inhabitants of these structures as gendered, Joan Acker (1990), Dorothy Smith (1989), and others urged us to consider the possibility that organizations themselves were gendered. This gendered character was evidenced by such phenomena as the persistent gendered division of labor within organizations and the symbols, images, and language that upheld such divisions. The image of the ideal worker in management and business literature was masculine; that is, only men tended to lack domestic and outside responsibilities, a precondition for "existing only for the work" as the business discourse demanded. Acker envisioned an alternative to masculine organizations, a type of firm that would value care work, have no hierarchy, and "where work and intimate relations are closely related" (1990, 155).

Some direct selling organizations, in particular those with a primarily female workforce, appear to be a type of gendered organization that is not masculine. For one thing, these companies explicitly and symbolically define themselves as feminine, and are "unabashedly women's worlds" (Biggart 1989, 93). Avon calls itself "the company for women." Mary Kay's signature color is pink, down to the Cadillacs awarded to top distributors. Tupperware is associated with a traditional domesticity centered on the kitchen and the feeding of the family. In the past few decades, these feminine organizational identities have left the companies open to criticism by feminists and satire by drag queens and others who enjoy toying with gender stereotypes (Vincent 2003).

In these organizations, as in Yanbal, the consumer is generally assumed to be a woman, as is the distributor. Yanbal actually requires that prospective distributors be female, although resourceful Ecuadorian men have found ways around this restriction (see chapter 2). Unlike many economic organizations, these DSOs are built on the assumption that the selling interaction is an all-female one, with a female seller and a female consumer. In the catalogs of cosmetics DSOs, most products are oriented toward adult women, with a much smaller selection of items for men and children. This hyperfeminine image obscures not only the actual involvement of men in the creation and distribution of Yanbal products but also the realities of the customer base, which, according to Yanbal Ecuador's general manager Robert Watson, is 54 percent male. According to distributors, male customers buy items for themselves (especially colognes) and for the women in their lives. Some sellers told me that they prefer to have men as customers because they pay more promptly; according to these distributors, male clients are embarrassed by the thought of owing money to a woman.

The working conditions of distributors for women-oriented companies seem to support Biggart's assertion that direct selling organizations are "feminine." Direct selling organizations that target women to be sellers stress the flexible nature of the work and the opportunity to combine income-generating activities with domestic responsibilities. As Biggart points out, "being able to care for family needs and work at the same time serves both the material and emotional needs of women" (1989, 58). Rather than supporting the traditional division of work from home, and public from private, DSOs "claim to offer an alternative to the model of separate spheres" (ibid., 72).

The appeal to women who need to earn money but feel obliged to take care of the home and children is obvious. In theory, distributors set their own hours, decide how much to work, and can work from home or have children accompany them to meetings or parties. It is easy and relatively inexpensive to become a distributor (Yanbal requires an initial outlay of $16 for the starter kit) in comparison with starting up another type of business, and there are few or no penalties for dropping out of the DSO. Rather than valuing "masculine" characteristics such as competitiveness, DSOs are said to promote personal qualities and interactions that women are socialized to perform anyway, such as nurturing, cooperation, and emotional expressiveness (Biggart 1989). In some ways, these organizations seem to approximate Acker's dream of a firm that will value and respect care work, mute rigid hierarchies, and meld the personal/social and the public/economic. As Biggart puts it, "DSOs have almost no rules and . . . few managers" (ibid., 5).

To some extent, my findings in chapters 1 and 2 challenge the image of DSOs as kinder, gentler capitalist organizations. Men are involved in Yanbal's operations at all levels, from its male founder to the men who, while not formal distributors, sell or "help" sell products. Many women in Yanbal's sales force have not reconciled the demands of the work with their domestic responsibilities, and some are living in situations of active conflict with male partners over their choice to work in direct sales. This conflict seems to stem from these men's opposition to the women working and from a rigidly gendered household division of labor, rather than from any particular dislike of direct sales or Yanbal. I also found that, despite the talk of nurturing and cooperation, competition between sellers and (especially) sales directors was encouraged by company officials and the women themselves. Yanbal Ecuador's top manager confided that he finds women to be even more competitive than men and that this is a major motivating factor for the members of Yanbal's sales force.

Despite the debatably "feminine" characteristics of DSOs, the question remains of whether direct selling empowers women. Ariel de Vidas correctly states that "the network of feminine social relations underlying the Tupperware sales system does not automatically make Tupperware a feminist organization" (2008, 274). Biggart (1989) claims that individual women are empowered by the self-affirming experience and the economic advantage gained through direct selling, but that the industry does not challenge macro-level gender hierarchies. Wilson (2004) shows how direct selling allows women to expand the boundaries of their social worlds beyond kin networks, but their local/domestic feminine identities are supplemented with cosmopolitan feminine identities that do not critique gender inequalities. Yanbal, Avon, and other cosmetics DSOs encourage women to take care of themselves and value their own needs (Vincent 2003, 184), but this could also be read as encouraging an oppressive preoccupation with appearance and the body that is already promoted by mainstream cultures.

In material terms, the chances of women radically improving their socio-economic status through direct selling are small, and although the success stories are real and are constantly retold by DSOs, the average distributor will not become wealthy through her work selling cosmetics or Tupperware. Even the most "feminine" DSOs and those with female figureheads are often run by men at the highest corporate levels. In Yanbal, the founder of the company and its general manager are both men from Peru, although the founder's daughter is increasingly visible in promotional material and at events in Ecuador. During the period in which I conducted fieldwork, men also tended to run the company's marketing division and led other departments as well. These men are formal employees of the corporation as opposed to the thousands of women who act as "independent contractors," and they reap the benefits of this more privileged position in the form of higher and more stable incomes and more social prestige. Of course, there are also many powerful women on the corporate side, whose incomes and prestigious jobs distance them from the women in the sales force.

In terms of the empowerment question, work as a Yanbal beauty consultant or director entails what I call "moments of empowerment," in which constraints of traditional gender roles are temporarily lifted. For example, promotional photographs advertising men's fragrances or other men's products always feature hunky male models. In group meetings, consultants frequently engage in objectifying these models and make loud, overtly sexual comments about the men's appearance, often at the goading of directors or Yanbal staff. These catcalls, and women saying that they would like to take the model home with them ("just for a night," as one Yanbal coordinator put it), lead to delighted laughter and help lighten the tone of the meetings. Such sexualized commentaries by women are highly censured in public speech, but within the confines of an all-female meeting, women are free to express sexual desire and frustration with the constraints of married life.

In another instance, in fall 2007, Yanbal held pop music concerts in Guayaquil and Quito for consultants and directors who had met a certain sales target. Prior to the concerts, consultants were explicitly told that only women should attend the event, and only those who had earned a ticket. Despite this, some women obtained extra tickets and brought their spouses to the concert. At the Guayaquil event, unsuspecting men were harangued by groups of women as they entered the concert venue. The women shouted things like "Go home and wash the dishes!" They were claiming the space as theirs by virtue of their gender and used their numerical majority to temporarily invert gender roles and show the men that they weren't wanted. These are examples of "moments of empowerment" made possible by women's involvement in the DSO. In general, however, it is up to individual women to construct their gender identities, devise gendered economic strategies (plans for economic action based on gender ideals and material conditions), and negotiate their place in their families and communities.

As gendered organizations, Yanbal and other direct selling companies often claim to provide opportunities for women to balance paid work and family responsibilities. This idea of the DSO as "the company for women" (Avon's corporate slogan) sets up expectations about valuing women's private and public work and helping women to improve their economic conditions. As is shown in the next chapter, the situation of women direct sellers on the ground is complicated by gendered norms of work and family and the multiple demands that are placed on them as wives and mothers.

NOTES

1. To provide some comparison: Ecuador's neighbor Colombia is ranked the eighth-most unequal country, and the United States is fifty-sixth on the list. In the early 1990s, Ecuador was the most unequal country in Latin America (Weiss 1997, 17), and Latin America is the most unequal region in the world (UNDP 2008).

2. Feminine genealogical terms are often used in direct sales, such that the woman who recruited Ligia into the direct selling organization is referred to as her "mother" director.

3. As I am writing this, Yanbal and the Correa administration have been negotiating over a new set of policies that negatively affects the direct sales company's ability to import products and prizes for sellers. What these debates show is that Yanbal is a big enough economic player to engage in direct dialogue with the national government. Since I did not ask Yanbal sellers or corporate officials about the relationship between the company and previous governments, I cannot provide a historical perspective on the events recounted here.

4. Although Colombia had the highest sales in 2007–2008, Ecuador had previously attained this position for several years in a row.

5. Ecuadorian scholar Felipe Burbano de Lara has argued that structural adjustment was "incomplete" in Ecuador, due to the political fragmentation that he characterizes as "lack of consensus and constant bickering" (2008, 274–275). Moser counted eight "distinct stabilization/adjustment packages" of policies implemented between 1982 and 1988 (1993, 178).

6. Even before dollarization, Ecuadorians had been telling researchers that, in the past, "*la plata valía más* [money was worth more]," reflecting both currency devaluation and rising prices/inflation (Weiss 1997, 24).

7. The academic literature on women and work in globalizing economies is discussed further in chapter 1.

8. "Maquiladora" is a term commonly applied to factories or assembly plants owned by multinational corporations and located in developing countries, often in areas designated as export-processing zones. These companies are attracted by low taxes and tariffs (incentives offered by the countries in which facilities are located) and the low costs of labor. Often maquiladoras are associated with predominantly female labor forces.

9. The earliest direct selling organizations in the United States followed in the door-to-door tradition of Yankee peddlers, according to sociologist Nicole Biggart (1989). By the early 1900s, such companies were growing rapidly and offering socially acceptable employment to American women (Peiss 1998). Female entrepreneurs, such as the first African American millionaire, Madam C. J. Walker, were at the forefront of developing large-scale, multilevel direct sales companies (Peiss 1998, 76). By the 1920s, direct selling was established and recognized as a legitimate enterprise in the United States, though not without some resistance by traditional retailers who felt threatened by this alternative form of distribution (Biggart 1989). During the Great Depression, direct sales recruitment shot up as "alternative forms of work were eliminated" (Biggart 1989, 33). When labor standards such as the minimum wage were beginning to be implemented by Congress in the late 1930s, most direct sales companies began to consider distributors as "independent contractors" (Biggart 1989, 40). By the 1950s, most DSOs used the multilevel or network structure that continues to be common today, and growth was steady through the 1970s (Biggart 1989). Some of the most recognized names in direct sales are those of cosmetics companies, including Avon (originally the California Perfume Company) and Mary Kay, whose charismatic founder Mary Kay Ash "reached out to displaced homemakers and other women rocked by the social and economic turmoil of the 1960s and 1970s" by combining "feminist economic aims with traditionalist ideals of womanhood" (Peiss 1989, 262).

In the 1970s and 1980s, DSOs began looking overseas for new markets and, of course, new sellers (Lan 2002, 166; A. Wilson 1999, 407). As direct sales, like many other industries, becomes a global—or at least transnational—enterprise, people living in Asia and Latin America have shown interest in becoming "cosmopolitan consumers and professional distributors" (A. Wilson 1999, 407). Just as direct sales recruitment soared in the absence of traditional employment during America's Great Depression, countries experiencing persistent economic crisis, the erosion of social safety nets as the result of neoliberal economic policies, and chronic unemployment and underemployment are prime candidates for a booming direct sales sector. American companies that are household names, such as Avon, Amway, and Tupperware, now count on new operations in developing countries to provide much (or most) of their profit (A. Wilson 2004).

Direct selling ideologies that emerged and evolved in particular social and economic contexts are always interpreted by sellers in the light of local understandings of economic activity, class, and gender. In Thailand, selling has long been seen as a feminine occupation, so direct sales seems to be a logical outgrowth of that tradition. On the other hand, the association of DSOs with a foreign and sophisticated modernity has allowed men (who would be ashamed to sell in the market) to become involved (A. Wilson 2004). In Mexico, people rejected traditional pie-in-the-sky direct selling pitches (showing how to earn a car, a vacation, etc.) in favor of a company with promotional materials that acknowledged their more immediate survival needs such as food and good health (Cahn

2006). While it may be expressly prohibited, both Thai and Mexican direct sales distributors often sell other items alongside their Amway or Omnilife products. Many Yanbal distributors I met also sold other lines, with most claiming to do so because it was what customers wanted. In Brazil and Argentina, Tupperware distributors eschewed the party sales method in favor of "one-on-one selling," although it is not clear whether for cultural, economic, or logistical reasons (Vincent 2003).

10. World Federation of Direct Selling Associations, http://www.wfdsa.org/. Figures are for 2009.

11. Ibid. The revenues for 2006 were $260 million with approximately 200,000 sellers. This represented a 37 percent increase in revenue and a 54 percent increase in the sales force since the previous year, 2005, when $190 million was generated by 130,000 sellers.

12. The cross-class appeal of direct sales is one of its most striking features, and, in the case of Thailand, Ara Wilson convincingly attributes this class diversity to the economic instability that affects both rich and poor and leads to the need for "extra income" (2004, 167). Of course, for many of the Ecuadorian women in my study, the income was not "extra" but vital to the survival of their households.

13. The general manager of Yanbal Ecuador, Robert Watson, told me that he knows that products leave Ecuador to be sold as "contraband" in the United States, but the exact percentage is unknown.

14. See England (2005) for an overview of the new scholarly work on "care" as a gendered form of paid and unpaid labor.

15. Although Benería and Floro (2006) use the term "degrees of informality" to classify women's jobs in Ecuador and Bolivia as low, medium, or highly informal, direct sales does not fit neatly into any of these categories. I am referring here instead to the closeness or distance of the seller to the transnational corporation or DSO, which has some connection—though not a perfect correspondence—to the degrees of informality that Benería and Floro define.

16. Factory work has been increasing as a source of female employment in many developing countries, including some in Latin America, but this trend is less pronounced in Ecuador, with some jobs created for women in shrimp processing on the coast and flower cultivation in the highlands, but no widespread maquiladora recruiting (Moser 1993, 182; Oscar García, interview with author, 2007).

17. Another intriguing feature of direct selling that social scientists have examined is the commodification of social relations, turning social links into economic links and vice versa. In direct selling, sellers' customers and fellow distributors are often their friends and relatives, blurring the line between business and personal relationships. DSOs like Yanbal, Avon, and Amway (which market products primarily to women and have a workforce that is 80 percent female) succeed on the basis of existing social networks that can be activated to sell products. In addition to the fact that distributors sell products to and attempt to recruit friends, family members, and acquaintances, relations among distributors are "highly personal" (Biggart 1989) and even "familiarized" (Lan 2002). The assumption that direct selling injects economic content into purely social or familial relations is based on a somewhat artificial distinction between the economic and the social; in many types of cash transactions, "social arrangements both prompt and channel economic activity" (Biggart and Castanias 2001, 471).

PART I

GENDER RELATIONS: WOMEN, MEN, AND WORK

MULTIPLYING THEMSELVES: WOMEN DIRECT SELLERS MANAGING PRODUCTIVE AND REPRODUCTIVE WORK

"This is a business that fits for all those of us who love our children, our husbands, and don't want to neglect that [no queremos descuidar eso]."

"I can spend all the time I want with my children. . . . [This is important because] I am a mother and father to them."
REMARKS FROM TWO DIRECTORS UPON RECEIVING
THEIR FIRST CAR FROM YANBAL

WOMEN'S INFORMAL ECONOMIC ACTIVITIES AND WORK-FAMILY CONFLICTS

A framed poster hangs on the wall in director Ligia García's office in northern Guayaquil. In it, a woman dressed in casual business attire and carrying an orange purse on her shoulder (orange is Yanbal's signature color) strides confidently down a city sidewalk, a broad smile on her face. She appears to be on her way to work. Holding her hand is a young girl of perhaps three, who is photographed mid-jog, her mouth open in what appears to be laughter. The text beneath the photograph reads: "YANBAL is the opportunity to begin the perfect career, for you and your family." This advertisement appeals to many women's wish to earn an income and spend time with their children, and it portrays choosing direct sales as something that a woman does not just for herself but also for the economic and emotional benefit of her family. The woman in the poster embodies this ideal of work-family balance, while also recalling Arlie Hochschild's image of "the woman with the flying hair," the working mother who makes it all look easy (Hochschild 2003 [1989], 2). While other posters and flyers came and went on the bulletin board across the office, this poster always occupied the same spot, a reminder of the promise of direct selling.

The global phenomenon of women's increasing incorporation into paid employment, especially with multinational corporations but also in the informal economy, and the accompanying degradation in working conditions, is often referred to as the "feminization of labor," a term coined by economist Guy Standing (1999). The term "feminization" refers both to the shift of hiring preferences in some industries from male to female workers and to the degradation in pay and working conditions for all workers as jobs come to be seen as women's work. These declines in pay and stability of employment are based on the assumptions that women's work is supplementary or "extra" and that women can depend on a male partner to bring in the lion's share of the family income (Elson 1999; Freeman 2000; Safa 1995).

Just as women in poor countries began to enter the labor force in large numbers, structural adjustment programs (beginning in the 1970s and 1980s) chipped away at existing state-sponsored social support networks, meaning that as women were increasing their paid work, their unpaid work in the home also increased, leading to a variety of household survival strategies (Benería 2003, 119; Lind 2005, 5; Moghadam 2005, 39). Scholars have shown how women in Ecuador have inhabited multiple roles in order to "moderate the effect of the economic crisis" (Pitkin and Bedoya 1997, 47). Class status does not protect women and their families from economic crisis, and both well-off and poor households experience "tension and anguish about making ends meet" (Benería 1992). This chapter considers women's perspectives, struggles, and strategies related to their paid work in direct sales and unpaid work in the home. I argue that, despite assumptions that the flexibility of direct selling allows women to balance income-generating activities with domestic responsibilities (housework and "care work"), many Yanbalistas struggle with the same types of issues that affect women working in the formal economies of wealthy nations. I also found that strategies for dealing with work-family conflicts differ by class, with better-off women able to hire domestic employees to help care for the home and family, and poorer women drawing on social and familial networks.

In the formal economy, women in developing countries tend to work in the service and manufacturing sectors (Benería 2003, 77), and academics have been particularly interested in the working conditions of women employed by multinational corporations in export processing zones (Fernández-Kelly 1983; Freeman 2000; Salzinger 2003). Aside from the excellent work that has been done on women market sellers (Babb 1989; Seligmann 2004), much less is known about the everyday lives of women working in the informal economy. Starting in the 1980s, women have become increasingly involved in informal employment without jettisoning their disproportionate or total responsibility for caring for the home and the family (Benería 2003; ILO 2002; Moghadam 2005, 7). Although direct sales organizations are formal economic institutions at the corporate level, their sales force is officially made up of independent distributors, who purchase goods from the company and resell them, meaning that sellers are not official employees and thus do not receive benefits aside from their earnings. Direct selling and other types of informal work are especially accessible to poor women, "hampered either by low marketable skills . . . or by other obstacles such as lack of mobility and the need to combine work with child care and domestic activities" (Benería 2003, 112). The growth in direct selling is thus related to the increasing "flexibilization" of labor that characterizes capitalist globalization.

While research has been done on "feminized" sectors of the formal economy (such as maquiladoras) and on traditional informal work (such as market vending), direct sales has been understudied relative to its economic impacts in places like Ecuador. Direct sales of cosmetics is a new "feminine" type of informal work, and I am interested in "the ideological construction of jobs and tasks in terms of notions of appropriate femininity, domesticity . . . and cultural stereotypes" (Mohanty 2003, 142). The examination of a single direct sales organization also allows us to test some of Acker's hypotheses (1990) about nonmasculine gendered organizations, specifically her assertion that such organizations would recognize and support workers' responsibilities to their families. Unlike some of the literature on the incorporation of women in developing countries into jobs connected to multinational corporations, I want to show the Ecuadorian women working for this Peru-based company as "agents rather than victims" (Mohanty 2003, 143).

The sizable and significant sociological literature on U.S. working women's attempts to juggle paid work in the labor market with unpaid work in the home emerged largely during the second wave of the feminist movement in the 1960s and 1970s. Such work led to popular books such as Betty Friedan's *The Feminine Mystique* (1963) and landmark works by sociologists, including Paula England, Kathleen Gerson and Jerry Jacobs, Naomi Gerstel, Alice Kessler-Harris, and Arlie Hochschild, most famous for her book *The Second Shift* (1989). Interest in the topic within the academy, primarily by sociologists and scholars of gender, continued into the late 1980s. At that point, U.S. feminist concerns with women's material conditions and disproportionate domestic burdens became somewhat eclipsed by postmodern scholarship, which focused on identity construction and embodiment, and by multicultural feminism, which drew attention to the simultaneous oppressions experienced by poor women and women of color.

Fascinating sociological work continues to be produced on women's (and increasingly, men's) work-family dilemmas, yet nearly all of this research focuses on families in the United States or western Europe. Here I echo Mohanty's critique (2003) of feminist research that takes the "First World," or "One-Third World"[1] (the portion of the world's population that enjoys relative economic stability), as its starting point. While women are certainly working for pay in developing countries, there are few recent sources of information on how they handle work-family conflicts or manage the unpaid work of caregiving, despite studies in the field of international development that explore income distribution in households (Dwyer and Bruce 1988) and women's experience of unemployment and poverty (Herrera 2006a; Moser 1989). The emerging scholarly discussion of women's care work (caring for children and other relatives) also tends to leave out the experiences of women in places like Ecuador and foreground women in industrialized nations (with some notable exceptions: Benería 2008; Folbre 1994).[2] This is true even though in Latin America "increasing female participation in the paid labor market is likely to intensify the pressures felt by families to deal with care work" (Benería 2008, 3). These pressures have been shown to have increased as a result of structural adjustment programs and other neoliberal economic reforms (Pitkin and Bedoya 1997, 34).

These gaps in the literature exist perhaps in part because of the lack of study of everyday life among women working informally both within and outside the "First World." Once the focus is shifted to women's formal and informal income-earning strategies in Ecuador and other poor countries, the questions we can and should ask are different, and the existing terminology becomes less useful. For example, how can we talk about a "second shift" when nearly 60 percent of Latin American women work in the informal sector (ILO 2002), and not in factories or offices where the concepts of "shifts" or separate work and family time exist? In the case of informal work, artificial conceptual boundaries between work done in the "public" sphere and work done in "private" become less relevant.

Some concepts developed by scholars of Latin America and the Caribbean, such as women's "triple burden" (work, home, and community volunteer work) or "triple shift" (formal and informal work plus unpaid domestic work) seem more applicable to the Ecuadorian context, yet they do not always capture the fluidity of women's strategies over time (Freeman 1997; Moser 1989, 1993; Ward 1990). It is important to note Moser's assertion that women's "coping strategies" are affected by the composition of their households, especially the number of income earners, the "stage in the household life-cycle" (i.e., whether there are young children or elderly family members to be cared for), and the number of people, usually women, assisting in reproductive work (1993, 176). Understanding these factors helps explain some of the variety in women's work-family strategies.

DIRECT SELLING: THE PERFECT WOMEN'S WORK?

Academics studying direct selling have often pointed to women's disproportionate membership in the ranks of salespeople, claiming that this type of work is preferable to other job options for women. As can be seen from the epigraphs at the beginning of this chapter, a similar position is taken by many within the world of direct selling. This assessment is based on women's primary responsibility for caring for home and family, regardless of whether they engage in paid work. The following description by sociologist Nicole Biggart is typical:

> Direct selling is infinitely flexible. Distributors sell when they want to, and as much or as little as they need or desire. Many women sell at night when their husbands can care for children, and they value being able to work around pregnancies and illnesses. . . . Being able to care for family needs and work at the same time serves both the material and the emotional needs of women. (1989, 58)

This portrait of direct selling makes some assumptions about the societies in which women live, assumptions that are worth examining. The U.S. women described by Biggart apparently have the freedom to go out at night and work without being looked down upon or endangering themselves, and without being hassled by husbands, who are willing to help out with child care while women are working. This description also assumes that women not only are able to combine paid work and family work but can engage in these two types of activities *simultaneously*. Much of the data I collected on women's direct selling work in Ecuador contradicts these assumptions.

Other scholars state that women are attracted to direct sales because of its low initial investment and low "entry barriers," and some have referred to a subset of these sellers as "trade-offs"—"those [distributors] who adopted the economic activity in question in an attempt to achieve a work-life balance of interests between economic and non-economic objectives" (Brodie, Stanworth, and Wotruba 2002, 68). Direct sales appeals to these women because "much of the activity . . . can be done in the evenings and the administration completed from home" (ibid.). The idea that direct sales is perfect for mothers looking to keep the home functioning while earning an income (which is usually viewed as secondary or supplementary) is not a new one. Biggart (1989) argues that American women began entering the workforce in large numbers in the mid-twentieth century in order to increase the household's ability to consume status-conferring goods and services. In a 1978 study of Tupperware distributors in the United Kingdom, Rex Taylor claimed that "the part-time nature of the work and the fact that most of the parties were held in the evenings, made it possible for many women to combine the job with their domestic responsibilities" (575). Similar claims are made about informal work more generally, with scholars claiming that "informal-sector work . . . often allows women more flexibility in balancing their domestic responsibilities with income-generating activities" (Pitkin and Bedoya 1997, 41–42). The truism that this type of work is perfectly suited to women's needs and schedules seems to be as accepted by researchers as it is by the direct selling companies.

In promotional materials aimed to recruit and train sellers, such as the poster described above, Yanbal emphasizes selling its products as the ideal resolution of the work-family conflict. Some beauty consultants (sellers) and directors featured in promotional videos explain that Yanbal originally appealed to them because it allowed them to spend time with their children. In one video, an actress portraying a consultant says that she loves Yanbal because she can decide her own hours and "that way I don't neglect my son or my family." Real-life Yanbalistas are shown performing housework and serving food to their families. Spouses and children are shown as grateful and supportive, and the image of the traditional family is promoted. For example, while the women who have achieved success as Yanbal directors are shown receiving the keys to cars that they have won, in the videos their husbands are always depicted driving the car. These images are a nod to traditional gender roles and cultural norms that place household work and child care in the domain of the feminine.

Women working as directors and beauty consultants with Yanbal are aware of the image of work-family balance that is used to characterize the work that they do. They also strongly identify with their roles as wives and mothers, which are a source of self-respect and respect from others. As Marjorie González, an upbeat and friendly consultant who was pregnant with her first child when I met her in 2007, told me, "I am a housewife . . . and I am also a sales executive." Betty Brigss Mantilla outlined her priorities and her efforts to keep a balance between the needs of her children and the demands of her job as a Yanbal sales director who manages a group of around forty active consultants. "First, God, [then] me and my children, my family, my home, then the work. I mean, I cannot do the opposite. . . . If they [sellers/directors] have their priorities straight, they can obviously do it, because for reasons of work I cannot neglect my son." Comparing work as a Yanbal consultant with her previous job in an office, Diana Hurel Molina, the mother of two teen daughters, explained the benefits of managing her own time: "In the office, I had to be there from nine until six in the afternoon, that is, all day outside the house. . . . My mother-in-law took care of the girls for me, and I only saw the girls when they woke up, [when] I took them to school, and then again at night." She is now able to spend more time with her daughters, aged fourteen and sixteen.

Although women agree that, in theory, direct selling allows them to balance home and work, the question is how to go about doing it all. When I asked twenty-nine-year-old consultant Érika Martínez García, flanked by the two youngest of her four daughters (aged one to nine), "How do you manage the work with Yanbal, your other job [she sold for another direct sales company], the housework, and the girls?" she responded with a chuckle, "Ah, yes, a lot of people ask me that. . . . How am I able to multiply myself?" I uncovered a wide range of strategies in response to this question and found that while some women felt that they succeeded in balancing their many responsibilities—or did not complain about this balancing act—others admitted to being under a great deal of stress. At least part of this stress resulted from their frustration with themselves for not being able to achieve the ideal work-family balance that Yanbal portrayed as attainable. In their effort to improve material conditions for their families, women had to reconcile their direct selling work with cultural norms of femininity and motherhood that placed the burden of running the household squarely on their shoulders. Dealing with the dilemma of how to multiply oneself can lead to different outcomes, depending on a woman's financial position and family situation, as well as her income-earning activities.

THE TYPICAL DAY

In *The Second Shift*, a groundbreaking work about the efforts of U.S. working women to juggle the demands of paid labor in the workforce and unpaid labor in the home, sociologist Arlie Hochschild was able to learn about this struggle by asking women to describe their typical day (Hochschild 2003 [1989], 289). I decided to use this question in interviews because I was also interested in issues of work and family and because, with the self-directed nature of direct selling work, I was curious about how the women actually structured their days and the types of work activities in which they

Direct seller, wife, and mother Marjorie González holding her youngest child, Gabriel, at her group's holiday party in 2009. (Photo by the author)

engaged. The women's first reaction to the request to describe their typical day was usually one of surprise, as if they thought I couldn't possibly be interested in the ins and outs of their daily routines. Once they saw that I was serious, most described in detail the ways in which they "multiplied" themselves, to use Érika's term.

Consultant Daniela Solís Nevárez lived in one of the nicer houses on a paved street in the poor and working-class neighborhood of El Guasmo

Sur. With her dark skin and tightly curled hair, she would probably be considered black in the United States, although she was referred to as "*morenita*" (literally, "little dark-skinned girl") by those who know her.[3] Because Daniela has a young daughter who is not yet in school, and because her husband has a relatively secure and well-paying job working for a government agency, her days, as she described them, were a bit more leisurely than those of some other consultants:

> Well, I get up at seven in the morning, I make breakfast for my husband, he goes to work and I keep sleeping [*laughs*]. . . . I go back to bed until nine thirty or ten o'clock when my baby wakes up, and then it's time to do things, clean, sweep, put the clothes in the washer, make lunch. In the afternoons sometimes I watch the [Yanbal training] video that they give us— it's a nice video—and then I start to look at the catalog and study it, because sometimes people have questions. . . . I look at that, taking advantage of the fact that my daughter is asleep in the afternoons. . . . After that, I go out in the afternoons. Sometimes I have to go out to collect money [that a client owes] or over there to show a neighbor the catalog.

From this description, we see that Daniela tends to devote the first part of the day to housework and child care, usually working on Yanbal tasks in the afternoon.

Vanessa Paredes Márquez lived in another part of El Guasmo and combined her work for Yanbal with a home-based selling business, caring for her two sons (ages five and two), and full-time studies as a law student at the University of Guayaquil. She claimed to spend around eight hours on Yanbal work each weekday:

> Okay, generally I always wake up at five thirty; I go to the university with the catalog always in my purse. . . . There I have classes, and as we come out of class I start to show the catalog, or to give people their orders, and collect money. . . . If lunchtime catches me out of the house, I eat on the street and continue on from there. I come to visit the Malecón 2000 [a downtown shopping center on the boardwalk overlooking the Guayas River], where I worked before, to visit my clients, [and] I show them the catalog, explain what's on sale, [and] go on like that until I arrive at my house in the [late] afternoon.

Work did not end for Vanessa when she arrived home in the afternoon, as she often tended a small store on the first floor of her mother's home, a business venture in which she was her mother's partner. They sold Yanbal products in addition to imported clothes (some of which Vanessa's mother brought from Venezuela), medicines, and other sundries.[4] When I asked Vanessa if she worked on the weekends too, she said yes: "Saturdays I dedicate to collecting money, just collecting or delivering orders . . . and Sundays I also dedicate myself to collecting and sometimes in between collection visits I go out to visit [clients], with the kids." Vanessa was one of the few consultants I spoke with who occasionally took her children with her to do direct selling work, and she did so only on Sundays, which are thought of as the day dedicated to family in many Guayaquilean homes.

Seller Ramona Delgado is tall for an Ecuadorian woman and looks like a different person when made up to attend a Yanbal meeting rather than relaxing at home. Ramona's children have both grown and migrated to the United States, and she is now raising her four-year-old nephew. As we spoke one hot afternoon at her dining table, over the din of a dozen baby chicks chirping in a box in her kitchen, she described her typical weekday:

> I get up in the morning and straighten up the house. I already know what I have to do. I say [to myself], "Now I am going out." I clear time, and I am going out to use the next two hours or so, two or up to three hours, to see if I am going to work now with Yanbal. . . . I say, "Well, I am going to go out right now before the 'baby' gets out [of school]," because also with him I sometimes can't go around carrying him. . . . [I work] always in the morning, so I grab everything, go out and go make my rounds. . . . I have to be back here before twelve [noon], because he gets out at twelve. . . . Afternoons I spend with him, teaching him how to do his homework.

Like many women raising school-age children, Ramona dedicated the hours that her young nephew is at school to selling Yanbal products and collecting money. Housework and cooking were distributed throughout the day, and afternoons were dedicated to helping the young boy with his homework.

One of the distributors whose work covered the largest territory was Narcisa Pazmiño, who worked around five hours a day as a Yanbal beauty consultant. Narcisa, a short, stout woman, has an infectious energy and a "what you see is what you get" mode of self-presentation. She habitually addresses the women around her as "*amiga*" (friend) or "*ñaña*" (an Ecuadorian term of endearment for sisters). She dedicated the morning to housework or helping her husband in their small store and sometimes traversed the entire city in the afternoons and early evenings, selling Yanbal products:

> [In the morning] I cook, wash [clothes], okay . . . and in the afternoon I go
> out to work. . . . Sometimes I am excited to go out because I work in dif-
> ferent parts [of the city]. One day I dedicate myself to going downtown,
> another day it's my turn to go to the *suburbio* [marginal neighborhoods
> in southwest Guayaquil], okay, and then another day I will go down like
> I was going to El Guasmo, not in El Guasmo, but close to there . . . in La
> Pradera. I have some clients there.

Narcisa described herself as "a little bit free," both because her son was grown[5] and because her husband was supportive of her working and did not mind her being out on the street until nighttime, although she always checked in with him by phone so that he wouldn't worry about her. On weeknights when her son didn't have class, the two men would eat together and leave her a plate so that she could eat when she got home.

Thus the way in which women schedule their days, dividing time be-tween work and family duties, varies, depending on several factors: whether they have school-age children; children's school schedules; whether they have a spouse; spouses' work schedules; whether they engage in other in-come-generating activities; and whether they have help with child care.[6] These are just a few dimensions of the diversity of the Yanbalistas' fami-lies, differences that affect the amount and type of work that they can do, as well as their ability to take part in activities organized by Yanbal or by their directors.

"ES CUESTIÓN DE ORGANIZARSE"/
"IT'S ALL ABOUT ORGANIZING YOURSELF"

When I asked women how they managed to fit so much into their days, working to earn money and also taking care of their homes and families, they often answered with the phrase "It's all about organizing yourself" (Es cuestión de organizarse). This is director Ligia García's response when her consultants "make excuses" (her words) about not selling because of lack of time or other responsibilities. When I asked her how she juggled work and home responsibilities, Quito-based director Jackeline Vivanco ex-plained: "The truth is it's all about organizing yourself. . . . I organize my-self and I am even able to do the one thing while I am also doing the other.

Generally more, I put a little more into my work. Sundays I do keep free for my family." Beyond just telling me about her work-family management, Jackeline was displaying it, as she alternately caressed and shushed her four-year-old son, who had accompanied her to Yanbal's main office in Quito. Although she claimed to prioritize work, except for Sundays, she was attentive to her son and at one point interrupted our interview to take him to the bathroom. Directors claimed to often spend more time working than with their children, and they either lamented this situation or found ways to justify it. Maryuri Palma Pico, a director since 2005, told me: "It is clear that one isn't with the children much, or the house, but they [Yanbal] have also taught us that you have to give them not quantity of time but quality of time." This explanation is reminiscent of the justifications made by working women in the United States when caught in the work-family bind (Hochschild 2003 [1989]).

Other sellers agreed that making it work was an achievable goal if they put their minds to it. Érika Martínez told me, "It's about making a time for everything." When talking about her work with Yanbal, Diana Hurel said that time management was the key to doing well and that the more time a distributor puts in, the more she sells and earns: "It's about time, organization, [and] one has more time for the house, and for oneself." Consultant Érica de la A, who usually did housework and cooking in the morning and went out to sell in the afternoons, said, "I organize myself well, and I haven't had any problems."

When I asked aspiring director Belén Vera Marín her secret to time management, she laughed and said, "I breathe deeply." Her plate was fuller than most, since she was on the path to becoming a director, which required enrolling many new consultants in a short time and making sure that they sold, while keeping up her own sales and attending trainings at least weekly at Yanbal's office in northern Guayaquil, quite a trek from her home in El Guasmo Sur. Belén, a redhead who at twenty-five looked all of eighteen, also had two young sons, ages five and three. In her words, "I organize myself. I mean, the time I have free, I go [out to work], I go out to make the rounds and enroll people or sell, and I have to keep in mind the time that I have to pick up the 'baby' from school." María Bustamante is a good-natured and friendly woman who is a daughter consultant of Belén's, with a mischievous sense of humor and a tendency to be the class clown in meetings; she lives right around the corner from Belén and near several other consultants in the same group. María tended to devote mornings to housework and cooking, except on Wednesday mornings when she took her order to her director's home office, about a ten-minute walk away. Perhaps because she only had one child, a high school student, living at home, she didn't claim to have difficulty managing her home and the work with Yanbal, telling me, "It's easy" (Es facilito). Single mother and Yanbal director Betty Brigss saw the ability to balance family and work responsibilities as something uniquely feminine:

> Where do I get the time to be able to contribute? I am mother and father to my children, but my children are not out on the street because of that; they are not bad kids, right? I can do it; I can make the child be a good boy who goes to school, who has family values. So women—we women have that capacity. Men don't.

While some women attempted to fit Hochschild's definition of a "super-woman" (2003 [1989], 25), trying to do everything themselves, many had a support network that made it possible for them to keep up with the housework, child care, and direct selling.[7] Although her youngest child is now nineteen, director Marjorie López (Ligia's sister-in-law and a whiz at recruiting because of her willingness to travel to distant towns and knock on more doors than the next director) remembers beginning her career in Yanbal when her children were young. Smiling as she spoke, she recalled her early days with the organization:

> I lived with my mom, so that made it very easy for me. Because my children—I came home and they had already eaten. Ah, [and] I have a sister who is a teacher, so she helped me a lot with the kids' homework. And they were set, the kids had eaten and their homework was done. So I always went around working, knowing that they were well cared for, full [i.e., fed], and with their studies and everything okay.

By the time Marjorie moved to Babahoyo, the capital of the province she lived in before moving to Guayaquil, she was earning enough to pay for a domestic employee to be with her four children in the morning, so that she was able to work during those hours and care for the children in the afternoon. The children were also older then, and Marjorie remembers that "the bigger ones took care of the smaller ones and that made the work easier."

Consultant Gioconda Ibarra Ruiz is a soft-spoken, heavyset woman who almost always wears her hair pulled back into a ponytail. She lives in a humble neighborhood in Durán, a satellite city just outside Guayaquil, and has help with the housework from her thirteen-year-old stepson:

The boy helps me out a lot also. Sometimes he straightens up the house, he washes the dishes for me, whatever. . . . I also have to check his homework sometimes, [and] I tell him, "While I check this, you go wash the dishes for me," and that's how we coordinate. Or if I go out, he knows that he has to sweep the house for me or something else, because sometimes, sometimes I am not able to leave everything neat; and I will always tell you, I am not a superwoman, I tell you.

Interestingly, she described his housework as being done "for her," implying that he was doing tasks in her place or tasks that were really hers. Nevertheless, she recognized that his cooperation allowed her to get work done, and she adamantly declared that she was not a "superwoman," because she needed this help. Narcisa Pazmiño also told me that her husband or twenty-year-old son would sometimes cook dinner if she was out late and that this freed her up to squeeze the maximum amount of work into each afternoon.

Gioconda and Narcisa spent much time talking about the helpful males in their families because they were aware of the uniqueness of their situations. More often than not, it is other women who pick up the slack when work and family collide;[8] when a woman is out working at selling Yanbal, it is usually mothers, mothers-in-law, aunts, older daughters, or female neighbors who fill the gaps.[9] This is especially true of child care, as can be seen in the story of Marjorie López, whose mother and sister helped her with her small children years ago. In a recent example, Vanessa Paredes had a substantial network that could be drawn on to care for her two young sons when she was working or studying; her mother always lived with the family or nearby, her in-laws lived just up the block, and she could even leave her children with neighbors if the need arose. Not surprisingly, the most common person distributors turned to with their child care needs was their mother; the second-most preferred caregiver was the mother-in-law. These are the patterns seen throughout Latin America, even when it comes to leaving children behind when parents emigrate (Dreby 2006; Hondagneu-Sotelo and Ávila 1997). Other help came from sisters or daughters. Directors who could afford it hired a domestic employee to help with both housework and children.[10]

These support networks can sometimes be precarious or easily interrupted. Marjorie González continued to work about half-time once her first son was born, leaving him in the care of her husband's niece in the mornings. But when the niece became pregnant herself and was confined to bed at her doctor's recommendation, Marjorie's child care arrangement ceased.

Previously one of the most successful consultants in her group, Marjorie told me that she had basically stopped working because of this development. Most of her clients were office workers, and when she attempted to visit them with the baby in tow, he would "start up with his crying concert" and she would leave, embarrassed and frustrated. This anecdote illustrates the conditional nature of female support networks. Since women have their own domestic responsibilities and are often mothers themselves—as in the case of Marjorie's niece—any change in their own health or home life can affect their ability to help relatives and friends care for their families and homes.

As can be seen from the descriptions above, women downplay the tremendous amount of work that they do in order to maintain the household, raise children, and engage in paid work, including selling Yanbal products. They claim that it all boils down to being "organized." The emphasis on organization could be seen as self-serving, as if the women were claiming that their superior organizational skills were allowing them to engage in paid and unpaid work and comply with their domestic obligations, but I do not think this is the case. Saying that it can be done if one is organized shuts down any critique of the disproportionate burdens placed on women due to gender inequality and cultural norms that make women responsible for the home and children. If the balancing act were perceived as impossible, women would be more willing to criticize men's lack of involvement in housework and child care (only three women claimed to have husbands who helped significantly with housework or child care). But since it is framed as something that anyone can do if she can just make a schedule, organize, and "multiply" herself, the only excuse for not making it work is that she is not trying or is not organized enough.

The beneficiaries of this ideology are men, who, with the exception of some more collaborative partners like Narcisa's husband, did not take part in the daily work of the household or in the day-to-day raising of children. This pattern of lack of participation in domestic affairs holds true whether or not the men are engaged in stable, full-time employment. The importance of men's reactions to women's work, and the range of stances they take in relation to their wives' income-generating activities, are explored in greater detail in the next chapter.

When asked why they thought Yanbal allowed only women to sell its products, several women used reasoning based on gender-segregated responsibilities and gender stereotypes. Some women believe that their role in managing the household translates into an aptitude for business and success in direct sales. According to Betty, Yanbal wants women to sell because "we women have the ability to do many things, without neglecting others. . . . For example, we can work without neglecting our children. . . . The Yanbalistas . . . have to be organized to do that." Gioconda agreed that women were the ideal choice: "We are better administrators in the home [than men]. . . . The owner of the company . . . thinks of women, because we know better how to administer the business, [and] we know how to administer money." She went on to give an example: "Sometimes, our husbands give us just five dollars, and we have to work wonders with that. Many times it's happened to me that with one dollar I have to make lunch and dinner . . . but you know that no one can eat with one dollar." Although women's disproportionate burdens in the home make it difficult to engage in paid work, there is the sense that some women "take pride in their ability to perform miracles with the family income" (Pitkin and Bedoya 1997, 41).

Sara Murillo Balladares, a pretty and talkative young mother of a two-year-old, who was a university student as well as a Yanbal consultant, claimed that God made women to be in charge of the home, adding, "Women have always known how to administer the home, and in this case, what is the home? It would have to be the Yanbal company." Despite this positive spin, Sara had renounced her position as a director because of conflicts with her husband over housework and child care issues and was working as a regular consultant at the time we met (she later stopped selling altogether and then returned to full-time employment with direct selling on the side; her story is discussed more fully in chapter 3). In this way, women did not view work and home as opposed or mutually exclusive spheres, but thought that their skills in multitasking and running the household were assets to them as they moved into the direct selling business, assets that were recognized as such by the architects of the Yanbal corporation.[11]

WORK-FAMILY IMBALANCE

For all the talk about organizing oneself and managing everything, several women were willing to talk about their anxiety, conflict, and stress over the difficulty of juggling their multiple roles as wives, mothers, workers, and, sometimes, students. These issues become intensified as women move up the Yanbal sales ranks, spending more time working and planning and attending scheduled events. When I met Carmen Carrillo in Quito in late October 2007, she was working as a Yanbal sales director while studying law full-time and raising three children. At the time we spoke, she was working on an internship-based thesis, the last step needed to graduate from law school. She told me: "My children are now complaining to me a lot [*Me están reclamando mucho*], because since I have to do the internship in order to graduate, I have been abandoning my children a bit lately." Each weekday, Carmen got up at five in the morning, fed her children breakfast and had them on their way to school by six. Then, before leaving the house around eight, she had to have their lunch prepared so that they would be able to eat when they came home. Her sister helped out by picking up the kids from school, feeding them lunch, and helping with their homework. Between her internship activities and her work with Yanbal, Carmen did not get home until eight or nine o'clock at night. She seemed stressed not only by her schedule but also by her children's complaints that she was not around enough.

Two years ago, Betty Brigss was running her Yanbal group out of a small room in her mother director's dental office, across the street from the Policentro shopping mall in northern Guayaquil. Around that time, her husband migrated to Spain to look for work, leaving her with the choice of following him to Europe (and potentially leaving their children behind) or becoming a de facto single mother. After spending some time in Spain, she decided against emigrating for good, and "because of mother's love" (*por el amor de mamá*), she decided to move her office into the ground floor of her home in the northern neighborhood of El Cóndor. She had bought the lot some years back, splitting the cost with her sister, and once she had completed the first floor of the house she was able to move her family from the *suburbio* in southwest Guayaquil, where she had been raised, into this more middle-class area. She lived in one part of the house with her three children—two boys and a girl, aged eight to thirteen. In an attached apartment lived her mother, Mercedes Mantilla Aguirre, and Betty's younger brother, whom everyone called El Chino. Betty's choice to work from home was due to her concern that her children needed her around more now that their father was gone. She felt that she should be there to "control" her children and make sure they were doing what they needed to do. Her mother, whom Betty refers to as her "strategic partner,"[12] began to take over the "street work" of the Yanbal group, such as going to the bank or meeting with consultants at their homes.

Although the intention of creating a home office was to be close to her children, Betty acknowledged that it was sometimes stressful having them around while she was trying to work. She took advantage of the morning hours when all three were in classes, but as soon as lunchtime rolled around and they started coming home, she had to "multiply" herself in order to act as both mother and Yanbal director. As each of her children entered, she asked them about their day at school, inquiring after any test results and ascertaining what their homework was for the day. The children's grandmother Mercedes made sure that they ate (she also did the cooking, which Betty claimed she disliked doing and was not good at), with no excuses accepted for not eating the soup that customarily precedes the lunch entrée in Ecuadorian homes. Between taking orders and talking with consultants in person or on the phone, Betty commanded the children to shower and dress and start their homework, and to turn off the television. Once homework was begun, she was interrupted periodically by her curious and precocious younger children with questions about this or that assignment. I even found myself recruited to check English homework one afternoon while at Betty's home office.

Ligia García, who is Betty's "grandmother" director, always advises against directors setting up their office in their homes, because she claims that the children distract the women from the work and that the work finds its way into what should be intimate family time. She spoke from her own experience of intrusive evening telephone calls from consultants and her husband's annoyance when women who were strangers to him dropped by the house unannounced.[13] Betty understood this perspective, but since she was "both mother and father" to her children, she opted for a different plan. When the second floor of her home was finished (it was under construction during my first visit), she moved the family upstairs. The office has now been physically separated from the living quarters on the first floor, which have been rented out to bring in some extra money. Whether or not the kids will stay upstairs to do their homework under this new arrangement remains uncertain.

AT WIT'S END: ANA MARÍA'S STORY

At the time of our first interview, Ana María Briones was a married woman of forty with three daughters, aged eight, seven, and five. She actively participated in the meetings and trainings organized by Ligia and her daughter directors; Anita, as she is called, is one of Ligia's granddaughter directors. She has an energetic and professional presence and could always be seen wearing Yanbal products and, often, a shirt with the Yanbal logo. She has cinnamon-colored skin and, when I met her in 2007, wore her brown hair cut in a bob; her middle-class status was evidenced by the braces on her teeth. Ana María had left a lucrative job as a corporate accountant just the year before, because the schedule was too taxing and she felt that she didn't see her children enough. She saw Yanbal as the solution to this problem, an avenue for earning good money and still being able to spend time with her daughters.

Yet, one year into her new career with Yanbal, she was feeling disillusioned. Her earnings were not what she had hoped, and she felt torn between caring for her daughters and putting in the time she saw as necessary to be a successful sales director. She wanted her group to grow and sell more, but she said, "I am noticing a lot of conflicts over my time, with my three daughters. I have to pick them up from school, I have to cook, I have to do everything in the home." I interviewed Anita one afternoon after a meeting at Ligia's office, and she complained about her lack of child care for her daughters, saying, "Right now they are home alone, because I don't have anyone to leave them with." For that upcoming Saturday she had originally planned an activity with her consultants, but then her daughter told her that she would be performing in a school program. Ana María had canceled the planned Yanbal event in order to be able to attend her daughter's presentation; she said that this kind of conflict was typical and that she felt that she had to choose her daughters over her work.

Ana María described her husband, a mechanical engineer, as being "*machista*" and overdemanding, saying that he complained if there wasn't enough money coming in but also if she was not home enough. "So what do I do?" she asked rhetorically. "I can't do this anymore. I am a normal, common woman, and he was making me crazy." In an argument with her husband, Ana María pointed to his failure to embody the ideal male provider role, saying, "If you don't like it [my working], then support me [financially]." This cooled things off, if only for a while. If she could just afford a domestic employee to help with the housework, Anita thought, she could dedicate time to growing her Yanbal business and handle much of the child care as well. As things stood, she said, "I can't do it, so I have an imbalance."

Part of the conflict that Anita experienced came from her image of herself as a person of middle-class standing. When she first began to work with Yanbal, she felt able to balance work and family because she had a domestic employee to help with housework and child care. But things soured when the household income dropped (because of her job change and her husband's mounting debts), and she "lost" the employee as a result.[14] Anita marveled at the success of other Yanbalistas she characterized as "uncultured" and uneducated and said that they were able and willing to work in a way that she was not: "They don't care if it's sunny, if it's hot, maybe if the kids stay home alone—they [still] go out [to work]." Aversion to walking around outside in the hot sun is the privilege of people who can afford to work indoors or not work at all; such preferences are also connected to ideas about the desirability of light skin and its link to high social class.[15] Although almost no one in my sample claimed to leave children home alone, perhaps Ana María assumed that this is what lower-class women do. In my experience, women in poor neighborhoods have a social network whose members provide them free child care within relationships based on solidarity and reciprocation. Perhaps middle-class women like Ana María do not have such tight social or familial networks, or perhaps her situation in this regard was unique. Yanbal appealed to women, she said, because they were oppressed in society and forced to act as "domestic employees," something that she saw as demeaning. Of course, only middle- and upper-class women are able to pay someone to take over these domestic tasks, so this comment also shows her relative privilege.

Stories like Ana María's show the cracks in the monolithic argument that balancing work and home is just about being organized. In her work with Yanbal and its concomitant frustrations, she had found that "it is not enough to be organized, to be a good administrator, to manage the finances." She hoped that the difficulties she was facing were due to her being relatively new to Yanbal. But the myth of easy living and working through being organized hung over her head: "I try to organize my time, but I think that, as with every beginning, when you start off, you have to work hard at everything." She said she would like to be in the position she saw her grandmother director Ligia as having; with daughter and granddaughter directors working, Ligia was earning well and was able to prioritize family and travel and relax a bit. Of course, Ligia works at least as many hours as most professionals, if not more hours, and her children are grown, which means that they can take care of themselves in a way that Anita's young daughters cannot.

Ana María's experience shows that Yanbal and, by extension, other DSOs, may not be as family-friendly as they are portrayed in their promotional materials or in the academic literature. As directors, women are expected to take part in meetings and trainings delivered by Yanbal corporate staff and to organize and attend similar activities for their consultants. This can be stressful and can add to the time crunch experienced by mothers of young children, like Ana María. She describes the demands on her time:

> Sometimes what I don't like about Yanbal [is that] there are too many meetings, too many. I see how it's like the time disappears, though they originally told us, "This is a business where you all will be able to manage your time." But after a while it's like the meetings are managing us

[*nos manejan*], because if I showed you my calendar, it is full, and today I filled it out and I said, "My God! And where's the time for my daughters? Where's the time for the family?" So I can't do it, I always have to sacrifice something, and so there have been times when it's happened to me that I don't come to the meeting and then they say, "Anita didn't come." . . . But maybe [it happened that] I had to take my daughter to the dentist, that I have to take her to the doctor, that my daughter said to me, "*Mamita*, don't go," and I stay with her.

Ana María frequently found herself in a position that obligated her to choose between paid work as a Yanbal director and unpaid work as primary caregiver to her children.

There are surely other women working with Yanbal, or in other types of jobs, in situations similar to Ana María's. This detailed analysis of her case is useful because it highlights the conflicts that many women find in their attempts to balance their need to earn an income and their cultural and social role as housekeepers and caregivers. As I discuss in the next chapter, and as this case shows, husbands can often exacerbate rather than ease this conflict. As for Anita, when I left the field in January 2008, she had not found a way to resolve the imbalance and stress in her life and did not see any hope for doing so in the near future. Referring to the "psychological chaos that I live every day," she said, "I don't know how many women it is happening to, but it is happening to me and I have not found the way out. I want to now, but I don't find it." In this reflection, Ana María exercised what American sociologist C. Wright Mills (2000 [1959]) called "the sociological imagination," generalizing from her personal troubles to the larger struggles of women as a group.

When I returned to follow up with the participants in this study in May and June 2008, I found Ana María a changed woman. She had cut her hair short, removed her braces, and was wearing more business suits and more glamorous makeup. 'I am working so much more now,' she told me after a meeting Ligia held to recognize the achievements of directors in her network. When we were able to sit down and chat in private, I asked Anita about the situation with her husband. Two major developments had led to an improvement in their relationship and her renewed dedication to her work with Yanbal. She explained that their frequent arguments had culminated in a weekend-long "discussion" during which she threatened divorce. Once she mentioned divorce as an option, her husband apologized for his behavior and promised to try to be less critical and more supportive. Shortly after this climax and fresh start, Ana María's husband lost his job, which threw him into a depression for about a month. He eventually decided to go into business for himself, selling insurance, which meant that now both partners would have flexible schedules. He started dropping off and picking up the three girls from school in the mornings, allowing Anita to dedicate weekday mornings to Yanbal. When she decided to expand her group outside of Guayaquil, recruiting and training consultants in other cities and provinces, he agreed to pick up the slack, caring for the children on the two weekends a month that she traveled.

Anita was feeling more positive about her ability to balance work and family as a result of these changes, and she said that once she and her husband hired a domestic employee, which they planned to do in the coming months, she would be able to work harder and grow her group faster. As we will see in the next chapter, men often have a change of heart regarding their wives' work if they themselves hit a period of unemployment or income instability. In this case, the combination of the husband's job loss and Anita's demand for change within the home caused him to rethink his earlier positions and to work on being more supportive.

The next chapter of Ana María's story is still being written. When I saw her in December 2009, she told me that her out-of-town travel, which her husband's willingness to watch the children had made possible, had been cut back significantly, and she complained that her husband would never really change, since he was "one of those men who doesn't like the woman to stand out [*destacarse*]." It seemed that although he valued her financial contributions more than in the past, he was still not fully supportive of her career goals within direct sales. So, although Ana María's situation had improved from when I first met her, her struggle to balance work and family commitments within the existing relations of gender inequality within her home was ongoing.

CONCLUSION

The material conditions of most Ecuadorian women's lives require them to work to help support the household, but this demand for income must be reconciled with cultural norms of gender that make women solely responsible for domestic tasks. In getting to know women working as Yanbal beauty consultants and sales directors, I was able to move beyond the idealized assumptions in both the promotional and academic literature about direct selling's ability to resolve women's work-family conflicts. Women are aware of this discourse and, because of the hopefulness that it represents, struggle to embody the perfect balance between work that is potentially financially rewarding and work that is unpaid but emotionally and socially rewarding.

Directors, despite their own personal difficulties in juggling work and family, continue to paint this idealized portrait of direct selling in their interactions with consultants and potential sellers.

This chapter argues that despite being a "gendered organization" (Acker 1990) that is feminine, the direct selling organization generally does not support women in their attempts to balance work and family responsibilities. It is not clear that Yanbal or other DSOs go beyond lip service to the importance of women's care work in the home. While Yanbal presents itself as offering mothers the perfect kind of job for their lifestyle, the activities involved are not necessarily family-friendly. For example, women are not allowed to take minor children into meetings or trainings held at Yanbal's two Guayaquil offices, a policy that many directors attempt to impose on their group activities as well (with varying degrees of success). Consultant María Bustamante, knowing of my relationship with Ligia, who hosted the monthly campaign launches for several groups within her family network, asked me to try to influence Ligia on the issue of child care during meetings. 'We girls [the consultants] could even rotate and take turns watching the kids in whatever space was available,' María told me. Although María did not have young children herself, her daughter consultant had never attended a meeting because of the lack of child care. When María brought up the issue with her mother director as the three of us chatted one afternoon, she did not encounter much sympathy. 'It's only once a month,' the director said. 'The women need to make time and make arrangements to be able to attend the meeting.'

The assumption is that arranging for child care is a possibility for each woman and is each woman's own personal responsibility. As shown in the stories presented in this chapter, however, access to child care varies, depending on a woman's economic resources and social networks. Although the work of selling and of running a group is largely unstructured and self-directed, almost none of the women I met actually had children with them while they worked, as Biggart implied American direct sellers did. When children were present, they were often viewed as a nuisance: Ramona didn't want to have to carry her nephew when she was working and he got tired of walking, so she went out to sell when he was in school; and Betty's children were routinely kicked out of the office so their mother could work (and I noticed that they had to remain in the back of the house during her group's Christmas party). So work and family responsibilities are not usually combined in the same time period; rather, women find ways to carve out a bit of time for each task that they need to do. The typical days described by the women give us an idea of how they manage their time.

Although women must work hard to find a time for everything and earn an income while not "neglecting" home and family duties, they tend to downplay this accomplishment and the challenges they face. If you ask them, they say, "It's all about organizing yourself." Self-discipline and a consciously planned schedule are seen as the keys to getting both productive and reproductive work done. Most women have help in their endeavor, especially with child care, usually from female relatives. The myth of being "organized" not only leads women away from questioning gender inequality and their disproportionate burden in the domestic sphere but also hides the real ways in which women help each other fulfill their social and economic roles. Behind every successful Yanbalista is a strong woman (or a team of women) helping make sure that lunch gets cooked and the kids get their homework done. In poor families, this woman is usually a relative; in well-off families, a domestic employee is paid to step in.[16]

Despite being "organized" and devising what I call *gendered economic strategies* that take into account both material conditions and gender norms, some Yanbalistas find themselves in active situations of conflict in their homes, the recipients of hostility from spouses, children, or both. The demands of direct selling work grow as a woman moves up the ranks, so directors are often the ones to feel the work-family squeeze most acutely. Although Ana María was unusually candid and open about her struggle to balance paid work and unpaid work, many other women experience similar difficulties. Part of Ana María's stress arose because her daughters were young and needed to be cared for all the time; these situations are not encountered to the same degree by women whose children are grown. Women with more resources are able to hire someone to care for their children in the family home, in a sense partially buying their way out of the cultural obligation of child care. Still, the anxiety caused by the family's need for a woman's income, coupled with her sole responsibility for housework and child care, must be taken seriously and viewed within the larger context of the lack of adequate employment and the ideologies of devoted motherhood in contemporary Ecuador.

In her study of one low-income Guayaquil neighborhood, Moser (1993) identified three groups of women, distinguished by their level of ability to cope with economic crisis. Women were either "coping" (with the help of male partners and female relatives), "burnt out" (unable to balance their multiple roles), or "hanging on" (defined as "under pressure but still trying to balance"); most of the women in my study, as in Moser's, fell into this last group (Moser 1993, 194–195). However, it is important to recognize that in the precarious balance between work and home responsibilities, women's feelings toward each of these "jobs," and their strategies for coping with their double (or triple) burdens, can change over time.

In some instances, such changes result from alterations in their support networks, as when Marjorie's niece could no longer care for her infant son and Marjorie had to drastically cut her working hours. More commonly, these changes come about because of changes in the relationships between women and their male partners. For example, Ana María was able to focus more energy on her work with Yanbal once her husband became willing to try out a different attitude and once he became aware of his own economic vulnerability upon losing his stable job in the formal economy.

In another case, Betty's husband returned from Spain for a visit in February 2008, when they "renewed their relationship," as she put it. She decided to try to make her group larger and more stable in order to hand it over to her mother and migrate with her children to Spain to reunite the family. When originally given the choice between a family unit that included her husband and her career with Yanbal, she chose the latter. When given the same choice a few years later, she was leaning toward sacrificing her job to be with her husband. But, she noted, with a twinkle in her eye, 'Yanbal is in Spain now, so after I get my work papers, I could start again and have my own group over there.' By 2009, she had decided to remain separated from her husband and continue living in Guayaquil, working as a Yanbal director.

The consistent demands of traditional gender roles, combined with the shifting conditions of economic life and the shifting emotional relationships between men and women, are the backdrop for decisions about work and family that are constantly being amended or renegotiated. As employment in both "developed" and "developing" countries becomes increasingly flexible and precarious and comes to involve more and more mothers of young children, gender scholars must find ways of making the experience of working mothers in the global South talk (or talk back) to theories of work-family conflict that emerge from and apply to the United States and Europe. In the different cases, different ideologies and practices of motherhood exist, and women are incorporated into the paid (formal and/or informal) labor force in different ways.

We must consider the applicability of Latin American theories of gender to the Yanbalistas' situations. For example, in her work on the Dominican Republic, Duarte (1989) claims that women are often able to escape the full burden of the "double day" (paid work plus domestic work) through class-based strategies. Indeed, I found that when it came to child care, as in Duarte's study, women with fewer resources relied on social and kin networks and those who could afford it hired a domestic employee. Yet this model does not fit perfectly, since (1) even women who rely on these strategies experience stress, guilt, and conflict related to the difficulty of achieving work-home balance, and (2) some women are stuck in the middle, with neither strategy being a viable option (they have no support network and no money to hire a domestic worker). Still, it is rare to see studies of work-family issues in occupations that involve women of a variety of class backgrounds, and direct sales, with its cross-class appeal, allows us to see these class-based strategies among women who do the same job yet have access to different resources.

As this chapter has shown, men are somewhat invisible yet important actors in working women's lives. Their attitudes, employment situations, and behaviors can have a marked impact on women's job choices and even on their mental health. In some cases, the spouses' gendered economic strategies complemented each other, whereas in other cases they diverged or clashed. The next chapter explores the most common stances of Yanbalistas' male partners toward their wives' work and shows how the men's engagement with direct sales can be a determining factor in the women's quality of life.

NOTES

1. The terms "One-Third World" and "Two-Thirds World" were introduced by Esteva and Prakash (1998), and the relative usefulness of these neologisms is discussed in detail by Mohanty (2003, chap. 9). While I find this new vocabulary a bit unwieldy, it does seem preferable in some ways to the alternatives, especially in highlighting that the majority of the world's population lives in "developing" countries.

2. For an overview of this emerging body of literature, see England (2005).

3. In Guayaquil it is generally offensive to call someone "black" (*negro/a* or *moreno/a*) to their face, regardless of their skin color or features. The use of the diminutive, as in *morenita*, takes some of the sting out of this pseudoracial classification and can make such a label into a term of endearment.

4. Yanbal consultants are not prohibited from selling other items or even selling for other DSOs. Only when a consultant becomes a sales director does she sign a contract promising not to promote products from other DSOs.

5. As Loscocco found in interviews with self-employed parents in the United States, "the ideal work-family balance" can sometimes result from "calculated synchronization of business and family stage"; those with grown children experience less conflict between work and home responsibilities (1997, 220). Moser also noted that the "stage in the household life-cycle" affected Guayaquilean women's strategies for coping with economic crisis (1993, 176).

6. Pitkin and Bedoya (1997, 34) found that poor women in Quito considered a similar set of circumstances as they organized their daily tasks.

7. For a discussion of the importance of familial support networks among the urban poor in Quito, see Pitkin and Bedoya (1997).

8. Here we see a difference from Biggart's description (1989) of direct sellers at the beginning of this chapter; Ecuadorian husbands are less likely than U.S. ones to help

with child care or housework or to accept being served prepared foods instead of home-cooked meals.

9. My having a young child with me during my research was a source of rapport and common topic of conversation with the mothers who sold Yanbal. Most of them asked me who watched my four-year-old son while I was working, and when I told them that my husband's aunt cared for him, their positive reaction showed that this was a socially acceptable and appropriate choice. If I had left Joaquín behind in the United States, I would not have been viewed favorably, but leaving him home with a female family member every day was within the bounds of good mothering. (See Mose Brown and Casanova 2009 for a discussion of the role of motherhood in researcher-subject relationships.)

10. None of the mothers of young children whom I interviewed employed domestic workers at the time of the study; at least three women whose children were older (high school age or above) employed domestic workers. I also knew of several sales directors not interviewed who had hired domestic help. I did not specifically ask questions about domestic workers: they either were mentioned spontaneously or I observed them directly.

11. Interestingly, women participating in Carla Freeman's study of Barbadian data entry workers (many of whom were also involved in informal sector work) also subscribed to the myth of self-organization. Freeman quoted one of her informants as saying: "'If you plan your life well . . . then it should be easy' to work and be a mother too" (2000, 132).

12. This term is taken from Yanbal's training materials and is part of the organizational lingo; it is usually, though not exclusively, used to refer to husbands of consultants or directors.

13. See Loscocco (1997, 209) for accounts of how self-employed men and women in the United States attempted to keep work and family separate.

14. In the case of Mexico, Benería and Floro identified the "reduction in [paid] domestic work" as one way of dealing with economic crisis by cutting expenses, noting the "subsequent perception of isolation, loss of social status, and downward social mobility" among middle-class women (1992, 96).

15. One of Freeman's Barbadian informants also invoked work performed in the sun (on sugar plantations) as low-class or low-status work (2000, 113). The term "cultured" is a loaded term here, since Andean hierarchies of race and class often operate in daily life as a "scale of inferiority and superiority that depends heavily on an assessment of whether one is 'cultured'" (Seligmann 2004, 149).

16. As Benería (2008) has pointed out, the "cushion" of the "still-abundant supply" of domestic employees keeps middle- and upper-class women in developing countries from experiencing the severe work-home conflicts common in wealthier countries. My findings show that whether or not a domestic worker is employed in the home, women experience stress connected to managing their work and family roles.

CHAPTER 2

MEN MAKE A DIFFERENCE:
OPPOSERS, SUPPORTERS, AND DRIVERS

WHY TALK ABOUT MEN?

One Saturday afternoon in December 2007, I found myself sending excited text messages to friends in the United States, saying that I had just met a man who sold Yanbal. I playfully referred to him as "Mr. Yanbal" because of his enthusiastic involvement in the company and his willingness to literally "put on the Yanbal T-shirt" (a metaphor used by Ecuadorian Yanbalistas to describe people dedicated to the company and their work). Before meeting this male seller, I had debated the usefulness of researching male direct sellers; could such unusual outliers tell me anything new about this economic activity? Over the course of my fieldwork, however, I realized that men were involved in the DSO indirectly and directly at many levels, and to tell the women's stories in isolation would mean that this involvement would remain invisible.

Part of what attracted me to study the direct selling of cosmetics, and Yanbal in particular, was the gendered character of the direct selling organization, which has been noted by scholars of direct sales in the United States and elsewhere (Biggart 1989; Vincent 2003; A. Wilson 2004). On the surface, this model of commercial capitalism involves women selling products designed for women, to women. The DSO thus seems to be a "gendered organization" (Acker 1990) that may, by virtue of its predominantly female participants, depart from the masculine prototype of the capitalist firm. The assumption that this is a social and economic activity by and for women may be part of the reason that this type of work and consumption are invisible in most national-level statistics and ignored by many social scientists. In studies of "feminine" DSOs, men are not usually seen as participants in this social world.

This chapter goes beyond such first impressions and omissions to show how men are involved in the DSO both as consumers and sellers, and how men's view of direct selling can affect their wives' livelihoods and work conditions. Ultimately, I examine the roots and contexts of this involvement and the resulting implications for gender relations at the micro level. In men's stances toward and engagement in direct selling of cosmetics and other personal care products, cultural norms of gender shape their decisions and interactions with female partners, but in ways that are moderated by the context of material conditions (including elusive employment), resulting in specific types of gendered economic strategies. This examination of the effects of men's attitudes toward and/or participation in their wives' direct selling contributes further to understanding women's work-family conflicts, because although "there have been many studies of work spillover into family life, there have been far fewer studies of the ways that family influences work" (Loscocco 1997, 206).

Regardless of their relationship to sellers, men are involved with Yanbal as consumers. As is evident in the Yanbal catalog content (discussed further in chapter 3) not all of the company's products are geared to women. The general manager of Yanbal Ecuador himself admitted to me in an interview that just over half of the clients are men, according to the company's internal marketing reports. Men are increasingly targeted by the company as consumers of fragrances, personal care products, and even women's and children's products that can be given as gifts. There is no question that men are buying Yanbal products, and many of the consultants I know say that the gender composition of their clientele is approximately fifty-fifty, with equal numbers of men and women buying. Men are also involved in selling, both directly and indirectly.

Most of the Yanbalistas I met in Guayaquil were either legally married or referred to themselves as *unidas*, meaning that they were in long-term, live-in relationships similar to what would be called common-law marriages in the United States. So most consultants and directors are part of a household in which a man shares in the decisions and contributes economically. Domestic relations matter not just because of their effect on how and when women can work but also because of the gender inequality that is built into the family structure (Benería 2003; Dwyer and Bruce 1988; Herrera 2006a; Salzinger 2003). According to one recent study, approximately 43 percent of Ecuadorian women living in urban poor neighborhoods say that they need their spouse's permission to work outside the home (Benería and Floro 2006, 164).[1] Women are often responsible for balancing the family budget, whether or not they are in the paid labor force, and information about and access to their husband's income can affect the financial outcomes of households (Dwyer and Bruce 1988; Safa 1995).

Women's work becomes more important as employment for Ecuadorian men becomes less stable (a trend seen in many developing nations). In 2004 an estimated 63 percent of Ecuadorian men were unemployed or underemployed (Herrera 2006b, 205). A total of 87 percent of Guayaquil residents are classified as living in poverty, and unemployment rates in many neighborhoods are routinely in the double digits (Floro and Messier 2006, 234; INEC 2007). The deterioration in both men's and women's formal employment means that, despite the culturally prized man-as-provider ideal (Safa 1995), men and women—and sometimes their children or other kin—must often work together to maintain the household (Pitkin and Bedoya 1997, 40). Many men have not accepted this state of affairs, however, and oppose their wives' efforts to earn an income working outside the home. Among Yanbalistas, these "difficult" husbands are infamous, and even those women who are fortunate enough to have "supportive" partners know of peers who experience conflict in the home as a result of their work with Yanbal. In general, the company remains silent on the question of how women can avoid such conflict and manage tensions with spouses. However, the narrative of husbands transforming from enemies of women's work to cheerleaders is a common one, emanating from both official company sources and women's experiences.

When I was conceiving of this research project, and even in my first couple of weeks in the field, I believed in the accuracy of the image of women selling to women in direct sales. I then came to find out that men sell Yanbal products, although the company does not allow men to be official distributors. Men's desire to sell demonstrates that although the company's recruiting pitch is to women, men are convinced that there is money to be made through Yanbal. The willingness of some men[2] to engage in a type of work that is seen as "feminine" and associated with women shows the direness of men's employment situation (cf. Agadjanian 2002; Seligmann 2004, 57). In Ecuador, men are accustomed to having the first choice of jobs. When confronted with a seemingly lucrative opportunity that is designated for women, some men simply ignore this restriction and move into the field.[3] While some social scientists have found that men move up the ranks faster in formal jobs that are seen as feminine (Williams 1995), advancement in direct sales is based solely on performance—sales and recruiting—which, along with the official prohibition on male sellers, makes such institutionalized advantage impossible. Men may, however, be stigmatized for their involvement in "women's work" (Agadjanian 2002; Seligmann 2004; Williams 1992, 1995).

Women Yanbalistas at all levels, from new sellers to corporate leaders, have varying responses to this incursion by men into what is socially constructed and officially designated as women's work. Many men who are active in Yanbal act as business partners to their wives or other female family members, working together to increase the household's income and status. The very existence of male sellers pushes us to examine the context of men's and women's employment in Ecuador, the assumptions about gender that are built into a "women's" DSO, and the question of how gender identity is constructed in everyday life.

Based on patterns in the data I collected through participant observation and interviews, men's involvement with Yanbal (in the sales force, not the corporate side) takes the form of one of three stances. Men can act as *opposers*, disapproving of their female partner's work and acting as an obstacle to their selling. They can be *supporters*, a variegated category that includes both those who silently tolerate their wife's work as well as those who help out a bit, taking catalogs to work with them or making bank deposits to cover orders.[4] Finally, there are the *drivers*, men who actively sell and grow the Yanbal business, either in partnership with a woman who is officially enrolled in the sales force, or on their own, using a woman's name and contact information while she remains inactive. As with all conceptual categories used by social scientists, these divisions are not etched in stone.[5] Individual men's behavior sometimes transcends these categories, alternating between oppositional and supportive stances. The narrative of men's miraculous transformation from opposers to supporters is also an important bit of Yanbal folklore, which many women I met claim to have experienced firsthand.

OPPOSERS

When I lived with that person [my ex-husband], he didn't want me to go out, but in light of the fact that he didn't give me money, didn't support me—because they [men] always give just enough for the food—well, okay, then, one does selling albeit in a hidden way. . . . [And] sometimes there were ladies [clients] who work and arrive home at seven at night, [and] I had to be waiting for them outside their house or inside the house until the time they came home, in the north of the city [I lived in the south]. . . . So I got home at ten, nine at night because I waited for them—well, I preferred the clients and since I know that the husband is out on the street,

going around with other women, I waited . . . so for that reason I also had problems [with him].
CONSULTANT NANCY TORRES ZAMBRANO

I always try not to give my husband any reason to talk [*Siempre trato de no buscarle la boca a mi esposo*]—"Well, you are always stuck over there [in meetings]; you don't attend to me." I always try to have his clothes clean, everything clean, so he doesn't talk.
CONSULTANT TANIA ZAMBRANO BURGOS

As shown by these two interview excerpts, husbands can affect women's ability to work as well as their quality of life as workers and members of the household. Whereas Nancy did not mind staying out late, because she knew her unfaithful husband was out anyway, she still had to argue with him when she came home, even though he either did not make enough or did not share enough of his income to support the family. Tania referred to the extra burdens that working women face, such as needing to have the house in order and to "attend" to their husbands with extra care so that their paid work cannot be blamed for any perceived domestic shortcomings. Consultant Érika Martínez, who is a neighbor of Tania's and belongs to the same Yanbal group, faced a similar situation with her husband: "He doesn't like it if he calls me and the food isn't ready because I've been in a Yanbal meeting. . . . If he calls and tells me 'at such-and-such a time I will be home,' I have to have everything ready for him." It is clear that the social and familial expectations of women are high and that these expectations can lead to conflict. Women in this study talked about difficult husbands in two ways: speaking generically or about other women's husbands, or speaking about their own personal experiences living with the men I call opposers.

The oppositional husband is a major component of the Yanbalista organizational worldview: a common enemy and an almost mythical figure capable of making or breaking a woman's income-earning potential. The image of the oppositional husband represents a real concern among many women direct sellers, especially considering the high incidence of domestic violence in Ecuador.[6] Within the context of an all-female gathering, however, husbands can sometimes be lampooned and painted as buffoons with great effectiveness and to the delight of the women present. When women at a recruiting event I attended complained about not being able to get the $15 inscription fee[7] from their husbands, a Yanbal coordinator[8] told them, 'I'll tell you how you can get the money tonight. Just go in his pants pockets when he's sleeping and take it.' The coordinator then asked a consultant in the audience how she had gotten the money to sign up. The woman explained proudly that she simply waited until her husband was drunk one night to ask him. The room filled with laughter at this story.

At a campaign launch event in early 2008 at Yanbal's Guayaquil headquarters, the same coordinator encouraged women to think about their goals for the new year, shouting, "New year, new husband!" Some women shook their heads and said no, others applauded, and everyone was smiling or laughing (including me). Similarly, in one of Ligia's group's meetings, a consultant brought up the topic of husbands' opposition to Yanbal. Another consultant jokingly advised her to "change husbands." Ligia said, 'I would agree with that advice, but you all always change your current bad husband for a worse one!' This accusation was met with laughter from around the room. Later in the meeting, Ligia returned to the subject of husbands to say that although women should try to get all the housework done and cook each meal to avoid trouble with their partner, "husbands complain for no reason sometimes."

It was Ligia who first encouraged me to look at the crucial role of husbands in women's participation in the Yanbal sales force. One day as we made the short walk from her office to the bank in the Mall del Sol (an upscale shopping mall) to make a deposit, she told me that many men did not want their women to work, and many women were so used to being submissive that it was difficult to convince them to join. Ligia's position on oppositional husbands is to tell the consultants (or potential consultants) that they cannot keep their work with Yanbal a secret[9] and that they must find a way to persuade their husbands to allow them to sell. She does not advise an adversarial approach, since she is aware of the possibility of verbal and/or physical abuse if women cross difficult husbands.

Sales directors have much indirect experience with oppositional husbands as they attempt to recruit women and guide active consultants. A longtime consultant of Ligia's came into the office one day in October, and Ligia invited her to sit down and chat. She asked the consultant why she had not been coming around the office or attending meetings. The woman said that her husband was "very jealous" (*celosísimo*) and had been giving her a hard time. As we sat in Ligia's interior office, separated by a door and a windowed wall from the main part of the office, Ligia told the woman and me that women always made their husbands out to be bad guys and that it was sometimes just an excuse for not working. The woman said that she sold Yanbal products mostly to the clients of her husband's business who came to the house; since she did not have to leave the house to sell, her husband "let" her work.

Men who are disengaged from the life of the household, or who abandon it altogether, are lumped together with opposers as people who make women's lives more difficult. Director Ana María Briones observed, "Most times when I interview people [potential consultants], I run across people who say that their husband left them, that the husband doesn't give her one dollar for food, that they have three, four kids at home, that they don't have money for food." In this description, men are seen as not upholding the role of family provider, a role traditionally assigned to them in Ecuadorian culture. It is not clear whether the husband who does not give "one dollar" for food is hoarding the money that he earns or simply not making money; however, the consequence is the same for the woman, who is charged with administering the household budget and feeding the family.

The statistics regarding women needing their husbands' permission to work are confirmed by the experiences of women as directors and consultants. The question of permission comes up when a woman is in the process of deciding whether to become a Yanbal seller, although opposition from husbands takes other forms once women join. One day I went out with Tía[10] Ligia and my husband's other aunt, Tía Fátima Casanova, to a woman's home in order to enroll her as a new consultant. The woman, a roughly sixty-year-old mother and grandmother, told us quietly that her husband had "a very strong temperament" (*un carácter bien fuerte*, often a euphemism for abusive behavior) and that he had never allowed her to work, although she had been trained as a nurse prior to getting married. Based on his reaction toward our presence, deducible from his grumpy greeting, piercing stares, and avoidance, he was not exactly thrilled that she was signing up to sell Yanbal. The only reason she was able to do so was because her son had encouraged her and given her the money to register. The situation of women whose partners do not allow them to work is especially difficult and frustrating for directors, whose income and status depend on recruiting women and keeping them active in selling.

Director Maryuri Palma noted, "Of course there are girls who don't join." When I looked at her questioningly, she stumbled over her words, trying to find the way to explain it to me, a foreigner and a Yanbal outsider. "Here in Ecuador," she said, "it is still—how do I put it? How can I say it?—the women, um . . . even to go downtown they ask their husband for permission. They don't join because they say that the husband says that he won't let them work. [*Imitating the women:*] 'No, it's just that, let me ask my husband if he will let me.'" This puts Maryuri in a challenging position, trying to recruit the woman, yet not being able to deal directly with the man because of the dictates of Ecuadorian gender etiquette, and not wanting to endanger the woman or worsen her quality of life. If faced with a woman who is afraid to join because she thinks it will cause problems with her spouse, Maryuri said: "I don't insist either, [because then they might] say, 'Because of Maryuri, my husband left me.'" Young married consultant Tania Zambrano interpreted men's opposition as a sign of their investment in the provider role: "There will always be obstacles, especially with the husbands. They always stand in the way, saying, 'No, you are not going to go out,' and one has to be there struggling [*luchando*], because there are men who just want themselves to be [working], and they don't let the women work."

Not only directors recruit consultants. Other consultants recruit as well, and it is the main way that they can attract the attention of their director (and eventually the company) and begin on the path to becoming a director. Érica de la A is a consultant who was brought in by Nancy Torres, a successful seller who was once up for director but didn't quite make it, and was working her way up the ranks again at the time of the study. Nancy knew that her consultants needed to recruit in order for her to move up, so she frequently worked alongside them to enroll new people. Érica explained that she was in the process of trying to re-enroll her cousin who had joined Yanbal when Érica did. The cousin had been a good seller, but Érica said that she did not want to join again because she had problems with her husband, who did not want her to sell. When I asked what it was that bothered him, Érica said that he didn't like her going out, which led the cousin to say (in Érica's words), "It's that I don't go sell because sometimes my husband doesn't let me." Érica interpreted the situation based on the husband's perception of himself as provider and the wife's need for him to share his income: "So I imagine that . . . since she doesn't work at all [outside the home], but rather her husband gives her money, then if her husband isn't going to help her [i.e., contribute to the household from his income] if he doesn't approve of her working, then how is she going to . . . ?" The ellipsis with which Érica ended that statement implies a world of unwanted consequences. The woman can't work because of her husband's opposition, because if she did, he would withdraw his financial support of the household, and then she would be hard-pressed to make ends meet.

Thinking about the reasons for this man's opposition, Érica offered a psychological analysis, saying, "I think it's because of jealousy, I think, no? Or that they must not have trust between the two of them." The idea of jealousy (*celos*) as motivating men's behavior came up repeatedly in discussions of husbands' opposition to women's work. Most of the women I knew agreed that husbands did not have a specific distaste for Yanbal or direct selling, but that they didn't like their wives leaving the house for any type of work. Director Marjorie López, who has been working with Yanbal for sixteen years, thinks that Yanbal allows only women to sell because the company anticipates this opposition by husbands. When I asked her why the sales force is (officially) all-female, she said, "Because there are men who are jealous. . . . [Husbands] have said to me, 'If there are no men, then enroll my wife' . . . or 'If men don't go [to the meetings], I will let my wife go with you.'"

Consultants who are married to opposers cite jealousy as a primary reason for their lack of support. Jacinta Menoscal is a petite, forty-nine-year-old woman originally from a rural part of the coastal province of Manabí[11] and has been working in Guayaquil as a Yanbal consultant for twelve years. Her then common-law husband (they have since married) runs a small store in the southern part of the city, and he has made clear his distaste for Jacinta's selling work with Yanbal and Avon. When I asked about his position, Jacinta explained, "He doesn't like me to go out on the street, because if I go to collect money, sometimes I have to go running out. . . . He doesn't trust me; he is not a trusting person." When she is out visiting customers, sometimes she has to stop and return home in case her husband calls or comes home, because if he doesn't find her at home, "he gives me trouble, and I don't like him to give me trouble."

Although her husband supports her work with Yanbal, consultant Micaela Vera Muñoz, mother of two school-age children, likes to speculate on why husbands might be jealous and act as opposers. She told me, "I think that they must be doing something when they're out of the house, something they shouldn't be doing. . . . What must they be doing in the street that they judge these ladies [*las señoras*]? . . . It's as if they [the husbands] were going around doing other things, and they are afraid that the wife will go out and find out about what they do."[12] It is difficult to know whether men tend to be more unfaithful in marriage than women, as Micaela implies (and as most Ecuadorians I know also believe), but I found her theory of jealousy as men projecting their 'bad' behavior onto their wives to be thought-provoking.

Sometimes men's opposition to women's work is not as blatant as prohibiting them from leaving the house. It can also take the form of eschewing domestic and child care responsibilities, which can sometimes make women's engaging in paid work very difficult or nigh impossible. Ana María Briones, whose story appeared in the last chapter, explained, "My husband . . . is hating Yanbal right now. He says that he can't stand Yanbal, that he hates Yanbal, that he is sick of Yanbal. . . . Here in our *machista* society, the man throws onto the woman all of the responsibility." In a recent argument with her husband, Ana María protested, "You blame me for everything: if [the kids] get sick, I am at fault; if they have bad grades, I am at fault; if they don't eat, I am at fault; if they don't bathe, I am at fault." Ana María's husband went beyond just expecting her to take care of the house and the children, by complaining about the way that she did these tasks.

Husbands may also oppose wives in a more subtle way, by expressing doubt in their potential to make money and succeed. This type of husband, in addition to telling his wife that she is "just for cooking," as Yanbalista Betty Brigss put it, undermines her goals and self-confidence by asking, "What? You're going to win a trip? What are you going to be able to make happen?" Other husbands display indifference toward their partners' work with Yanbal, which can sometimes be nearly as painful as explicit opposition, especially as women progress through the ranks. Having your husband not show up when you are presented with a car that you earned with your hard work can be demoralizing and embarrassing, but some directors contend with such apathetic spouses.

I do not mean to give the impression that male partners of Yanbalistas can always be grouped into either the opposer or the supporter categories. The real social world is more complicated than social scientists' orderly depictions of it, and of course some people's behavior can be classified as both oppositional and supportive. For example, Jacinta's husband, who gets angry if she isn't at home during the day, also allows her to display some of her Yanbal products in his store. People sometimes come by asking for specific products and he sells them, although Jacinta says, "He calls me right away, [saying,] 'How much is this, and how much is that?' . . . since I don't leave the prices with him." Érika Martínez's husband, who complained that she neglected her domestic responsibilities to sell, also helped her sell, asking her to buy an extra catalog that he could take to his co-workers or their wives. Sometimes he took Érika to his friends' homes so that she could offer them Yanbal products. These combinations of opposing and supporting actions indicate a tension between men's ideas about gender relations and women's place, and their realization that Yanbal can be a valuable source of supplemental income that can ease the pressure on them to provide for the family. Thus oppositional attitudes and behaviors may be part of a gendered economic strategy on the part of men that also allows for some practical help with their wives' selling. It is important to remember that these arrangements can change over time, sometimes in the positive direction described as a transformation (discussed later in this chapter).

LIVING WITH OPPOSERS: DIANA AND MARYURI

Several Yanbalistas discussed the difficulties of having a partner who did not approve of their work, but two women were especially frank and eloquent when speaking about their experiences. According to them, the challenges they have faced do not include some of the more extreme possible consequences of men's displeasure, such as domestic violence. These husbands do not attempt to impede their wives from working with Yanbal, but they find ways of letting the women know that their work is not supported or appreciated, even though, in both cases, the women's income is needed to sustain the household.

Diana Hurel is an opinionated, expressive woman of forty who lives in northern Guayaquil with her husband and their two teenage daughters. Diana is on the plump side, and she takes special care with her appearance: her thick curly hair is either pulled back or expertly styled, and she wears Yanbal jewelry, business attire, and makeup in tones that complement her clothing. She has worked as a Yanbal consultant for the past six years, ever since her sister (an active consultant in Ligia's group who recently became a director) recruited her. When Diana joined Yanbal, it was over the objections of her husband, who told her it would be a waste of time. He works as a dentist for a mobile dental clinic that travels to the most disadvantaged areas of the city to provide dental care for the poor. His employment is stable (one reason many people covet government jobs), but the paychecks are small. One reason that Diana said he opposed her selling was that it often set her scrambling to cover the cost of an order. I witnessed such a situation firsthand a few days after Christmas in 2007. I was helping to distribute catalogs to consultants in Ligia's office when Diana came huffing into the room to ask about a check of hers that had bounced. On the phone and in conversation with the secretaries, she was obviously upset and aggravated, and part of this stress, she explained later, came from the potential for conflict with her husband because of the bounced check. Despite these *apuros*, or stresses, Diana asserted:

> [Selling Yanbal products] helps me because, although he tells me it isn't any help, I can at least pay the telephone bill, I pay De Prati [a department store credit card]—he pays one month, I pay the next—I buy my things, and when the girls fall in love with something new, I buy it for them. And that is a savings for him although he doesn't recognize me for it.

Diana thus defined her income as supplemental, for use in covering bills and for pleasurable consumption. Her husband did not acknowledge the help that Diana brought to paying bills, and thought that the "fun" things she spent some of her money on were not important.[13] These enjoyable expenses included the cost of keeping Diana and her daughters looking good, according to middle-class standards of appearance, as the following interview excerpt shows.

> DIANA: If I go get my hair done, it's with my money. If I get the girls' hair styled for some [event], it's with my money. But he doesn't see any of that; that is, to him that's not helping [financially]. . . . Maybe he thinks that . . .
> ERYNN: Those things are extras. They aren't . . .
> DIANA: Yes, well, yes. . . . So he says, you spend on those foolish things for no reason, so . . . since he doesn't have to get his hair styled or anything . . . [*laughs*].

Despite her husband's opposition, feisty Diana had no plans to quit selling Yanbal; she felt that he was all talk and that she actually had the freedom to work. "I go out just the same, even though he gets mad. I go out just the same, because he's also not one of those [who says,] 'I'll hit you if you go out.'" Diana's gendered economic strategy was to ignore her husband's dissatisfaction and work for the money she felt she needed, but without overtly challenging him. Despite her adamancy about her right to work, she still tried to be home by 6:30 p.m., "because around that time my husband gets home, so to avoid problems I prefer to be there before he gets home, and although he sometimes doesn't say anything [when I'm late], he still goes around with his grumpy face [*anda con su cara de mal genio*], so it's better to avoid problems." Although she said that he denied being jealous, she thought that jealousy underlay some of his opposition to her work. When she worked in an office, he did not complain, so Diana thinks that her having to move around the city to sell and collect money is what bothers him.[14] "He doesn't prohibit me anything," she told me, "but all the same he goes around in his bad mood. . . . But sometimes it's like you have to give him his fifteen minutes [of being mad], and then he's fine." While her working is tolerated to an extent, Diana made it clear that "it's not like he helps me." She often finds herself trying to pull together the money needed to cover her order, but, she says, "I prefer to borrow from someone else with interest. I take him as the last resort."

I wondered if Diana's husband had always been opposed to her work with Yanbal, and she said that he had. She said he used to blame her sister for "getting me into this mess." Diana said that she sometimes tried to reason with her husband and show him how her work benefited him and the family—for example, emphasizing how she helped pay bills and buy things for herself and her daughters from her earnings. She claimed that only by being enrolled in Yanbal was she able to purchase her personal items, like perfume and lotion (benefiting from the consultants' discount), because her husband was not the type to say, "Come on, I'll go buy you something." So Diana often told him, "'If you want me to get out [of Yanbal], then give me . . . well [*pues*], give me everything that I want, that I need,' and that's when he gets quiet." By challenging her husband's ability to fill the gendered role of economic provider, she was able to stop his verbal opposition to her income-generating activity, at least temporarily.

Yanbal sales director Maryuri Palma lives at the opposite end of the city from Diana Hurel, in El Guasmo Sur. She is a petite woman with curly brown hair and braces, who often dresses casually in jeans and whom no one would suspect has a sixteen-year-old son at home, since she looks so young herself. In meetings and interactions with other Yanbalistas, Maryuri is enthusiastic, intense, and friendly. Behind the scenes, she is strategic and ambitious, modeling her work style and career path after her mother director, Ligia. Once in a meeting I sat in on, between Ligia and four of her daughter and granddaughter directors, Ligia asked a new director, 'Do you want to be the best director in Yanbal?' No sooner had the woman quietly answered yes than Maryuri energetically said, 'No! Because the best director will be me!' This type of energy inspires and motivates Maryuri's thirty or so active consultants, who are known for turning out in full force when invited to participate in events along with Ligia's group.

In an interview, Maryuri spoke at length about women in her group who had had difficulty with their husbands over Yanbal, including Maryuri's sister, whose husband told her to "choose Yanbal or choose me." Maryuri saw oppositional husbands as a common concern among Yanbalistas and as an obstacle that prevented the women from succeeding or making as much money as they could. She guessed that the majority of the women I interviewed had had trouble with husbands who didn't want them to work, and this may be true even though some women did not indicate opposition by the men in their lives. When I asked Maryuri why her husband did not like her work, she told me,

> Because he says that he works, and as long as we have what the children need [the pair have four children between six and sixteen], then why do I have to . . . why do I want to work, that I should stay home taking care of the kids. . . . That has always been his opposition; it's always been about

the kids. . . . Even right now he tells me, "You leave and the kids stay here alone." So we're still going on. . . . It has not been resolved.

The children are not generally alone, since a domestic employee helps out during the day and Maryuri tries not to schedule meetings or events at night. She said her husband stays out late most nights anyway, and so she wonders how he can claim that she is not around enough. Maryuri's husband defines her appropriate role as that of housewife and mother and sees her work in Yanbal as superfluous. He feels this way even though Maryuri is advancing through the ranks of Yanbal's sales force, earning prizes, and pulling in a good income.

Part of the reason that Maryuri's husband can downplay her financial contributions is that, instead of buying items that could be used immediately, Maryuri earmarks most of her earnings for a home she is having built in a new middle-class subdivision in northern Guayaquil. Her reason for buying a new house is that she wants to leave El Guasmo, for fear that her sons might get into trouble in a low-income area known for crime and delinquency. (Maryuri's cellular phone was stolen from her right in front of her home during the time that I was doing fieldwork in Guayaquil, likely confirming her belief that this was no place to raise children.) But like Diana's husband, Maryuri's husband does not feel that she contributes to the family.

Speaking of oppositional husbands, Maryuri said, "We have to make them change that idea that Yanbal means that the woman is out on the street all day, that Yanbal just means that they [the women] are indebted." She believes that the company could help ease tensions between husbands and wives by acknowledging that most sellers are in domestic partnerships and by occasionally inviting husbands to participate in Yanbal activities. She envisioned special trainings geared toward what Biggart (1989) called "co-opting husbands": making them see the value in the direct selling work their spouses were doing.

> They could show them . . . all the good in the business. . . . I think that then the husband would, like, become aware and permit the consultants to work very well from the beginning, because in the beginning they [consultants] do not work in that way, like full speed ahead. . . . Because of that attitude on the part of the man. . . . [Because] people outside the business say, "It's that they separated because of Yanbal," [but] it's not because of Yanbal. That is the excuse that the man always looks to: "Because you were going around out there, more dedicated [to work], you have neglected here

[home and family]." That's a lie, a common lie. So I think that, yes, we have to sort of educate the man.

At present, Yanbal has no formal policies or engagement strategies geared toward the husbands and partners of women working in the DSO's sales force, and some directors and consultants told me that they wish the company would engage these men directly. Individual directors or high-level consultants often devise ad hoc methods for dealing with skeptical or difficult husbands whose behavior affects sellers' ability to work. For example, directors Marjorie López and Ligia García occasionally talk to husbands at the request of their wives, but in most cases they leave negotiations to the couples themselves. Consultant Elizabeth Contreras encourages her daughter consultants to invite their spouses to Yanbal events, with the thinking that if the men's objections stem from jealousy, they will soon see that they have nothing to worry about. She told me, "I tell the new people that want to enroll, 'Invite them [their husbands]. Take them [to meetings/activities], and you will see that he realizes that, where you are going, it's not that you are going to do [bad] things.'" Elizabeth suggests this strategy because taking her own husband along to a beauty session (the Yanbal equivalent of a Tupperware party) helped ease tensions between the two of them over her selling. "He ended up getting bored," she told me, "because imagine being in a beauty session. A man in the midst of four, five women, he gets bored. . . . And then he let me go [after that]."

Maryuri's and Diana's husbands' opposition took the form of verbal attacks and trying to make the women feel that they were neglecting their duties at home. The men also made light of what the women felt were real financial contributions to the well-being of the family. Neither woman saw her struggle as unique, and most Yanbalistas can tell a story or two about opposers who stand between women and the work that they want to do. The same men can alternate between opposing and supporting women's work, and some women claim that their men have permanently changed from opposers to supporters.

SUPPORTERS

ERYNN: What does your husband think of your work with Yanbal?
PATRICIA: Well, up to now he hasn't said anything to me. I imagine he must approve, no?
ERYNN: But he does know that you're in Yanbal?
PATRICIA: Of course, yes, he knows.
ERYNN: He hasn't said anything to you?

PATRICIA: No.

ERYNN: And he's not involved in any way? Does he buy from you?

PATRICIA: Of course, I mean the first perfume when I started, I sold to him.

INTERVIEW WITH CARMEN PATRICIA PÉREZ ÁLAVA

[My husband] even enrolled one [*laughs*], one he enrolled because he had talked with his friends, and the lady had told him, "Well, I want to enroll my daughter." [And he said,] "Okay. Well, that's no problem. I'll tell Martha to come by later." So he told me, and I went straight there. . . . He helps me sell too.

CONSULTANT MARTHA BERMEO BERMEO

The preceding quotes present two possible positions that men may take within what I call a supportive stance. In the case of Patricia, her common-law husband supports her by buying products and not hassling her about her selling, which, as we can see from the stories of opposers, is no small matter. Martha's husband takes a more hands-on supportive role, selling products in the small store that he runs and even arranging for a new consultant to enroll. While it is clear that Martha is still in control of her Yanbal selling, her husband recognizes that this activity increases household income, and he helps direct people to Martha to become clients and, in at least one case, consultants. Many women who had supportive husbands described themselves as lucky, a description that highlights how opposition is perceived as the default stance for male partners.

Women I spoke with listed a variety of behaviors as forms of support from their husbands. For example, Vanessa Paredes, a thirty-year-old law student living in southern Guayaquil, benefited from her husband's having a motorcycle and working as a messenger. She said, "When I tell him, 'Go leave this with Betty [her director]' [or] if I have to send her some document, to Betty, and I can't do it, he goes—or to deliver a product, he goes. He's never told me no."[15] Many husbands are willing to help out in this way, and especially at the beginnings of campaigns, quite a few men show up to director Ligia García's office to buy catalogs, drop off orders, or pick up prizes. These men often included a businessman who worked in Ligia's office building on a different floor, a uniformed policeman, and other male partners, dressed casually or in suits, whose body language and demeanor ranged from awkward and rushed to comfortable and communicative.

There can be limits to this type of support, however, and women are careful not to push it. One Wednesday afternoon, a consultant's husband dropped by director Betty Brigss' office to deliver a check; he was also supposed to pick up a product to take home to his wife, but Betty and her staff forgot to give it to him. Betty's secretary called the woman to find out if she could call her husband on his cellular phone and ask him to return. When the wife spoke with him, about ten minutes after he had driven away, he said he didn't feel like going back. Even while in the act of helping his wife with her Yanbal work, a husband can shift into a less supportive stance.

Many consultants claim that their husbands buy products. Belén Vera, who does not live far from Vanessa but belongs to a different Yanbal group, told me that her husband encouraged her to join the company, since she had been able to make money helping her mother sell in the past. While he is not actively involved in selling or recruiting, Belén told me: "He is the first client of each campaign [*laughs*]. I tell him, 'Buy this perfume from me,' and he buys it from me, and . . . he pays cash up front [*al contado*]." That Belén's husband pays cash for an expensive item in the beginning of the campaign is important, since most customers do not pay 100 percent of an item's cost upon ordering and so Belén must cover at least part of her order by using her own capital. Her husband is likely willing to wait a week or two for his cologne, so Belén can use the money he has paid her to place her other orders; then she can deliver those products and collect payments from those clients, always keeping the money flowing.[16]

HAVING A SUPPORTIVE HUSBAND: DANIELA, ÉRICA, AND GIOCONDA

Daniela Solís, the young mother of a toddler (and a new baby born in 2010), is known within her Yanbal group for having an especially supportive husband. Daniela's director, Maryuri, marveled at his willingness to help his wife. Not only does he give (*regalar*) Daniela the money to cover orders, but he also goes to the bank to make the necessary deposits in Yanbal's account.[17] In addition, Maryuri claimed, and Daniela agreed, that Daniela's husband was emotionally supportive, motivating her to work hard and do well. Daniela said with a chuckle that her husband is "really vain" and can always be counted on to buy a fragrance or a deodorant from her. Daniela's husband has a stable government job, and it seems he views her job as a necessary distraction to get her out of the house, allow her to meet people (one of her favorite aspects of the work), and help her earn a few extra dollars. When I met Daniela, the family was not dependent on her income, which may have defused any potential conflict over her work. However, around March 2008, when her husband's paychecks were withheld for several months due to some political restructuring and budget issues, and their young daughter was so ill that she had to be hospitalized, it was Daniela's earnings from Yanbal that pulled the family through. "Thank God for Yanbal," she told me with a smile; she described her husband as even more supportive after these difficult months.

When seller Érica de la A told me that her husband was a clown, there was an uncomfortable pause during which I tried to figure out if she was joking, insulting him, or telling me the truth. I decided to take her words literally, asking nervously, "Like at kids' birthday parties?" She confirmed that this was what she meant. Érica and her common-law husband have a unique relationship in which they work together (she paints faces at some of the parties he works), pool their money to pay household expenses,[18] and communicate openly about financial and other matters. When she was presented with the opportunity of joining Yanbal, she said that she talked it over with her husband first, as is her "custom" with many personal decisions. As she recounted the conversation, she was not asking for permission so much as sounding him out on the matter and asking for his advice. According to Érica, the discussion went like this:

> ÉRICA: Look, this is what happened. They are selling me Yanbal, [and] they told me that I could join. What do you think? [¿*Qué tal te parece?*]
>
> HUSBAND: If you think you'll be able to do it, do it.
>
> ÉRICA: But you are going to help me too? Because you also have to help me sell.
>
> HUSBAND: Okay. If I can, I will help you.

Using this negotiation as an example, Érica told me, "We understand each other; we understand each other on everything." She described Yanbal as being good for her marriage, saying, "I become closer to my husband, because my husband helps me to sell, and in the economic aspect also, because I like to help out in my home [financially]." Érica's husband helps her identify new clients, and he tells people he knows and meets that his wife sells Yanbal. He also takes clients' orders, delivers products, and collects money that he later turns over to Érica. Despite his involvement, he always makes sure to tell people that it is his wife who is selling Yanbal. This type of active support, and the open and communicative relationship that allows for it, seem relatively rare among the sellers and directors I studied. That Érica's husband has an unstable job seems to have made him more invested in her succeeding with Yanbal and thus more supportive than many other husbands. Her income is crucial to the household's survival, and the two treat each other as partners in keeping the home going.

Consultant Gioconda Ibarra echoed other supporters' wives when she stated that she was lucky to have a husband who did not oppose her work.[19] Her husband also gives her the emotional encouragement that she needs to work hard and continue selling: "The good thing is that I have a husband, thank God, well, who supports me in everything and . . . [he always] says, 'No, you have to go on. You already got into this, and you have to go on.' He gave me energy [*ánimos*] to continue." Gioconda's husband, who works at a banana company, has her order an extra catalog each campaign for him to take to work, and he calls her to place the clients' orders. He has been more active in selling in recent months, helping Gioconda reach higher total sales amounts. As for the money arrangements, Gioconda said, "I help him to pay his debts, and he sometimes covers me when I don't have enough money. And we help each other like that." According to Gioconda, her husband is not just concerned about her earning money but also sees emotional and spiritual benefits to keeping busy:

> Yes, he is happy because, above all, he says that if I feel happy there [working in Yanbal], then I should stay. Maybe what he doesn't want is, if I am in my house, you know that when we have our minds empty, so many things come to our mind . . . negative ideas. . . . So it's always good to have your mind occupied with work, and he . . . he realizes how I am developing myself in every aspect [*me estoy desenvolviendo en todo*], and he supports me. He says that he wants me to be even more than a director [*laughs*].

Although Gioconda did not connect this shared attitude to her family's Protestant faith, the above quote reminded me of my own Evangelical upbringing and the emphasis placed on hard work and keeping the mind busy, since "idle hands are the devil's workshop," as the saying goes. Perhaps the supportive position of Gioconda's husband was informed by this belief in the inherent value of hard work. In any case, her gendered economic strategy was based on the financial need for her to work and on a flexible rather than traditional idea of gender roles that did not preclude women working and in fact seemed to encourage it.

THE NARRATIVE OF TRANSFORMATION

In one Yanbal training video, an attractive young actress playing a beauty consultant claims that her husband was not supportive when she first decided to join Yanbal, but that once the money started flowing in, he changed his mind and now stands behind her and encourages her in her work. In pro-

Beauty consultant Tania Zambrano and her husband in their house in El Guasmo Sur. (Photo by the author)

motional videos, successful directors are frequently shown with their husbands and children, whose presence symbolizes support for the women's income-earning efforts. The narrative of oppositional husbands metamorphosing into supporters is familiar to many Yanbalistas; some women claim to have experienced this transformation in their own homes, and a few more know of others who have witnessed this phenomenon.[20] The narrative of transformation is an important motivational weapon in the corporate arsenal: it gives hope to women living with opposers, that someday he may turn around and that she can win him over by being a successful seller. Of the thirty-one consultants and directors I interviewed who had been married or were currently married, eight claimed that their partners had undergone a transformation similar to the one idealized in the Yanbal video.

Consultant Tania Zambrano said that her husband originally opposed her work with Yanbal because of jealousy (*celos*). When she first joined Yanbal, her husband was "like very angry," especially because of all the meetings and activities that she attended. A geographic coincidence allowed his suspicions to be allayed somewhat. As I should have guessed from the huge motorcycle occupying nearly half of the room that served as living/dining area and kitchen in Tania's mother-in-law's home (behind which Tania, her husband, and their son lived in a small house made of a bamboo called *caña guadúa*), Tania's husband worked as a motorcycle messenger. His employer was Porta, Ecuador's largest cellular phone company, and it happens that Yanbal's Guayaquil offices are headquartered in the "Porta building,"[21] where his work was based. Since he had a motorcycle, he would drop Tania off and pick her up from meetings and trainings, and because he had access to the building, she says, "he realized that I was in the meetings and not somewhere else." In addition, Tania said, "Now he doesn't say anything because he is seeing that I am earning." Having her economic contribution recognized helped her to gain her husband's support, especially considering his low-wage job. He was later laid off and Tania continued to sell Yanbal.

Vanessa told a similar story of her husband's original objections being overcome by the bottom line. In an example of the instability of men's employment and a tale that was echoed by other consultants, Vanessa said, "The time that he was without work, I was his financial support . . . [and] from then on, he didn't say any more [to oppose my work]." Though traditional cultural norms of gender are on the side of the opposers, the precarious nature of men's employment in contemporary Ecuador, and their realization that their partners are making money in Yanbal, can work to break down objections and lead to (sometimes reluctant and passive) support.

TRANSFORMATION STORIES: ELIZABETH, MARJORIE, AND MARJORIE

Elizabeth Contreras describes her Yanbal career as a battle of wills between her and her husband. Several years ago, when she was selling Yanbal and working in a factory to make ends meet and supplement her husband's work as a security guard, he was jealous and made it clear that he opposed her working. At one point, he even stalked her at work, standing across the street and watching to make sure that she went right home when she got off. Elizabeth said her co-workers would tell her, "Niña Eli [an affectionate nickname], your man is over there." She told me that this would make her nervous. She felt as if he was trying to catch her doing something wrong or talking to the men who came into work as her shift ended. When Elizabeth quit the factory job to tend to her mother, who was dying of cancer, her husband still opposed her selling, complaining that she was out all day and that she was "lazing around." According to Elizabeth, he could not get used to the idea of his daughters attending to him at home; he thought that this was Elizabeth's job and that she should be serving him his meals and doing the domestic chores.

Two events resulted in Eli's husband becoming supportive—albeit sometimes grudgingly—of her work with Yanbal. First, he was fired from his job when many longtime personnel were let go, and Elizabeth's income supported the family until he could get together the money to buy a truck and started earning income serving as an informal taxi and delivery service. Second, the couple's son, a Protestant pastor, sat his father down and told him that Elizabeth was considering leaving the marriage because of his bad treatment. These incidents brought the man's attention to his wife's economic contributions and the emotional damage his behavior had caused in the family.

Elizabeth said that now her husband not only doesn't complain about her selling Yanbal but actually helps out from time to time.

> He helps me, he accompanies me . . . [and,] for example, *la señora* Ceci [Cecilia García], my director, she pokes fun at him [*laughs*] . . . because when we have to do our orders, he goes to drop me off with the order . . . and *la señora* Ceci tells him, "If *la señora* Eli [Elizabeth] gets to be a director someday, you will have to do this." "Ugh, no," he says. "Let her do it alone, because this is too much" [*laughs*]. . . . So she [Cecilia] has realized that he is more helpful.

When I accompanied the ladies on a neighborhood canvassing activity near Elizabeth's home in Los Vergeles, Cecilia laughingly referred to Elizabeth's husband (in his presence) as "the secretary." That Elizabeth's husband can joke around with her director about his helpfulness is a major sign that his attitude has changed. However, his personality has not been completely transformed, and his grumpiness can still set the tone for his interactions with Elizabeth and her clients. For example, he goes to clients' homes to collect money if Elizabeth asks him to, but if they don't have the money ready, "he comes home furious [*laughs*]. . . . 'Don't sell that stuff anymore,' he says. 'All they do is make you waste time!'"

Elizabeth's husband confirmed this account. Riding back to my aunt's house one day with Elizabeth and her husband in his red pickup truck, I asked him how he felt about his wife's selling. He said it was okay, except when he had to make a trip to pick up money and the client didn't have any to give him. He found this frustrating and a waste of time and gasoline, he told me. Elizabeth laughs off these outbursts now, sure that he will continue to help her out from time to time. She told me, "I sometimes use my husband as my planner [*agenda*]." She asks him to remind her to go see a client, and he tells her, "Hey, weren't you going to go see so-and-so?" If he is free "and not going around in one of his bad moods," she will ask for a ride to the client's home. He tells her, "Okay. Will you take long? No? Okay, fine." In the spectrum of supporters, then, Elizabeth's husband is not as enthusiastic as Érica's or Gioconda's husbands, but she and others can see that he has come a long way from his former opposer persona. His gendered economic strategy involves allowing his wife to work and even helping her get work done, yet not showing any pleasure in doing so.

Marjorie López cannot imagine her life without being a Yanbal director. Yet when she first joined the sales force, her husband was not happy about her decision. She referred to him as her "first obstacle." He gave her an ultimatum, saying, "Choose either Yanbal or your family, because you're only out in the street all the time." Because of Marjorie's family support network (her mother and sister helped with child care, as described in chapter 1), she didn't worry about the children, but her husband thought that she should be the primary caregiver. I asked Marjorie how her husband changed his mind about Yanbal. She told me that he just began to get used to it, once he saw that she wasn't going to quit.

Marjorie saw her husband as financially "irresponsible" and as falling short of the male provider ideal. "When I would ask him for money," she said, "he never had any. [But once I started with Yanbal,] afterward I forgot to ask him, and then I guess he realized, 'Well, then, this one isn't asking me for anything anymore. Now with Yanbal she is resolving the whole [money] situation.'" For this reason, Marjorie claimed, he stopped objecting to her work, even when it carried her far from home or kept her out late at night. It seems that Marjorie's husband, always somewhat uncomfortable with the provider role, was relieved that she took charge of putting bread on the table. Once she won her first car as a prize for her work with Yanbal, Marjorie told me, "'Wow,' he must have thought, 'and this one, look where she's headed!' And since then he never again told me to leave Yanbal."

Marjorie's husband did not work at the time of this research; she referred to him as her "strategic partner," helping her with her Yanbal business. She said, "I give him circulars [newsletters for consultants and directors], and I send him here to Guayaquil [they live just outside the city] to distribute them." She also sends him to pick up documents or checks. He sometimes accompanies her when she has to work around town or take a road trip to visit daughter directors outside Guayaquil. When he doesn't drive her, she often takes one of her children along. "Because now," she said with a smile, "I tell you that now they are taking care of the goose who lays the golden eggs!" Marjorie's work with Yanbal is putting the couple's children through college, allowing them to live in an exclusive gated community in a high-status suburb, and paying for cars and other luxuries. This situation is just fine with her husband, who has made the pragmatic decision of going from being an opposer to being a supporter, a change of gender strategy that benefited the entire family.

Marjorie González, a successful consultant in Ligia's group who was recruited by Diana Hurel, was five months pregnant when I met her in the fall of 2007. She is a pretty woman with light brown skin, long curly hair, and an engaging smile, who exudes confidence and friendliness. Ligia called her one of her best sellers, a claim that her sales figures bore out. Ligia often tried to persuade Marjorie to become a sales director, but Marjorie, who also sold products from other DSOs, didn't want to give up her other lines and devote herself solely to Yanbal (as is required of directors). Marjorie attended college for three years, specializing in auditing, and then went on to work in offices in Guayaquil, always selling some products on the side.

When Marjorie quit her full-time job to concentrate on direct sales, her husband was unhappy for "the first few years," because his wife was frequently arriving home later than him in the evenings. He did not take her work seriously; she laughed as she told me, "Maybe since he knows me—that I'm cheerful, friendly, and chatty—maybe he thought that I was dedicating time to gossiping about celebrities and not to working." Many other sellers and directors also told me that their husbands did not consider their work important, viewing it as more of a hobby.

Things changed between Marjorie and her husband when "there was a moment in which he found himself without work and could not find work for about eight months, nine months, so then it was my turn to show him that I did dedicate myself to working [*me dedicaba a trabajar*]." This experience changed the way that Marjorie's husband perceived her and her work in direct selling, and he accepted her shift into the provider role. Marjorie says that even after he returned to the workforce, his positive attitude toward her work remained:

> When that emergency, that need happened, then I told him, "Look, take this money to pay this, take this to pay that." I bought the food, [and] then he—it was like I put a patch over his mouth [*laughs*]. . . . Never again did he prohibit me [from working], never again did he bother me, never again did he give me trouble, because from that moment on he realized, because

he saw money, he saw money, and he could sustain himself during that time, that long time. . . . One might say eight months is nothing, [but] no, it's almost a year.

Now Marjorie's husband congratulates her when she wins prizes and recognitions from Yanbal or Avon (two of the DSOs for which she sells); he has made the transition from opposer to supporter. Marjorie took pride in her work, in her ability to support her small family single-handedly, and this pride was bolstered by her husband's newfound appreciation for her hard work and sales skills.

DRIVERS

Yes, there are men too, and I got a kick out of it in the beginning. . . . When I would go to drop off my order at the [Yanbal] offices in the Policentro [a shopping center in northern Guayaquil], there were some men with a pile of order forms. There are men who . . . well, apparently it is the wife [who sells] but the one who manages [or drives] everything [*él que maneja todo*] is the man. . . . How could I not find that entertaining? It was entertaining to see those men there with the [price] list, with a pile of order forms . . . [because] most men are *machistas*, including mine [*laughs*].
CONSULTANT DIANA HUREL

Most men adopt an oppositional or a supportive stance toward their wives' direct selling work, or a combination of these behaviors. A few Ecuadorian men, however, become active and enthusiastic Yanbalistas. This active engagement, while unofficial and somewhat discouraged by the corporation, takes two main forms. First, men may work in partnership with their wives to build a business under the Yanbal umbrella, usually after these women experience some success in selling and recruiting. These men's involvement is acknowledged and accepted by Yanbal, which calls them *socios estratégicos* (strategic partners).

In one meeting director Ligia García held for her daughter and granddaughter directors, she asked the group, 'Who has a partner [*socio*]?' Among the few women who raised their hands was a young director whose husband had actually accompanied her to the meeting, which is quite unusual. Ligia acknowledged his work, saying to the woman, 'Your husband is your partner. He is very involved and helps you with your business.'[22] These men are generally seen as taking an assistant role, while the woman remains the primary face of the partnership and the more active member. Director Maryuri Palma referred to it this way: "How many women are helping their families progress? I tell you that the women are progressing, because the husbands are not even working anymore, and they dedicate themselves, or to say it better, they join with the woman and help them." At the time of my study, at least two directors in Ligia's "family" (directors she had recruited or who had been recruited by her directors) had spouses who acted as partners. In one case, the woman's husband was an illegal migrant to Ecuador who could not obtain formal employment. In another case, the woman's husband owned a retail store but helped her with all aspects of the business, including secretarial duties such as returning telephone calls. This director once told me, laughing, that when her office was robbed two years ago, the thieves asked her, not her husband, for the money. Her amusement came from the reversal of traditional gender role expectations because Yanbalistas are officially women. These women are the main providers for their families, yet they work together with their husbands, devising gendered economic strategies that sustain such partnerships.

The second way that men become involved is as the primary seller. Men who want to become Yanbal distributors are usually turned down by directors, as director Carmen Díaz Baldeón told me: "I had one [who said,] 'But I want to join Yanbal, *madrecita* ["little mother," a term of respect].' 'No,' I told him, 'you can't.'" But she informed him that his wife could join and that "if she doesn't like it, then you are the one who sells." She added, "So, well, that's how they did it." These relationships can change over time: one consultant in Ligia's group, whose husband had been doing all the selling and ordering (under her name and consultant code[23]), had recently left her job in the formal economy to become more involved in the business.

According to Ligia, one successful director who is featured in a Yanbal promotional video is a member of such a family; her father manages the business, including administration and recruitment. He has actually stepped on more than a few Yanbalista toes in Guayaquil with some questionable recruiting strategies that some people see as being shady or unethical. In some cases, women are merely a name on paper, not being involved in Yanbal at all, as their partner or male relative does the work. This was the case for one young man whom I met in a neighboring province; he worked under his sister's code and had risen to the rank of director. The man's gender did not prevent him from working and being mentored and encouraged by his mother director and the Yanbal coordinator (implying corporate approval of his work). However, when directors at a recruitment meeting I attended were asked to come to the front of the auditorium and give their testimonies, he remained seated in the back of the room.

One of the most well-known men in Ligia's group (whose wife was en-rolled) was in the military and did a brisk business selling to his fellow sol-diers in the barracks and on base. The wife was not involved, as became ap-parent when the man was transferred to bodyguard duty for the president of Ecuador, and the code he had used to order became inactive because he did not have time to sell. He continues to be a bit of a legend in the group; several consultants spontaneously mentioned him when our conversations touched on the subject of men selling.

A consultant named Mary Sánchez, whose husband was an officer in the navy, told me that several men in his unit also sold Yanbal products to their fellow sailors, so it is possible that the military is an especially good sell-ing environment. If that is the case, this fact challenges conventional as-sumptions that direct selling is women's work and that buyers and sellers are women. In fact, direct selling of cosmetics in the military could be seen as representing the incursion of a feminine-gendered organization into a masculine-gendered organization and masculine space, an interesting sym-bolic challenge to existing gender regimes.

If women's paid work is viewed as a path to their social and economic empowerment, as many experts on women and development believe,[24] then the involvement of men in a "women's" occupation (especially as autono-mous sellers) becomes problematic. Are men using their greater freedom to go out and sell in order to horn in on an activity that has the potential to benefit women and increase their power within and outside the home? This is a question that is open to debate, since no previous academic research on "feminine" direct sales organizations has broached the topic of men sell-ing. Most Yanbal consultants and directors whom I know are not bothered by men selling, and most look favorably on men who help their wives by acting as "strategic partners." Some claim not to understand the restriction on men enrolling as consultants, while others see Yanbal's focus on women as an almost charitable act that should remain gender-specific and exclude men. In interviews with corporate staff, only one manager told me that she thought men should be allowed to sell, although all the corporate employ-ees I spoke with acknowledged that men do sell, though not as official dis-tributors. Men's work is thus not completely invisible within the organiza-tion, and mixed views exist as to its appropriateness.

Despite the presence of male sellers, the majority of Yanbalistas are still women, and the DSO is still achieving its stated mission of allowing women to increase their incomes and is still benefiting from the inclusion of a seg-ment of the population that tends not to be employed in the formal labor market. A profile of one "driver" will help give an idea of the work that these men do, showing how one man views his selling in the context of employment alternatives, gender relations, and links to the company.

MR. YANBAL: CARLOS'S TABLE

After meeting a male Yanbalista, whom I will call Carlos Zambrano,[25] I found that the unique situation of male sellers can be used to illuminate the (gendered) norms of work with a women's DSO. I met this unassuming and talkative single man of thirty-five through a female consultant who lived near him in a small town located about a half hour by bus from Guayaquil. This consultant helped me arrange a meeting with him, on the sidewalk where he set up a table in front of a relative's store on Saturdays and Sundays to display his Yanbal products. The table faced the street, and he sat behind it in a white plastic chair. He was dressed casually in jeans and an orange polo shirt with the Yanbal logo and the number of the group with which he was associated.

Carlos had been a bit of a jack-of-all-trades, earning an automotive technician certificate and completing three years of law school, but he felt that he had found his niche with Yanbal. He told me that he was the seller in his group with the highest total sales for 2007 ($18,000), an achievement for which he would be publicly recognized by his director at their group's upcoming Christmas party. Carlos was working full-time in Yanbal in order to support himself and his mother, with whom he lived and who was in ill health. Why did he decide to join Yanbal? He quoted accurate figures on Yanbal's market share relative to that of other DSOs, which he said proved the superiority of the product and the business model. He also told me, "Men can't sign up, but there are many men who work in the company because it is a company that really gives recognition to the people who work in it, incentives in the form of prizes, products." This statement shows how the organizational culture of direct selling, based on effusively rewarding performance and motivating sellers—a style of management associated with these "feminine" organizations—can seem preferable to the traditional capitalist firm, generally perceived as less congratulatory and celebratory.

Carlos had sold other types of products, including shoes and clothing, but he echoed the assertions of other Yanbalistas that Yanbal products sell themselves because of the catalog and the other advertising put out by the company. Interestingly, he also responded positively to the idea that direct selling is flexible work that can be combined with family responsibilities, a pitch usually directed at mothers looking to combine child care, home management, and income-earning activities. Since Carlos was the primary caregiver for his elderly mother, the ability to work during whatever hours he had free appealed to him. He also responded to the rhetoric of entrepreneurialism that Yanbal incorporates; like many Ecuadorians, he believed that formal wage employment not only was scarce but also did not allow for socioeconomic mobility. He said that the only way to move up was to own and grow a business.

Carlos, who is known around town as *el joven de Yanbal* (the young man from Yanbal), strongly identifies with the DSO and sees it as the path to a more stable economic future. Despite being unable to enroll as a consultant because of his gender, Carlos told me, "I feel part of the Yanbal family, and my goals for the future are based on Yanbal. . . . I believe in the company." During our conversation, he coined the neologism "*consultores*" to refer to male sellers like himself, a male adaptation of the word for female consultant, "*consultora*." Carlos explained that Yanbal had decided to have only women in the sales force based on the subjugated position of women thirty years ago, when the company entered Ecuador. Now that gender equality had been achieved, he argued, he saw no reason why men could not sell as well. He viewed himself as an expert on perfumes, although he admitted with a smile that he did not know much about makeup, that it was not his strong area. Because makeup is a product that is designated as solely for women, it did not surprise me that a male seller would claim not to be interested in or good at selling this type of product. He also told me that he did not attend his group's meetings and events, insisting that this was not because he would be embarrassed to be the only man in attendance. When I asked Carlos whether being a man selling Yanbal was an advantage or a disadvantage, he applied a gender-neutral logic (cf. Agadjanian 2002, 337), emphasizing the seller's personality and, secondarily, appearance: "Being a man doesn't make it easier or more difficult to sell a product. I mean, it depends on you. It depends on you and on what you're like."

Despite Carlos's insistence that his gender did not matter in terms of his relationships with customers, some of his selling methods differed significantly from those employed by most of the female consultants and directors I met. While some consultants may have two or three people working with them to help them sell, Carlos had a relatively organized network of ten to twelve women who used the catalog to sell and then placed their orders through him. This arrangement meant that Carlos put up the capital to place the orders and counted on his team to help him sell and collect money from clients. He passed on to his helpers a percentage of the difference between his discounted product price and the price paid by the client, yet kept all the prizes (earned according to the total sales amount) for himself. The women who helped him sell were not officially enrolled as consultants, although he was considering making them official to help him move up the ranks and eventually gain the rank of director. The title of director would officially be given to his mother, under whose code he worked. He also planned to open a storefront where he could sell his Yanbal products and possibly products from other DSOs, although the company prohibits the sale of its products in fixed retail locations.[26] Carlos routinely sold products for prices lower than those in the catalog, a strategy that had gotten him into hot water with other directors, who told him that this was unethical. According to Carlos, he was simply introducing the products to people who normally could not afford them, helping to create a client base and increasing the number of clients and thus total sales amount. This technique is frowned upon by the company.

CONCLUSION

In terms of the economic and interpersonal relationships between Ecuadorian couples, the context of declining employment and wages for men and more "flexible" work options for women (i.e., direct sales) must be seen as a new strain on domestic partnerships that are already subject to rather rigid cultural norms of gender and family. This context influences both women's work decisions and men's responses to these decisions: the individuals' gendered economic strategies take into account both economic needs and cultural prescriptions of gender. These strategies are themselves flexible and can and do change over time in response to changes in the material conditions affecting the household. Sometimes, even when men are not earning, they oppose their wives working outside the home, in an assertion of traditional male dominance. Other times, men who are out of work see the value in their wives' economic contributions and make the pragmatic decision to place cash flow above their need to fulfill the provider role.

It is important to acknowledge the variety of ways that money (income and expenses) are handled by contemporary Guayaquilean couples. There was great variation among my interviewees in terms of who shared their income and who paid which bills, and whether there were two separate bank accounts or one joint account. Most commonly, in fitting with the traditional breadwinner ideal, the husband's income is viewed as primary (Elson 1999, 616; Safa 1995), whether or not it is larger than his wife's. The husband's income, or a portion of it, goes toward the household bills, such as rent and electricity. Women are usually responsible for actually paying bills, regardless of whose money is used. This pattern has been referred to as the housekeeping allowance model (Roldán 1988, 232). In these situations, wives' incomes are seen as supplemental and secondary and are generally used to purchase personal items, such as clothing for wives and children, or to pay down debts.[27] A majority of the women I interviewed had their own bank accounts, separate from their husbands, and claimed to use their earnings however they pleased. Less frequently among the families in my sample, wives and husbands pooled their income, combining it in a single account and using it for all household and individual expenses. This model has been called the pool pattern or the common fund (Roldán 1988).

Most women agreed that either of these arrangements is acceptable, provided that husbands make enough and/or turn over enough of their income to cover basic expenses and that husbands do not demand that wives relinquish their wages. While women are seen to have a claim on husbands' earnings, the reverse proposition is not generally accepted by the Yanbalistas I met while conducting this study. Research on developing countries has shown that women are more likely to use more of their income to support their children's nutrition and education (Dwyer and Bruce 1988), and several women told me that their earnings with Yanbal paid for their children's schooling. When men were not contributing enough to the household, the idea that they were irresponsible became conflated with the lack of adequate income-earning opportunities, so that it was sometimes not clear to me (or to the women) whether men did not bring enough money home because they could not or because they would not. In any case, women's incomes, especially in poor and working-class families, are crucial to maintaining the household.

The symbolic importance of the oppositional husband and the narrative of transformation cannot be underestimated in the organizational culture of Yanbal sales. The opposer is both larger than life and a part of everyday life, yet the corporation and many sales directors do not give consultants much guidance on how to handle difficult partners. Likely because of the unspoken threat of domestic abuse, these representatives of the DSO would rather not get involved in intracouple negotiations, preferring to let women find their own way. Some consultants and directors are dissatisfied with this state of affairs and take it upon themselves to try to win over husbands. Many agree that the company should acknowledge the very real problem of opposers and provide communication tools for the women or orientation for the men. Although I understand this point of view, I also see why Yanbal might not want to get involved in the marital relationships of its distributors.

One question that I raised earlier in the chapter is how we are to interpret drivers and especially solo sellers (men who sell on their own). Biggart (1989) wrote that in Tupperware, primarily a women's DSO, husbands are encouraged to take over the business once their wives reach a certain level. In Yanbal, the image of a successful director is that of a self-made woman whose family supports her emotionally, but not in the practical day-to-day operation of the business, which the director herself is in charge of. Are husbands who become strategic partners, or men who sell in place of a woman, cutting off chances for women's economic and social empowerment through direct sales? In the strategic partner model, it seems that this is not the case. The man generally takes a backseat to the woman, and she receives the accolades for the pair's success. Men who sell on their own are making what seems to be a practical and reasonable choice in light of the lack of adequate employment opportunities for those of all educational levels. In so doing, these men challenge the cultural norms of gender and of "men's" and "women's" work. Despite a gendered economic strategy that moves them into a "feminine" line of work, these men do not see themselves as women's competition, and I think that they may be right. In Guayaquil, a city of nearly three million people, there should be enough customers to go around, and as Ligia often says, it is impossible that all of those people already have a Yanbal consultant regularly offering them products.

NOTES

1. Urban Mexican women in Roldán's study (1988) also claimed to need their husbands' permission to work. In the Mexican context, men oppose their wives working "because it calls into question men's ability to support their households and . . . undermines men's ability to control their wives' movements" (T. D. Wilson 1998, 115, citing Mummert 1992).

2. Since men are not officially distributors, there are no statistics on how many men are actively selling Yanbal products. In my research, I encountered more than I expected, but I estimate that (at least in Guayaquil) only a handful of active sellers are men.

3. In his study of men becoming street vendors in Mozambique (traditionally an occupation seen as feminine), Agadjanian (2002) identified a similar lack of formal employment opportunities as a key motivating factor. In that context, as in Ecuador, "women's employment in the formal sector still tends to be seen as unusual, whereas for men, formal sector jobs constitute not only the most appropriate and desirable type of work, but also part of their masculine identity" (ibid., 334). I would note that in Guayaquil, these expectations vary somewhat by class, as highly educated middle- and upper-class women are expected to work in the formal sector if possible, at least until they become mothers.

4. Director Ligia García de Proaño, who has been in Yanbal for twenty-two years, once estimated that in 40 percent of cases husbands are involved in their wives' work with Yanbal in some way or another (i.e., buying products, providing capital, picking up

catalogs). Based on my interviews, I would say that the percentage is a bit smaller, but this is all guesswork since there has been no comprehensive survey of the Yanbal sales force.

5. I should note that these are terms that I have created to describe patterns in men's behavior rather than folk categories used by the research participants.

6. According to a report made to the United Nations by CONAMU, the Ecuadorian government agency responsible for women's affairs, eight out of ten Ecuadorian women have been victims of violence, of which the most common type is domestic violence (CONAMU 2004). Another source states that 60 to 80 percent of women have experienced violence, which came from husbands/partners in 95 percent of cases (Radcliffe 2008, 289).

7. The entrance fee, $15 at the start of my research, has since risen to $16.

8. Coordinators are formal paid employees of the DSO, who run trainings and other events and advise directors on how to run their groups.

9. A coordinator who had worked as a sales director for Yanbal in Mexico City told me that difficult husbands were more of an issue there. She said that many of her consultants had to sneak out of the house to place or pick up orders, working without the knowledge of their husbands. This coordinator described Ecuadorian machismo as much less intense and characterized Ecuadorian women as more gutsy and hardworking.

10. The Spanish word "*tía*" means "aunt." It is often used alone to address one's aunt and is combined with a first name when talking about the aunt in the third person.

11. Jacinta poetically described her town of origin as being located "*de Jipijapa pa'laaaaante, dijeron la gente del campo*," which roughly translates as "waaaay past [the town of] Jipijapa, the country folks used to say."

12. One of Pitkin and Bedoya's informants in a study of urban poor families in Quito described her husband's jealousy and anger about her working in this same way, saying that he was afraid that "she will 'do what he does' when he is away from home (i.e., have affairs)" (1997, 40).

13. In her study of self-employed men and women in the United States, Loscocco encountered a similar dynamic in one couple, in which "his perception that his wife was a spendthrift, and that her money was for 'extras' cushioned his disappointment that he could not provide well enough to obviate the need for her income" (1997, 217).

14. While many women thought that opposers would object to their partners working anywhere outside the home, some women living with opposers had held office or factory jobs before joining Yanbal, without complaint from their husbands. There is something about the need to be "on the street" in order to find clients, sell, and collect money that leads to a special disdain toward direct sales among some husbands. In a study on Mexican immigrants selling flowers in New York City, Robert C. Smith found similar ideas about male and female public space and concern for the respectability of women selling in public (pers. comm.).

15. When I returned to visit Vanessa in June 2008, her husband's motorcycle was broken and he was without work. They separated later in the year; she asked him to leave at least in part because he was not contributing economically to the household. "He only wants to work at what he wants to do," she complained, saying that he was too picky about jobs. They have since reconciled, and he is working; Vanessa's work with Yanbal has become more sporadic.

16. For more about distributors' collection strategies, payment policies, and cash flow management, see chapter 7.

17. This is the way that many new consultants pay for their orders, since they have to have a certain amount of time with the company before being able to obtain credit or pay with personal checks.

18. Fapohunda (1988) explains why we should not assume that members of a household pool money and how this unexamined assumption has limited theories of household economics. I found both pooling and nonpooling patterns among the families of the women in this study.

19. See Chant (1991, 158) for a discussion of Mexican women who felt similarly lucky to have "tolerant" husbands.

20. Although men's transformations from supporter to opposer are less commonly discussed, I encountered one woman who had experienced this change. Her husband originally encouraged her to sign up as a consultant, but when she became a director and her time commitments and responsibilities increased, he began to oppose her work with Yanbal. She eventually fell from director status, working as a consultant again, and later quit the DSO.

21. This large office tower, situated in the historically wealthy Kennedy neighborhood in northern Guayaquil, is actually called the Centrum Building, but since the largest tenant is Porta, whose name is emblazoned at the top of the edifice in big red letters, it is commonly known by *guayaquileños* and *guayaquileñas* as the Porta building (*el edificio Porta*).

22. This director also brought her husband along to the directors' Christmas party, even though Ligia had designed it to be women-only. They sat far in the back of the hall, and I thought he looked slightly uncomfortable as the disc jockey led the women in chants of "Long live women!" and "Who's in charge here? The women!"

23. Each consultant and director has a unique code number, which they must use to place orders or make claims with the company. The number can also be used by Yanbal and the directors to look up a consultant's registration and ordering history, as well as outstanding debts. If a consultant leaves the sales force and then returns, she is generally given the same code number. Directors accept orders from men as long as the orders are associated with a registered woman's code.

24. In the 1995 Beijing Declaration on women's global status, for example, "economic independence" is all but equated with "employment" (UNDAW 1995).

25. Although he gave me permission to use his real name, I decided to give this informant a pseudonym, since he is technically going against Yanbal policy by being a male seller and also by setting up a stand to sell products.

26. Here, like the Mozambican men in Agadjanian's study, Carlos engaged in "blurring the subjective status differentiation between large-scale commerce, traditionally a man's realm, and petty street trade, traditionally a women's lot" (Agadjanian 2002, 337). Aspiring to upward mobility and what Agadjanian calls "higher-volume trade" may be a way for Carlos to distance himself from the work of most women direct sellers (ibid., 339).

27. According to a study by Floro and Messier (2006), regardless of whether loans or other forms of credit are sought out by male or female members of a household, women are more likely to be the ones who pay off these debts with their earnings, despite their generally lower incomes.

PART II

THE LOOK: IMAGES OF BEAUTY, PROFESSIONALISM, AND SUCCESS

HOW PRODUCTS SELL THEMSELVES: PICTURING GENDER, RACE, AND CLASS IN YANBAL'S CATALOGS

WHY THE CATALOG MATTERS

It was a few days after Christmas, and the launch event for the first campaign of the new year had just been held in a crowded meeting room in the building where sales director Ligia García de Proaño has her office.[1] After the meeting ended, the office was mobbed with consultants picking up catalogs; even with me and two other women assisting, people had to wait for their catalog. Outstretched hands held bills and coins to pay for catalogs, and collected change along with the shiny magazines. Some women were purchasing one or more catalogs; others had earned a free catalog by reaching their sales goal in the previous campaign (a prize offered by Ligia), and their names had to be crossed off a list. Others waited around to ask questions of the office staff after getting their catalogs. There were probably more than fifty people in the office, and the level of activity and noise was impressive. A few women had brought their young daughters with them, although this practice is generally discouraged. A couple of teenage girls giggled as they admired a photograph pinned to the bulletin board, of a male model representing one of Yanbal's colognes.

Ligia was moving through the crowd, congratulating those who had won prizes in the previous campaign and putting women on the spot to name their sales or prize goal for the new campaign. A few consultants who had already received their catalogs were picking at the remains of a cake that had been served upstairs to celebrate December birthdays. My husband, visiting for the holidays, stood by the door, looking bewildered as he surveyed the throng of excited women packed into the modestly sized office. If the rush had lasted five more minutes, he would have probably been pressed into service behind the counter. Versions of this scene are repeated after every campaign launch, indicating the importance sellers place on the catalog in their work.

Like most direct selling organizations, Yanbal publishes a catalog that distributors use to sell products directly to customers. Since DSOs do not operate in fixed retail locations, the catalog is an efficient way for sellers and clients to get to know the products that are available. Yanbal operates on the basis of four-week "campaigns," with a total of thirteen campaigns per year. My main period of fieldwork in Ecuador touched on eight of these thirteen campaigns over seven months between September 2007 and June 2008.[2] The product offerings and special prices for each campaign are included in the catalog and also featured on Yanbal's website.[3]

In this chapter, I argue that the images, text, and themes that appear in direct selling organizations' catalogs matter because they illustrate common cultural understandings and aspirations in ways that motivate customers to buy products. Clients who buy products upon seeing a sales catalog are symbolically consuming the lifestyle represented in the catalog's photos, which overwhelmingly present glamorous white women and men taking part in activities associated with the wealthiest members of Ecuadorian society. It would be a mistake to assume that those who see the catalog are never critical of the gaps between its representations and the lives of most Ecuadorians. In previous research in Guayaquil, I have found that even young people, thought to be the most gullible media consumers, are able to analyze media images critically (Casanova 2004). Nevertheless, the images that predominate are similar to images found in many other cultural products in the country and in contemporary Latin America more generally and are thus worth examining in the context of the social and economic realities of people's lives. The glossy, full-color catalog is important for sellers not only because they see it as an indispensable tool for their work but also because the glamorous images on its pages strengthen their claims to a professional identity and an enviable association with a respected transnational corporation.

THE CATALOG AS WALKING DISPLAY CASE

Before getting to know people who sell and buy Yanbal, I was skeptical of claims that this or that product "sells itself." But this does seem to be the case with Yanbal products. Rather than needing to be persuaded to buy, clients leaf through the current catalog and choose the products they want. Consultants and directors alike stated that the catalog was a necessary tool for selling the products. When asked how important the catalog was for sellers' work with Yanbal, director Ana María Briones emphasized its visual impact on clients:

Ooh, it's fundamental, it's fundamental, because people fall in love when they see the product in the catalog, above all with the jewelry . . . [and,] for example, the lipstick that's shown on the cover girl, or in the middle page of the catalog a girl is made up with that one—that's the one they want. And it runs out [during] that campaign, but that lipstick was for sale in the last campaign and nobody bought it.

Consultant Gioconda Ibarra echoed many of her fellow distributors when she said, "If we don't have the catalog, we cannot sell anything." Jacinta Menoscal agreed: "If I don't carry the catalog, the client doesn't buy from me." Consultants and directors often recalled with amazement Ligia's stories of selling with only a price list and some product samples in the days before Yanbal produced a catalog. Some sellers and directors used language from Yanbal training materials, referring to the catalog as a walking display case (*la vitrina ambulante*) of the company's products. Clients have become accustomed to the catalog, as Narcisa Pazmiño explained: "[When I visit my clients,] they ask me right off the bat, 'Did the new catalog come out yet?'" In my observations and conversations with consultants, I learned that they differ in how they use the catalog. Some consultants will never leave a catalog with a client, for example, and some clients want to be walked through the special offers and new products, reviewing the catalog in the consultant's presence. Other sellers prefer to buy multiple catalogs, drop them off with big-spending clients, and then pick them up along with the list of products the client wants. Many consultants who sell to office workers prefer to leave catalogs to be passed around the office and then return a couple days later to collect the orders.

Many of the women I came to know, despite embracing the catalog, argued that the only way to sell perfumes is with samples, since customers have trouble buying a new perfume based simply on a printed advertisement. Applying the fragrance to the skin and inhaling it are crucial for perfume purchasing decisions and are part of what makes the buying experience pleasurable. Carlos Zambrano used samples to sell more than just perfumes:

When you want to sell a product, of course, I mean, the magazine helps you, but I think just going around with the magazine and seeing the product just in the magazine doesn't really have an advantage. I prefer to sell with the product, yes, and then at the end if they ask how much it costs, I show them the magazine: "Look, it costs this much."[4]

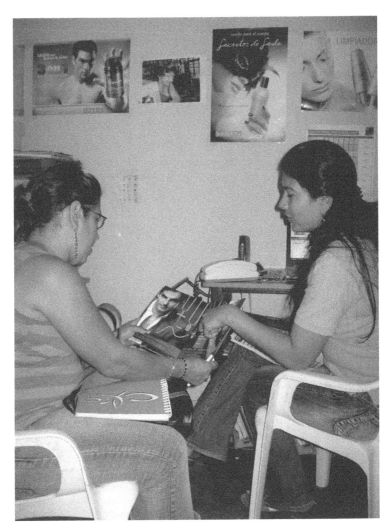

Sales director Betty Brigss (*right*) helps one of her consultants place an order in her home office in northern Guayaquil. (Photo by the author)

Sellers can buy samples of perfumes and other products along with their orders or receive them as prizes for meeting sales targets. Consultants who attend meetings at Yanbal headquarters or their directors' offices may also receive samples as prizes for answering questions correctly or through raffles. A prize that Yanbalistas were quite excited about in late 2007 was a boxed set of thirty fragrance demos in celebration of Yanbal Ecuador's thirtieth anniversary.

Regardless of whether or not they use samples, most consultants claim that they always carry a catalog with them. As women move up the ranks of the sales force and become responsible for other sellers, they tend to buy more than one catalog (the price per unit during my fieldwork was $1.70, or less if more catalogs were bought). Then-aspiring director Belén Vera described how she used the catalog: "I sometimes tend to work with five catalogs. . . . Sometimes the consultants [her daughter consultants] say, 'Sell me a catalog,' and I give them a catalog, and so I keep several catalogs. For the clients who keep a catalog for a day, I let them look it over calmly." Consultants can obtain the next campaign's catalog at the end of the current campaign. If they place an order in the last week of Campaign 3, for instance, they will receive one Campaign 4 catalog for free; they can order additional catalogs then as well. Alternatively, consultants can purchase catalogs from their mother director. As described at the beginning of this chapter, this often takes place immediately after a monthly meeting called a campaign launch, an event designed to get consultants informed and excited about the upcoming campaign.

Using qualitative content analysis, this chapter explores the visual and textual representations in eighteen Yanbal product catalogs from campaigns between January 2006 and February 2008. These catalogs were collected in the field or downloaded and printed from the Yanbal website. Because jewelry products change each campaign yet often remain available for sale, most consultants and directors zealously guard old catalogs, which made my task of collecting as many catalogs as possible a bit difficult. In Campaign 12 (November 2007), most of the directors I knew inadvertently ordered too few catalogs and scrambled to borrow from each other in order to cover the needs of their consultants. As selling products was a higher priority for these women than my data collection (and rightly so), it took me some time to track down an extra catalog. After asking around for months, I was finally able to buy one from a consultant just days before returning to the United States. Because they cost money, catalogs are treated as a precious resource, and consultants get upset if clients or family members borrow and do not return these "tools."

Beyond the catalog's utility for sellers, I am interested in the image of Yanbal that is embodied in the catalog's pictures and text. According to sellers, this image is so positively received that it allows the products to "sell themselves," and customers claim that the images in the catalogs inspire them to purchase products. Because the catalog is so crucial to sales and is the most accessible representation of the DSO to the public, I examine the messages that it contains about beauty, class, race, and other themes of cultural and social relevance. The catalogs draw on cultural norms and ideals in order to sell upscale products that allow customers to tap into a lifestyle that is beyond the reach of their material resources. Other scholars have fruitfully used studies of advertising to understand marketing and consumption within a variety of industries, including L. Cohen (2003), Miller (1997), and Peiss (1998).

ABOUT THE CATALOG

The Yanbal catalog that comes out thirteen times per year in Ecuador is a full-color publication of approximately 150 pages, resembling a fashion magazine in terms of its production quality and imagery. Officially, the catalog is to be used only by registered consultants and directors, but copies find their way into other hands as well. The glossy pages feature glamorous female and male models photographed in exotic or otherwise exciting settings (such as beaches, yachts, and mountains); the text and images emphasize what is new and trendy.

The catalog is divided into the following sections, whose order varies: women's jewelry, men's jewelry (not always included), makeup, women's fragrances, men's fragrances, skin care, youth makeup (geared toward teen girls), youth fragrances (not always included),[5] personal care products (body treatments, lotions, hair care, sunscreen), and products for children and babies. Catalogs also include an insert with candles and other home fragrance products, and a few times a year a bridal supplement features costume jewelry targeted at women planning a wedding. The best sale-priced item is generally featured on the back cover of the catalog. Some images or product campaigns appearing in the catalog are also featured in Yanbal's advertising: television and print ads, the website, and billboards.

MAJOR THEMES

Content analysis[6] of a sample of eighteen catalogs yielded four major themes, connected to and reinforcing cultural ideals that are communicated visually and textually to readers. These themes are repeated throughout many or most catalogs and are drawn upon to promote products. The messages about social class and race or skin color were similar to those that I found in a previous study of Ecuadorian women's magazines (Casanova 2003). Two themes that had not been relevant for that study were also prominently represented in the Yanbal catalogs: *latinidad* (Latinness) and motherhood. Taken together, these themes resonate with mainstream Ecuadorian (and more broadly, Latin American) conceptions of the social order and desire for status. Even though similar or identical themes appear in Yanbal catalogs distributed in other countries, I am most interested in the ways in which the words and images support or challenge the common-sense understandings of everyday Ecuadorians. These understandings are activated to market and sell products, and they provide the cultural base for the livelihoods of the women whose work I studied.

CLASS AND LUXURY   The association of beauty products with an upper-class or elite lifestyle is a familiar marketing strategy that is not unique to Yanbal, direct sales, or Ecuador (Peiss 1998; Santa Cruz and Erazo 1980). These tropes draw on associations between class standing and appearance (discussed further in chapter 4). Repeated symbols of upper-class status promote the idea that a socially acceptable appearance, and perhaps even socio-economic mobility, can be achieved by consuming the products displayed. The emphasis on the desirability of high socioeconomic status is both ironic and predictable in a country like Ecuador, where around 40 percent of the population lives below the poverty line and the richest 10 percent of urban households consume 35 percent of available goods and services (*World Factbook* 2008; statistics are from 2006). Despite this emphasis on the trappings of wealth, however, Yanbal makes luxury-like items available to the masses despite their low incomes (see chapter 7).

What do rich folks have that regular folks want? Money, for one thing. And Yanbal catalogs literally show customers the money. One advertisement featured a men's leather wallet that could be purchased for $10, after a minimum purchase of $35 in men's products. The wallet is shown with a $20 bill and a $10 bill projecting from the billfold (Campaign 11–2007, 127).[7] The promotion was repeated the following year, with two $20 bills and three credit cards visible in the wallet (Campaign 4–2008, 133). A wallet promoted in the *juvenil* (youth) section of the catalog showed that even young people can have money. The wallet, made of silver lamé, was shown with a $20 bill and a $5 bill peeking out of the billfold pocket (Campaign 13–2007, 105). A similarly metallic wallet had been promoted, also in the youth section, in a previous campaign. The imaginary owner of that wallet was doing quite well for herself, with three $100 bills in the billfold and credit and/or bank cards from Citibank, Visa, American Express, and Banco del Pacífico (an Ecuadorian bank) visible in the smaller pockets (Campaign 1–2006, 83).

These images must be placed in context in order to fully appreciate their meaning. When I began my fieldwork, the monthly minimum wage in Ecuador was $170, which was raised by the government to $200 in 2008.

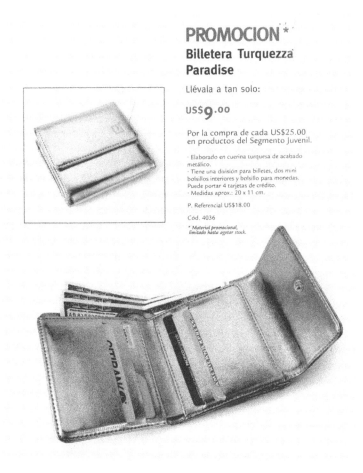

PROMOCION *

**Billetera Turquezza
Paradise**

Llévala a tan solo:

US$**9**.oo

Por la compra de cada US$25.00
en productos del Segmento Juvenil.

· Elaborado en cuerina turquesa de acabado
metálico.
· Tiene una división para billetes, dos mini
bolsillos interiores y bolsillo para monedas.
Puede portar 4 tarjetas de crédito.
· Medidas aprox.: 20 x 11 cm.

P. Referencial US$18.00

Cód. 4036

* Material promocional,
limitado hasta agotar stock.

A photo of a wallet featured in the Yanbal catalog for Campaign 1 of 2006 in
Ecuador, p. 83. (Courtesy of Yanbal International)

The monthly "breadbasket" (*canasta familiar*)—that is, the minimum of
basic foods, products, and services needed to support a family of four for
a month—was estimated to be $469 at the end of 2007 (Ecuavisa 2007).
With food prices rising worldwide, this figure had jumped to $503 by June
2008, when the average four-person household had an income of roughly
$373 per month (*El Universo* 2008a). The mismatch between wages and
average expenses meant that families were overextended, and those who
could manage to make ends meet depended on credit, loans from friends
and family, or other strategies to keep the household afloat. The average
Ecuadorian, regardless of age or gender, does not have $300 in cash in his

or her wallet (I have actually never seen a $100 bill in ten years of conducting research in Ecuador) and would perhaps be pleased to have the $25 shown in one of the wallets.

Another way that class is symbolized in the catalogs is through images of travel. Urban Ecuadorians, including residents of Guayaquil, travel every day. They travel across the city to get to work or school or perform other necessary tasks. Many are internal migrants, who initially traveled to Guayaquil from the countryside or from another city and continue to travel back home to visit. For less than $10, a person can travel by bus to basically any part of the country. And some have experienced, or know family members who have undertaken, international migration to various other countries, whether by plane, boat, the dangerous overland route to the U.S. border through Central America and Mexico, or a combination of these strategies. Geographic mobility is thus a part of life for many *guayaquileños*. But the type of travel that is associated with the upper class is fundamentally different from these other ways of moving through national and international space. This type of expensive luxury travel is a practice involving the most elite members of Ecuadorian society, as can be seen in media portrayals and ascertained by speaking with people at varying socioeconomic levels. The catalog from Campaign 1 in 2006 revolves around a beach vacation theme, and the destinations are far-off locales: the Caribbean, Puerto Plata (a resort town in the Dominican Republic), Mar de Plata (a beach in Argentina), and the "Riviera" (an unspecified coastal location). These locations are the settings for models photographed in beach gear and are portrayed as "a dreamy paradise" and "*tu destino esperado*" (your awaited destination, or your hoped-for destination).[8]

The catalog for the campaign that coincided with Mother's Day in 2007 featured mothers and children engaging in luxury travel together. A fashionably dressed mother and son pose on the Fulton Ferry Landing in front of the Brooklyn Bridge in one photograph, which bears the caption "Remember our first trip together?" The text at the margin of the two-page spread is an imagined note from the son to his mother, which reads in part: "When you chose that trip filled with fragrances and enchantment, you didn't just stay in the most marvelous places, but you also stayed in the best of all: my heart" (Campaign 5–2007, 32). It is obvious that this photograph is showing a pleasure trip to New York, not the migration journey that so many Ecuadorians have made to that city over the past decades. Another catalog features a bracelet called Destinations, with golden charms symbolizing luxury travel: a tiny Arc de Triomphe; the Statue of Liberty; a cruise ship; a suitcase with stickers reading "Paris," "New York," "Rome," and

"Tokyo"; a jet plane; a pagoda; and an Egyptian pyramid. The description of the bracelet tells readers: "This year give free reign to your adventurous spirit and prepare yourself to take that trip you always wanted to. There are no limits; New York, Paris, or whatever city you want will be a new world, waiting for you to discover it" (Campaign 13–2007, 23). The image and text imply that engaging in luxury travel is simply a question of deciding to go (or where to go); interestingly, mostly urban destinations were featured here, as opposed to the beach vacations described above. The catalog for the first campaign of 2008 took luxury travel as its unifying theme: on page after page, women dressed in simple yet expensive-looking clothing or bathing suits were shown posing on yachts in the water, often with shirtless men lounging nearby (Campaign 1–2008, front cover).

As Maureen O'Dougherty (2002) showed in her work on Brazil, international travel is often associated in the popular imagination with elites and is increasingly sought after by middle-class people throughout Latin America. Her research on the iconic status of the family trip to Disney World among middle- and upper-class Brazilians rings true with Ecuadorian perceptions and cultural ideals. To obtain the tourist visa necessary to travel to the United States, Ecuadorian citizens have to be able to show that they have money in the bank and reasons to return home (i.e., owning property or a business). Thus, taking pleasure trips to New York City, like that of the fictional family featured in the Yanbal catalog described above, is a symbol of upper-class status, a symbol with which most Ecuadorians viewing the catalog would be familiar.

Yanbal is aware of the association with travel and upper-classness, and this knowledge is not only utilized for marketing products. One of the biggest perks of being a successful sales director in Yanbal is the chance to win trips to destinations near and far. In Yanbal's promotional videos and in interactions with consultants or potential recruits, directors tick off a list of glamorous destinations that they have experienced courtesy of their work with Yanbal. These include Latin American countries such as Brazil, Colombia, and the Dominican Republic, as well as countries outside the region, like Greece, Italy, and the United States. By sending successful members of the sales force on trips of the type associated with the very rich, Yanbal is symbolically conferring a desirable class status on them, despite their income level or social origins. The influence of these shared symbols on women considering joining Yanbal or trying to move up the ranks should not be underestimated.

Another aspect of class that is communicated in the catalogs is the connection between an upper- or middle-class appearance and consumption. The use of certain beauty products and practices is associated with high-class status (discussed further in chapter 4), and this type of consumption is seen as having the potential to obscure humble origins (when performed "correctly"). An advertisement for nail color proclaims: "Class . . . it's written on your hands" (Campaign 1–2006, 24). For women, caring for and painting nails is an outwardly visible indicator of class. In an advertisement for a men's fragrance, an elegant young man is shown dressed in a tuxedo and holding a glass of champagne, both traditional symbols of luxury and wealth. The slogan of the cologne is "It's about knowing how to choose" (ibid., 118). The choice being referred to is, of course, the decision to buy the cologne, which costs $52 in this catalog (an amount equal to nearly one-third of the monthly minimum wage at the time).[9] The association between consumption, appearance, and class is obvious in this appeal to customers.

A similar image with a female model appeared in a holiday catalog in 2006. A formally dressed woman, with upswept hair, glittering makeup, and crystal jewelry shining like diamonds, holds a flute of champagne. The caption reads, "Celebrate with class" (Campaign 13–2006, 7). Another advertisement promotes a jewelry set as "the selection of an elegant woman." The accompanying photograph shows this elegant woman wearing all the pieces of the jewelry set, with expertly coiffed hair, a velvet top (velvet being a traditional symbol of luxury), and a patrician air (Campaign 3–2007, 27). The catalog for Campaign 8 in 2007 features women in fanciful Victorian-inspired dresses, hairdos, and headpieces. On the first page of the jewelry section, a caption describes the jewelry offerings: "The maximum expression of elegance. Collections that transmit luxury in every detail . . . Jewels that reflect the meaning of opulence and good taste" (Campaign 8–2007, 35). The text directly defines the social role of jewelry as signaling the class status of the wearer.

Despite the catalogs' emphasis on class, wealth, and elite status symbols, Yanbal makes some concessions to the economic realities of the countries in which it does business, and the material conditions in which clients live. One symbolic indicator of this is that Yanbal sells engagement rings and wedding bands, made of sterling silver and cubic zirconia instead of the traditional gold and diamonds. Although these rings are portrayed as luxurious rather than bargain products, their cost (just under $50 for the engagement ring) makes them more accessible for the average Ecuadorian than "the real thing." In an urban environment, where flashy jewelry can set up a person as a robbery target, having a $50 ring as opposed to a $500 one may make sense for women of all class levels. I know one wealthy lady who has taken to wearing just such a ring so that if she gets mugged, her losses are limited.

RACE AND SKIN COLOR   If I were to show one of my undergraduate students images from the Yanbal catalog and ask them in what country they thought the publication was produced, they would most likely guess the United States or some European nation. This is because the models featured tend to be light-eyed, light-haired, thin Caucasian types or else some version of what I have called the "generic Latino" type, a dark-haired, dark-eyed but still thin and light-skinned person who looks vaguely Latin (Casanova 2003, 2007). Most Ecuadorians would probably say that the women and men featured in the catalogs and Yanbal's other advertising do not look particularly Ecuadorian (cf. Casanova 2004); of course, the same models are featured in catalogs in all eight countries, which represent a wide range of racial population compositions.

The racial reality of Ecuador has been the subject of study, although percentages are always up for debate and the national census cannot be completely trusted, because of people's desire to disavow nonwhite ancestry. It is generally agreed that the numerical majority of Ecuadorians can be considered mestizo, implying a mixture of indigenous and European heritage. People who identify themselves as indigenous and are associated with various tribes, nations, and communities are found primarily throughout the Andean highland and Amazonian regions of the country. In Guayaquil, indigenous people are few but are highly visible when they wear traditional dress, and they often work informally in markets or other public spaces. Blacks, known as Afro-Ecuadorians, make up a small percentage of the population (5–10 percent) and are concentrated in Guayaquil and the northern coastal province of Esmeraldas (Halpern and Twine 2000; Whitten and Quiroga 1998).

Quite often, the Ecuadorians located at the highest levels of industry and government, and those featured on television and in other cultural products, are white and European-looking. The whiteness of the models in Yanbal's catalogs fits in with a larger Latin American and Caribbean cultural logic of valuing that which is perceived as European, especially when it comes to physical appearance and beauty (Casanova 2003, 2004; C. B. Cohen, Wilk, and Stoeltje 1995; Miller 1997; Rahier 1998; Twine 1997).

The default image for beauty and physical perfection in the catalogs is the light-haired, light-eyed, white model. The models used to promote Yanbal's Sentiva line of skin care products uniformly fit this ideal, symbolizing perfect skin and a clean, fresh appearance. An advertisement for a makeup line called the Perfect Woman Collection visually represents the perfect woman as an ivory-skinned blonde with light green-blue eyes (Campaign 3–2007, 6–7). Advertisements for Yanbal sunscreens imply a white-skinned (or at least light-skinned) customer; the training materials aimed at consultants and directors cite the incidence of skin cancer only among people with white skin, for example. An ad for bronzing powders assumed an audience of white-skinned women seeking a tan, promoting "color that gives life to your tan!" (Campaign 1–2006, 10). Because of the value placed on light skin, many Ecuadorian women are more concerned with avoiding a tan than obtaining one; as Peiss (1998) showed in her history of U.S. beauty culture, suntans are the luxury of women whose racial identity is unquestionably white.

Pointing to the overrepresentation of white, blonde, light-eyed models in the catalogs, relative to the demographic realities of the Ecuadorian population, is a useful exercise that could take up an entire chapter. Here, however, I am more interested in complicating this "beauty ideals" approach by looking at the exceptions, and the complex ways in which Yanbal acknowledges its mestizo or brown-skinned consumers. That the corporation markets products for different skin tones shows a practical adaptation or tempering of cultural ideals in light of the phenotypical variations found among Latin American women.

In the earliest catalog in my sample, from January 2006, cosmetic foundations or bases are grouped into just three categories, represented by a table with skin color labels at the top and products down the y-axis: one shade for "very white skin"; three for "white skin"; and two for "brown skin" (*piel trigueña*) (Campaign 1–2006, 23). The darkest shade was called (in English) "classic tan," and appeared to be made for a light brown shade of skin. In the youth line of makeup from the same campaign, only two colors of base were available: "ivory" for "light skin," and "beige" for "medium skin" (ibid., 84). Young women with skin darker than "medium" were simply out of luck.

What is interesting is not that Yanbal limited the range of makeup choice to the lightest skin colors, but the way in which the foundation offerings have changed over time. By Campaign 4 of 2007, the skin color categories were still only three, but their names had changed to "white skin," "light medium skin," and "dark medium skin" (62). Just one shade of concealer, base, and powder was available for those with "white skin," and just one shade for those with "dark medium skin," implying that most consumers should be in the middle category. One shade that had previously been classified for "brown skin" moved into the "light medium" category, which had the most hues to choose from, in quite a range of shades. Surprisingly, a shade of foundation featured in this advertisement was actually called "dark 1," which represented both a change from previous terminology and the introduction of a new darker foundation.

Just two campaigns later, there were four options for skin colors, with the addition of "dark skin" (Campaign 6–2007, 90); however, there were only two foundations available for dark skin, and no concealer or powders. By the very next campaign, this situation was remedied, with four new products for "dark skin" (Campaign 7–2007, 37). The skin color/makeup product matrix in this catalog introduced close-up photos of a chunk of a model's face (cheek, nose, and lips) so that customers and sellers could see what was meant by "white skin," "light medium skin," "dark medium skin," and "dark skin." Although the white skin is indeed quite pale, the other photos do not seem to match their labels. The skin color of the faces shown seems lighter than the skin of the majority of Ecuadorian women I have come into contact with, such that the "dark"-skinned model might not be read as dark-skinned in social interactions. Someone with brown skin along the lines of model Naomi Campbell or even someone with lighter brown skin (whom *guayaquileños* might call *"trigueña"*) would likely find the "dark" foundation too light. Yanbal continues to tweak the foundation color options; in late 2007 the poetic names of previous products (e.g., "classic tan," *"beige antártico," "café pacífico"*) had been replaced by numbered colors: "light 1" for light skin, "medium" numbers 1 through 5 for "light medium" and "dark medium" skin, and "dark 1" for "dark skin" (Campaign 11–2007, p. 99).

The changes in makeup colors may indicate some confusion over skin color among the Yanbal marketing and product development staff, reflecting the shifting sands of people's racial identities and the politics of skin color in everyday life. What we see by examining the products advertised in the catalogs over time is an expansion of color options, most likely in an effort to serve as many customers as possible in a diverse society like Ecuador. At the beginning of 2006, the darkest skin colors mentioned were *"trigueña"* (brown) and "medium skin," even though the existence of a medium tone implies both light and dark tones at either extreme. By the middle of 2007, however, a "dark skin" category had been introduced, with a mostly new lineup of products associated with it. Although the skin and foundation colors called "dark" were not all that dark, the introduction of the previously taboo word "dark" showed some acknowledgment of the range of skin color among Ecuadorian women. It remains to be seen if newer, darker colors will continue to be introduced.

The inclusion in the catalog of products aimed at "dark"-skinned women, however, does not translate to individual women's embrace of this label. In a society that highly values whiteness, there are not many incentives to call oneself dark-skinned (regardless of phenotype). An interaction between Yanbal director Betty Brigss and one of her consultants illuminates this dilemma. The consultant had come into Betty's home office one Wednesday afternoon to place her order for the week.[10] She had promised a client a certain powder and wanted to see if Betty had it in stock, so that she wouldn't have to wait for her new order to come in to give it to the client. This is a common request among consultants who have close relationships with their sales directors. The consultant and Betty live near each other, and Betty knows the client in question personally. Based on this knowledge, Betty questioned the client's request of a foundation in the color "medium 2." Both Betty and the consultant agreed that the woman was "very dark" (*bien morena*) and would be better off using one of the shades prescribed for those with "medium dark" skin tone. But, the consultant explained, she doesn't want "medium dark" foundation. This discussion shows two things. First, customers may be reluctant to buy the darker makeup colors, since this implies selecting for themselves one of the darker skin color categories outlined in the catalog. Second, although Betty and the consultant both disagreed with the clients' self-classification as having light medium skin, beauty consultants are relatively powerless to advise clients on what shade is best, for fear of offending them by classifying them as darker than they see themselves.

Despite the overwhelming whiteness of the models featured in Yanbal catalogs, there were two issues that portrayed nonwhite ethnicity as somewhat fashionable. The first was the issue for Campaign 1 in 2007, whose cover and inside photographs elaborated a Polynesian-inspired theme through text and images. The cover photo showed a woman with light cinnamon skin lying on her stomach in the sand. The image conveys sensuality, from the model's wet hair covering one eye to the large flower in her hair and the way her shirt is loosely hanging off her shoulder. The model's racial identification and national origin are visually ambiguous, but her appearance evokes a tropical, South Pacific theme, underscored by the caption "A paradise of beauty." Similar photos appear within the catalog, and the same model is used in an advertisement for a makeup set called "pearls of Tahiti." The text claims that "the exotic landscapes of Tahiti are the inspiration for a collection in which the eyes [*las miradas*] become tropical" (Campaign 1–2007, 4–5). The Polynesian look is used throughout the catalog, and even a light-eyed, blonde model uses a flower behind her ear in the youth makeup section. These images show that although the model with light brown skin seemed to be racialized, this idealized pseudoethnicity or ethnic look can be put on by anyone. The women's bodies are not permanently marked as Asian or Polynesian or nonwhite; they just seem to be trying the trappings of these ethnic identifications on for size.

More relevant for the Ecuadorian context was the visual theme of the September–October 2007 catalog (Campaign 10), which featured white models in Andean indigenous settings and toyed with markers of indigenous ethnicity. Readers familiar with the social construction of race in Ecuador and throughout the Andes will know of the frequent association of indigenous people with the primitive and traditional; the opposite symbol is the white or mestizo, representing modernity and progress (Pequeño Bueno 2007). Although lip service is paid to the glorious Incan or aboriginal roots of Ecuadorian culture, actual contemporary indigenous people are often viewed as being stuck in the past and unable to join modern society (Meisch 2002; Whitten 1981).

The cover of the catalog references these popular understandings of the racial order by presenting an oxymoronic photo and text. The model is posed in front of what could be read as a town or city in the Ecuadorian Sierra (Andean region); the Sierra is strongly associated with indigenousness, both historically and presently, and is the region where most indigenous people live. The model has white skin and brown hair that is styled stick-straight, with heavy bangs. Indigenous people are associated with thick, straight, dark hair, and the model's hairstyle, combined with her whiteness, could be viewed as a play on this stereotype. The caption reads: "Encanto Original / Lo último en la belleza" (Original Enchantment / The latest in beauty). This juxtaposition of (indigenous) origins (as in "original") with the "latest" or the most modern is intriguing, as is the way that symbols of indigenous ethnicity appear throughout the issue.

The jewelry section proclaims the arrival of "ethnic glamour," words that are also set against the background of a mountain town (Campaign 10–2007, 4). Ethnic-looking textiles similar to those produced by indigenous people in various parts of Latin America appear throughout the catalog. Yet the stance of the models recalls the apostle's admonition to be "in the world but not of it." It is obvious that these ladies are tourists in this indigenous-identified landscape, as shown in the photo that prominently features a hostel with various foreign flags and the caption "Un paseo por tus fantasías" (A trip through your fantasies) (ibid., 14). The model is thus a visitor on a trip, rather than someone who belongs in or to this space. In a photo titled "Hidden Treasures," a light-skinned, Latina-looking model shops in an artisan market: indigenous textiles are hung behind her in a scene that brings to mind the famous market in Otavalo, Ecuador, a major domestic and international tourist attraction (ibid., 24). Most striking, however, is the photograph whose rural background includes indigenous women as part of the scenery. Although their images are blurred, they can be seen sitting on the ground, wearing elements of traditional dress (fedora hats, shawls) and with their hair in braids. The model in the foreground is distanced from these modestly attired women, both by her strapless top (contrasting with the covered-up style of the women in the background) and by the text, urging her to "live in the moment" (ibid., 26). The trope of indigenous identity as belonging to the past and its rejection as being equated with modernity is at work here.

In Ecuador's recent history, as in other Latin American countries, indigenous people have become increasingly visible in popular culture and on the political scene, and many mestizos have begun to accept this situation (see Hale 2006 for similar developments in Guatemala). However, as with the depiction of Polynesian visual elements, ethnicity in these representations of indigenousness is something to be consumed rather than a basis for identity or political mobilization. Ecuadorians can show their cosmopolitanism and tolerance by traveling to centers of indigenous culture or shopping in artisan markets, but this does not necessarily translate into better treatment for actual indigenous people in everyday life. These visual and textual representations of indigenousness place indigenous people in the past, whereas the Yanbal woman is evidently not a part of that world but simply a modern visitor enjoying local color.

LATINIDAD   Much has been written in recent years on the concept of *latinidad*, which can be understood as a set of discourses about what it means to be Latino or Latina. These discourses do not exclusively address or refer to people of Latin descent in the United States and can be traced to Latin American thinkers and political figures such as José Martí and Simón Bolívar. Pan-Latino images or slogans are commonly used to market products to Latinos in the United States and to Latin Americans throughout the hemisphere (Casanova 2003, 2007; Dávila 2001), and Yanbal also makes use of this strategy. Because Yanbal operates in seven Latin American countries and in Spain (with its growing numbers of Latin American immigrants), it makes good business sense to focus on the similarities between Latin Americans rather than create completely different marketing campaigns for each country. Indeed, the recently stated mission of the company was to "elevate the standard of living of the Latina woman," although the word "Latina" no longer appears in the mission statement on the website. The company does, however, define itself as a "Latina corporation." In the catalog dedicated to Yanbal's thirtieth anniversary in Ecuador, a letter from company founder Fernando Belmont and his daughter, Janine, referenced "making the dreams of Latina women [*la mujer latina*] reality" (Campaign 7–2007). The next year's anniversary catalog claimed to be "a celebration of Latina women" (Campaign 7–2008, 5).

The following excerpt from my interview with Robert Watson, the general manager of Yanbal Ecuador, describes in more detail this Latino corporate identity.

> ROBERT: It is difficult to find anyone who wants to argue with the vision of the company, because it is, on the one hand, to be the most prestigious direct sales beauty company (initially) in Latin America. Now it has changed recently, and it is to be the most prestigious *Latin* direct sales beauty business . . .
>
> ERYNN: What is the difference between those two terms?
>
> ROBERT: It's subtle but very big, because before the focus was Latin America and now it's not anymore, because we are selling in Europe also and we are thinking of opening in the United States, so the fact that we are Latinos and our Latino character are important, but we are no longer a business based and dedicated exclusively to Latin America but rather we have opened ourselves up to the world.

Stereotypes connecting *latinidad* to sensuality, similar to the hypersexual depictions of Latinos in the U.S. media, appear in Yanbal marketing materials. The perfume Osadía, for example, is promoted by the company as being "inspired by the nature of the Latina woman," and the face of the product's campaign is former Miss Bolivia, Desirée Durán (Campaign 1–2006, 49). The advertisements for this fragrance, whose slogan is "subtle provocation," are overtly sensual. So are the advertisements for the men's version of Osadía, which is described as "Latin provocation." The male model featured in the promotional materials for this scent has white skin, brown hair, and green eyes; that is, he is not strongly marked as Latino by his appearance. In the advertisements, however, he is featured with his black shirt unbuttoned and wearing a black and silver rosary (Campaign 11–2007, 128). This symbol of Catholicism could be seen to represent Latin America, where most people are Catholic (in Ecuador the figure is 95 percent; *World Factbook* 2008).

In some advertisements, the same male model is shown with a woman who fits the "generic Latina" type (Casanova 2003, 2007). With long, wavy black hair and dark eyes, she is dressed in a peasant-inspired look: an off-the-shoulder ruffled blouse and an ethnic-print skirt. In a particularly sexy ad (Campaign 2–2008, 130), this woman is seated or kneeling and the male model is standing over her, leaning on a wall. His trademark black shirt has come off and her hand is dangerously close to his enormous metal belt buckle. Despite the overtly sexual overtones of this image, the two are not touching, and the cross from his rosary hangs between them, a symbolic reminder of Latin American moral codes governing sexual relations. In another Osadía ad, a woman visible only from the chest down, dressed in a cropped top and sequined hot pants, caresses the face of a seated, open-shirted male model, who looks directly into the camera (Campaign 7–2008, 92).

A makeup campaign that began in 2007 focused on Latin beauty as a marketing strategy. The face of this campaign was Colombian actress Angie Cepeda, who became famous in Latin America for her roles in soap operas such as *Pobre Diabla*. On the cover of the Campaign 2 catalog, a glamorous photo of Cepeda is overwritten with the quote: "Las mujeres latinas tenemos algo que nos hace diferentes" (We Latina women have something that makes us different), with her signature below. Whether the difference is racial/ethnic, cultural, or of some other type is left a mystery. The catalog featured a new line of makeup called Latino Color. In the advertisements, Cepeda, who has hazel eyes and long, curly dark hair, is depicted with heavily lined eyes, smoky eye shadow, bright blush, and red lipstick and nails. She is also featured on the Campaign 3 catalog cover, with the text "International Women's Day/We Celebrate Your Latina Beauty." In another catalog, Cepeda's image is used to promote Hydra-Lip lipstick, described as "innovative and modern . . . to create a unique style that marks the difference of a woman who has it all . . . the Latina woman" (Campaign 4–2007, 46). Another ad for the lipstick urges consumers to "live Latino color!" (*vive el color latino!*) (Campaign 5–2007, 56). The equation of Latin women with sensuality continues in a page displaying eye shadows: "Latin passion/fall in love with the most seductive colors." During the time of my fieldwork, the campaigns involving Angie Cepeda were featured in print and television ads, and her face and the words "Miradas Latinas" (Latin Looks), the name of an eye shadow set, were visible on billboards throughout Guayaquil.

A major event planned for 2008 was a makeup workshop for directors and members of the "beauty specialists club," which Yanbal had called "Color Latino/Mujer Latina" (Latino Color/Latina Woman) (*EntreNos* Campaign 2–2008). The text of an announcement of the workshop in

A Yanbal billboard in the Kennedy neighborhood of Guayaquil promotes the "Latin Looks" campaign. (Photo by the author)

the Yanbal trade magazine for consultants and directors read: "Without a doubt Yanbal has transformed Ecuador into the country of fashion, highlighting femininity in an extraordinary way. . . . Yanbal creates color and specializes in tones for the Latina woman" (ibid., 5). The workshop was to feature lessons and makeovers by a world-renowned makeup artist who has done makeup for contestants in Miss Universe and many other pageants. The success of Latin American representatives in international pageants is well documented, and Yanbal seeks to capitalize on this global image of Latina beauty. For example, the company was the major sponsor of the Miss Universe Pageant when it was held in Ecuador's capital, Quito, in 2004. Among the things that students in the makeup workshop would learn was "how to make up the four types of eyes most common in the Latina Woman," with the types illustrated in small photos. They would also learn how to "recognize skin tone" and "highlight the expression of your Latina face" (ibid., 6–7).

While the language of *latinidad* is present in Yanbal's marketing and training materials, in my experience and observations it was not repeated often on the ground among sellers. If anything, directors were likely to reference Ecuadorianness rather than Latinness as an aspect of group identity. It remains to be seen if the pan-Latino thrust of recent Yanbal campaigns will become part of Yanbalistas' and clients' everyday interactions and interpretations of the social world. The choice of Latino images and descriptions seems a logical one, given the countries in which the company does business and the popularity of pan–Latin American/Latino advertising appeals worldwide.

MOTHERHOOD   There may be no other image more associated with femininity in Latin America than that of the devoted and self-sacrificing mother. Discourses of long-suffering motherhood stem from reverence for the Virgin Mary in Catholicism and have been called *marianismo* by some scholars. It is not surprising that Yanbal features images of idealized motherhood in its promotional materials, since most of the company's sales force is composed of mothers, as is much of its customer base. According to consultants and directors, the campaigns around Mother's Day are usually some of the most profitable, as people rush to buy gifts for their mothers. Although images of mothers and children are featured in Yanbal catalogs throughout the year, as are appeals to moms to buy products for children, this theme is ubiquitous in April and May catalogs. The image of mothers that emerges from these catalogs is as desexualized, religious keepers of tradition. This image is consistent with portrayals of women and mothers in Ecuadorian popular culture and advertising more generally.

In an advertisement for Unique Woman perfume, a baby's hand is shown clutching a woman's perfectly manicured index finger. The text reads, "For today's mom, a symbol of the modern woman" (Campaign 4–2007, 10). In an interesting juxtaposition, the facing page features another perfume, Sexy Unique Woman, which is described as "seductive" but makes no reference to mothers as destined recipients. Unlike many of the products in the catalog, this perfume bottle does not feature a "Happy Mother's Day" gift tag (ibid., 11). In the same catalog, Aie-né perfume is described as "soft, sweet . . . the essence of Mom"; the perfume bottle and deodorant, in a pale pink, are shown surrounded by rose petals of the same color. In addition to being sweet and soft, the ideal mother as portrayed in the catalog is self-sacrificing. According to an advertisement for children's perfume and shampoo, "his [the baby's] happiness is your best gift" (ibid., 138). I found this slogan a bit confusing, as it seemed to imply that mothers should buy something for their baby because it is really a Mother's Day gift for themselves.

The Campaign 4 catalog was just the warm-up, however, for the catalog completely dedicated to Mother's Day. That cover features a woman and a boy, supposed to be mother and son. They are dressed formally and are seated in the kind of red velvet seats that might be found in a theater for opera or ballet. The boy smiles, resting his head on the mother's shoulder, and the text reads: "With you, every day has a happy ending / Happy Day, Mom!" (Campaign 5–2007). On the inside cover, an elegantly dressed woman effortlessly carries an equally fancy little boy, who is apparently asleep; "Mom gave us everything," reads the caption. A similar sentiment is used to market hand cream: "Her hands cared for you. It's time to care for Mom's hands" (ibid., 93).

In this same issue an entire two-page spread is dedicated to a rosary necklace and bracelet (Campaign 5–2007, 10–11). Featuring this product in the Mother's Day catalog implies that ideal mothers are religious devotees, referring us back to the cultural logic of *marianismo*. The ad for Unique Woman perfume in this catalog proclaims it as "a modern fragrance for a modern mom" (ibid., 47). Once again, the "sexy" version of the perfume is not pushed as a Mother's Day gift, and neither is another perfume that is advertised with a photo of a man and woman passionately kissing in the rain.[11] While sexuality and passion are symbolically off-limits for Yanbal moms, these women are seen as embodied subjects suffering from gender-specific problems. An anti-aging cream features the text: "Don't let hormonal changes affect Mom's beauty" (ibid., 88). Apparently nothing says "Happy Mother's Day" like a message that mama is getting old.

In a catalog that came out prior to the holiday season, mothers are portrayed in another stereotypical role: as keepers of traditions, in this case, traditions related to Christmas. They are also symbolically teaching daughters to carry on this role, as in the photograph of a well-dressed mother and daughter in which the mother wraps a gift as her daughter looks on intently (Campaign 12–2007, 12). On the following page, the mother is shown guiding the daughter with a hand on her back as the young girl carries a gift. The present doesn't seem to be for the girl; instead, it appears as if she is on her way to give it to someone. The young girl looks up at her mother, seemingly seeking approval, as the mother looks straight ahead (ibid., 14). Overall, despite the text's emphasis on modern motherhood, mothers are shown in quite a traditional light in the Yanbal catalogs: as religiously devoted, self-sacrificing, and asexual and as keepers of tradition.

OTHER THEMES

Other themes appeared less frequently in the Yanbal catalogs, but they are worth mentioning because they are rooted in cultural attitudes toward gender and the body.

- Foreignness: In addition to the international travel destinations discussed in the section on social class, there is another obvious marker of prestige in the catalogs. A plethora of Yanbal products have names in English, and a few in French. Products with English names include Hydra-Lip (lipstick), Unique Woman (perfume), Prolong Color (nail polish), Glossy (lip gloss), Titanium (men's skin care), Irreverent (men's fragrance), and many others. Despite their English names, these products are referred to by most sellers using coastal Ecuadorian Spanish pronunciation, so that Hydra-Lip sounds like "eedra-lik" and Titanium becomes "tee-tah-nee-oom."[12] A few product names feature a mixture of Spanish and English spellings, such as "line correxion [sic]" wrinkle cream and "maq-off" makeup remover. French-sounding products include Exfoliage (skin cleanser) and Petit Pon-Pon (a line of children's grooming products). It would be a mistake to think that this use of foreign labels is unique to Yanbal or the types of products the company sells. These names must be viewed in the context of fashion and style in Latin America and Ecuador generally. T-shirts, both new and secondhand, commonly carry English slogans, and people are familiar with foreign designer labels and brand names such as Guess, Tommy Hilfiger, and Diesel. Fashion is still defined as that which comes from outside Ecuador, be it from the United States or Europe; domestically produced products are perceived as inferior.
- Youth marketing: Given the tight restrictions on many Ecuadorian youth (especially girls), relative to social norms in the United States, Yanbal products marketed to young women make use of sexuality in a way that may seem daring and irreverent. Young men and women are portrayed in some ads in a physical proximity that most Ecuadorian parents would deem inappropriate for their children, where such cross-

gender touching in public is frowned upon and opposite-sex friends are usually limited to the living room of the home. Despite this, young girls are urged to be "fresh" and "daring" (Campaign 1–2006, 82) and to "conquer him" (ibid., 86). They are told, "You are how you kiss" (ibid., 89) and "Your lips provoke" (Campaign 11–2007, 121). Whereas the ideal Ecuadorian girl is taught not to draw attention to herself through manners or dress (Casanova 2004), Yanbal tells girls to "enjoy being the center of attention" (Campaign 13–2006, 84). Words such as "daring," "rebellious," and "freedom" appear frequently in advertisements for youth products (Campaign 6–2008). The makeup and nail polish advertised in the youth section feature brighter, more sparkly colors than those in the general makeup section; their use seems destined to get more than a few young girls in trouble with their parents.[13]

• Masculinity: Yanbal's product offerings for men are growing as men's concern with their appearance is becoming more socially acceptable in Ecuador (as in other societies).[14] Stereotypes of idealized masculinity are used to promote products: advertisements often feature muscular male models in various states of undress. Dendur cologne is marketed to "the man who handles extreme situations and lives adventurously" (Campaign 1–2006, 125). The Oxygen fragrance is "the perfect complement for the man who chooses a life outdoors [al aire libre]" (ibid., 128). Another cologne, called Diez (Ten), targets sports fans (the number "10" is usually worn by the best player on a soccer team). Its metallic spray bottle features a soccer ball, and descriptive text references "energy" and "passion." Men are assured that it is all right for them to be concerned about their appearance and to use skin care products: "It's not vanity, it's pleasure" (Campaign 1–2007, 130). Men's audience is implicitly female: according to one perfume advertisement, "He uses it and she enjoys it" (Campaign 1–2006, 126). In a plug for an under-eye skin cream, the text reads: "Wrinkles, bags, dark circles . . . you don't notice them, but she does" (Campaign 6–2007, 27). Men and products for men are featured in all catalogs, but more heavily in the sixth campaign of each year, which coincides with Father's Day.

• Typical beauty themes: These themes have been exhaustively described in studies of the business of marketing beauty and research on women's magazines (Casanova 2003; Peiss 1998; Santa Cruz and Erazo 1980), so I will not devote much space to them here. One common theme is that of physical perfection; the word "perfect" appears in nearly every catalog, most often in connection with skin care and cleansing products. Another common trope is the equation of beauty with health and nutrition, which associates personal beauty practices with self-care rather than self-indulgence. This language of beauty as health is increasingly common in the United States and elsewhere and has become so accepted that even cosmetic surgery is often portrayed as a strategy for health and wellness (Pitts-Taylor 2007).

CONCLUSION

Why examine the words and pictures that appear in the Yanbal catalogs? Why focus on these representations in a study primarily on the work and lives of the sellers of the products? It is precisely because of their crucial role in the process of selling that the catalogs deserve scholarly attention. When a majority of people working with Yanbal tell us that the products sell themselves and that the catalog is their most important tool of the trade, we must take these claims seriously. If the catalogs are so good at per-suading clients to buy, regardless of the actions of the seller, then the im-ages and text contained within these pages convey powerful messages that are largely accepted by their recipients. Rather than assuming that repre-sentations in the catalog show the "real world" and the conditions of peo-ple's lives, I see these images and words as aspirational and symbolic of cul-tural values and ideals. It is precisely because the images are generally not a part of the everyday Ecuadorian's life that they inspire people to buy. By purchasing products that can help present a socially acceptable (often mid-dle-class) appearance, clients can consume—in some small way—elite life-styles, whiteness and foreignness, or idealized motherhood. By practicing consumption that is in line with cultural ideals, some customers can mo-mentarily escape their material conditions and lack of resources.

The emphasis on "class" and luxury in the catalogs is especially interest-ing in light of the Yanbalistas' efforts to portray the products they sell as necessities used by the masses during the public debate over ICE, the lux-ury tax on perfumes and other "special" purchases. In that instance, the company's argument, communicated by the sales directors, was that the elites bought foreign perfumes and brands and everyone else bought do-mestically produced Yanbal products. While this may have been true, the pages of Yanbal's catalogs are filled with visual and textual references to elite lifestyles and consumption practices (including international travel), which were designed to appeal to customers at all socioeconomic levels.

The elements of race and skin color, and the valuation of foreignness, that have been discussed in this chapter bring to light an interesting ten-sion between cultural norms and material conditions that is reflective of contemporary Ecuadorian society. Yanbal has expanded its makeup options to include shades for darker-skinned women, acknowledging the phenotypical realities of Ecuador. At the same time, models promoting Yanbal products continue to embody the blonde, light-eyed Caucasian ideal or a light-skinned, "generic Latina" ideal, both of which are culturally glorified but disconnected from what the majority of real-life Ecuadorian women look like. As in other spheres of Ecuadorian life, whiteness and foreignness are portrayed in Yanbal materials as desirable and as sources of status and prestige. This theme of foreign superiority directly contradicts the corporation's explicitly stated identity as a "Latino" company that aims to promote improved living conditions for Latin American women. Interestingly, the message of Latin pride is interpreted on the ground in Guayaquil as a valuation of Ecuadorianness rather than a pan-Latino identification.

So women (and men) are receiving and transmitting mixed messages: it is good to be white, though most Ecuadorians are not; it is good to be Ecuadorian, but not to be brown- or dark-skinned. Nevertheless, most Ecuadorians *are* brown-skinned, and in order to make money, Yanbal needs to sell them products that they can and will use. This is much simpler in theory than in practice, as shown by the case of the client who insisted on buying makeup that was a few shades too light for her skin, and the distributor who, because of complicated racial and skin-color politics, could not challenge the woman's decision or her implied racial self-classification.

Of course, the themes discussed here are not limited to Yanbal catalogs; they are often echoed in publicity campaigns for a wide variety of products and in the marketing materials of other DSOs. In this study, which aims to understand the social world in which directors, sellers, and clients are immersed, the contents of the catalogs are an important piece of the puzzle and should be viewed as catalysts in the processes of selling and recruitment.

NOTES

1. Campaign launches are held each month to introduce the products and special offers featured in the next campaign's catalog and to inform consultants about potential prizes and any other news that affects how they go about selling.

2. The catalogs I collected included the major gift-giving holidays in Ecuador: Christmas, Valentine's Day, Mother's Day, Children's Day (El Día del Niño), and Father's Day. Fieldwork covered the Christmas holiday period, seen by directors and consultants as one of the most profitable times of year.

3. I was unable to obtain permission from Yanbal to reproduce most of the catalog photographs discussed in this chapter, due to the company's contractual obligations to its models. I would suggest that readers take a look at the company's website (www

.yanbal.com), where many of the visual and textual themes that I discuss here can be observed.

4. Explaining prices to customers became more difficult in the first few campaigns of 2008, when the new tax on perfumes forced Yanbal to paste a new price list on the inside cover of the catalog. According to consultants I spoke with afterward, some clients did not trust that the new, higher prices were legitimate, suspecting the sellers of trying to scam them. Beginning in Campaign 6 of 2008, all taxes were included in the catalog prices, helping to resolve this issue. The political antecedents to this tax, called the ICE, are discussed in the introduction.

5. Beginning in early 2008, products geared toward youth (jewelry, makeup, and fragrances) were collectively presented in a minicatalog, called *Clic*, within the regular catalog.

6. For more information on the methods employed in this and other chapters, please refer to the methodological appendix.

7. The dollar was adopted as Ecuador's official currency in 2000.

8. The Spanish word "*destino*" can also be translated as "destiny."

9. People are able to afford such expensive items because of the flexibility offered by most Yanbal consultants in terms of payment. While coming up with $52 at once may be impossible, it is much easier to pay $5 per week until the total amount due is met. For a full discussion of the arrangements I call "flexible consumption," see chapter 7.

10. All ordering for Guayaquil and surrounding areas takes place on Wednesdays. Directors place orders for their consultants through an online (Web-based) system; those who do not have computers with Internet access at home must make several trips each Wednesday to the nearest Internet café to place orders. Some new directors have their mother directors place orders for their group's consultants. Consultants get the orders to their directors by telephone, in person, or by e-mail, instant message, or text message.

11. In the Father's Day catalogs, a bifurcation between images of fatherhood and perfumes generally advertised with sensual male models was not apparent. In one such catalog, all of the men's cologne ads featured men with children, in nurturing or playful poses, except for one cologne, Irreverent, which portrayed a young shirtless man with a prominent bicep tattoo (Campaign 6–2008). In advertisements featuring fathers, "sexy" product slogans (such as "provocación latina," or "Latin provocation") remained unaltered, whereas sensuality and motherhood never mixed in the catalogs I examined.

12. See A. Wilson (2004) for a discussion of how Thai direct selling organizations also adopt English product names and refer to them using Thai pronunciation.

13. It seems that most young women buy products rather than their parents selecting them for them; of course, the money generally comes from parents as gifts, lunch money, and so on. There are quite a few young women selling products who are not officially allowed to be Yanbal consultants because they are under eighteen, but whose mothers or sisters are enrolled. One of the subjects of my interviews was a high school student whose clients mostly consisted of her schoolmates.

14. There is a growing popular and scholarly literature on the changing expectations of men's appearance in the United States (Bordo 2000; Luciano 2002), but to my knowledge this subject has not been explored in reference to Latin American societies.

CHAPTER 4

EMBODYING PROFESSIONALISM:
CONSTRUCTING THE YANBALISTA IMAGE

The body/work nexus is crucial to the organization and experience of work relations, and . . . people's experience of embodiment is deeply embedded in their experiences of paid employment.
CAROL WOLKOWITZ, *BODIES AT WORK*

APPEARANCE AND SOCIAL CLASS

One day, an aspiring director from Cecilia García's group came in to pick up some catalogs, and Ligia called the woman into her office. Ligia asked her, 'Why don't you put on some lipstick?' The woman, smiling nervously, explained that she did have on eye makeup (taking off her glasses to prove her point), but that her lipstick had come off a little earlier when she drank a coffee. Ligia asked the woman if she wanted to borrow her palette of lipsticks, and began to rummage around for it on her shelves. 'No,' the woman said. 'I have a lipstick in my purse in the car.' Then she asked Ligia, 'What, do I look a little "manly" [*machita*]?' I was a bit uncomfortable witnessing this interaction, and I felt that my aunt was perhaps being too harsh. But she kept on going. 'Fix your hair, and straighten your collar,' she said, pointing to the woman's pink suit. After running her hands through her hair, which might not have been uncombed so much as thin, the consultant replied that it seemed that the woman who had made her suit had made the collar too wide. When the woman left, Ligia told me that she couldn't remember her name. I was taken aback by the directness of Ligia's interventions and the way that she had no qualms about delivering such direct instructions to someone who was not in her group but rather in her sister's, and whose name she couldn't even remember. I witnessed many similar interactions during my research, in which directors were especially harsh in their comments on the appearance of other directors and poten-tial directors.

This anecdote, and other similar scenes I observed, highlight the em-phasis on physical appearance and self-presentation within this DSO sub-culture, not just at an abstract, corporate training level but also on the ground, among members of the sales force. Why was this woman's appear-ance of such importance, leaving her open to a sort of hazing by a senior sales director? Partly because she was on the path to becoming a director, an official representative of Yanbal. As women move from being consul-tants to being directors, their responsibilities change from mostly selling to mostly recruiting and interacting with Yanbal corporate staff. Appear-ance, already culturally valued, becomes more important in this new, pro-fessionalized setting than it was when women were "on the street" sell-ing, because the presentation of an acceptable appearance is an outward sign of corporate belonging. The outward image of a successful Yanbalista is similar to that of the "Avon Lady, the embodiment of the modern public world," who is marked by "business clothes" and the use of a car (A. Wil-son 2004, 169). Though all of the direct sellers I came to know were aware of this image, they responded to it in different ways.

This chapter explores the perceived connections between cultural norms of feminine appearance and social class or status in Guayaquil; the ways in which the direct sales organization and its members use stereotypes about appearance to construct an idealized, "professional" image of the Yanba-lista; and the ways in which appearance and class often do not match up in everyday life. This disjuncture challenges accepted ideas about the link be-tween appearance and class and shows what happens when cultural norms must be adapted to material conditions. I argue that the focus on appear-ance within the social world of the DSO is tangled up with ideas about gender, work, and social class and that the class-appearance connection is not as straightforward as it may seem at first blush. The image of the Yan-balista is actively constructed by sellers and the company, and people adapt these ideals to the practical needs of their everyday lives, resulting in a va-riety of gendered economic strategies. An examination of the place of the body and appearance in direct sales, a newly growing, "flexible" type of work that combines elements of formal and informal employment, is over-due. In general, "the direction of ethnographic research still lags behind the sectoral shifts in the location of paid work" (Wolkowitz 2006, 12).

In a society where appearance matters (especially for women) and com-municates class status to others, people assume that they can read social class by just looking at you. Social scientists and cultural critics have discussed how physical appearance and dress can reveal or conceal class status and have shown how surface judgments based on appearance affect social interactions (Bettie 2002; Blum 2005; Bourdieu 2007 [1984]; Cerbino, Chiriboga, and Tutivén 2000; Root 2005; Sutton 2010). In Ecuador, where clothing has historically been a marker of ethnic identity, visually separating indigenous and mestizo people[1] and stereotypically associating indigenousness with poverty and a lack of sophistication, the stakes of bodily self-presentation are raised (Crain 1996; Pequeño Bueno 2007). While appearance has social significance for all women, those engaged in selling beauty products could be expected to be more concerned with the image they project than are women in other occupations. Yanbal corporate training materials, and the sales directors who use them, stress the need to present an appropriate, professional appearance, one that is in line with the practices of the middle and upper classes. No matter where you are from or what your current financial situation, the message is that you must present yourself in a certain way in order to succeed in Yanbal.

The image of the Yanbalista builds on cultural ideals of appropriate feminine appearance in urban Ecuador, ideals that are associated with the middle and upper classes. In popular stereotypes, humble neighborhoods are associated with a style of self-presentation that communicates a lack of interest in appearance. Director Betty Brigss, who grew up in a poor neighborhood in southwestern Guayaquil, always begins her testimony (a story told to recruit new salespeople) by saying that she never used to wear makeup at all. Makeup is associated with middle- and upper-class women, or women whose jobs require them to have a professional appearance (e.g., office workers). In this way, makeup can serve as an indicator of status.[2]

In my prior study of two groups of adolescent women in Guayaquil, one wealthy and one poor, I found that the practice of making up was much more common among the girls from well-to-do families and neighborhoods (Casanova 2004). Thus, social class is associated with bodily practices such as using makeup, which become a visual cue of status. This earlier research highlighted the emphasis placed by young women not on beauty or physical perfection but on being *arreglada*, a term meaning "well groomed" or "well put-together" (Casanova 2004). For women who are officially affiliated with Yanbal, being *arreglada* implies a variety of beauty and self-care practices, including careful hairstyling, the use of makeup, manicuring and painting nails, wearing matching jewelry, and using professional—or what the women call "executive"—dress.[3] As Yanbal director Ana María Briones put it, "Beyond being pretty or ugly, I think [we have to] simply go around *arreglada*, go around well-presented . . . go around made-up, perfumed, so that people see that we have a pleasant appearance." Although these products have a global, cosmopolitan stamp, they are used to conform to norms (of appearance) that are ultimately local (cf. Ariel de Vidas 2008, 279).

Items or aspects of appearance that were frowned upon by Yanbal directors and consultants I came to know included shirts that showed the wearer's cleavage or belly button, T-shirts, flip-flops or casual sandals, jeans, sweats, sparkly or flashy clothes, and messy hair. All of these "looks" can in certain situations be read to mean that a person is from a lower-class background. These standards are not particular to women working with Yanbal but are a more narrowly defined version of ideas about appearance that are common throughout the country. To express the social pressures and cultural norms that obliged them to arrange their bodies in certain ways, the women and men I met during my fieldwork used a cultural or sociopsychological explanation, saying that Ecuadorians (and especially Guayaquileans) are vain (*vanidosos*). Some people expressed to me that Ecuadorians saw perfumes and personal care products as necessities on the level of food; this perception was shared by directors, consultants, and others who were not associated with Yanbal.

Despite the seeming universality of this focus on appearance, the Yanbal image implies a certain level of income to allow for the use of sometimes costly products, which can be made more affordable for low-income women by becoming a consultant and purchasing at a discount. That Yanbalistas see themselves as "selling beauty" adds to existing social pressures to look good. As distributor Gioconda Ibarra told me, if a consultant does not present an acceptable image, "the first thing that they are going to say is that you are with Yanbal, but look how you go around all sloppy-looking [*toda desarreglada*]."

Since people categorize others and decide how (or whether) to interact with them based on appearance, self-presentation can be an important marker of middle-class respectability. For example, some sellers think that "careless" dressing can impede a Yanbalista's access to people of higher class standing. One seller summed this idea up with the old saying "*A uno como lo ven, lo tratan*." This phrase is difficult to translate, but it implies that people will treat you based on how you look or how you present yourself. Micaela Vera is a consultant with Ligia's group; she is almost always smiling and loves talking about Yanbal, although she told me that she used to be quite shy. Micaela said: "We have to worry [about our appearance] because you know that in the street you meet every kind of person. You meet professionals. You also meet from the most humble up to those . . . So yes, it is important to go around well groomed."

When consultants and directors begin thinking about recruiting other women, appearance can become even more important to them. Aspiring director Nancy Torres, a single mother in Cecilia's group, was one of the people who emphasized this point: "It [appearance] is important because if we are going to talk about a good product, where there a lot of earnings, then if they see us poorly dressed . . . they aren't going to think that we earn good money."[4] Nancy saw looking successful as key to attracting new sellers.

Although the narrative of women's appearance "improving" as they work with Yanbal was commonly repeated by Yanbalistas, many directors and consultants believed that potential recruits should already have a certain look. While assisting director-in-training Belén Vera in prospecting for new consultants in southern Guayaquil, director Maryuri Palma reinforced this idea. After Belén approached an overweight woman dressed in a tight tank top and bicycle shorts who was waiting for a bus, Maryuri questioned her consultant's judgment: 'Why would you talk to her? She is dressed like she's going to the beach!' When I asked Maryuri about the criteria for selecting people to approach, she hedged, saying that it depends, but that someone dressed like that would not make a good consultant. A probable explanation for Maryuri's impassioned reaction is that the woman's clothes connoted low social class and a lack of effort to disguise these social origins.

THE COMPANY LINE

Yanbal portrays a particular look in the training and promotional materials designed to initiate consultants. The actresses playing consultants in the training videos look like they have stepped out of a *telenovela* (soap opera) with their good looks, light skin, professionally styled hair and makeup, and fashionable clothing and jewelry. One video urges consultants to check their appearance before going out to sell: an actress portraying a consultant examines herself in a full-length mirror, focusing on her makeup, jewelry, and nails. The video also counsels sellers to make sure they are using Yanbal products (jewelry, makeup, and perfumes) when going out to sell. At one recruitment meeting, a Yanbal coordinator[5] said that the good thing about selling Yanbal is that "it obliges us to fix ourselves up and take care of ourselves, because how can we sell beauty if we go around looking all scruffy?" In this instance, she was implicitly comparing the image of a Yanbalista to the image of a woman who keeps house, a function that is not seen as requiring any particular image or self-presentation (unlike a professional or office job).

In one Yanbal manual for consultants, image was the focus of several pages. The manual urged women to remove hair from their faces, legs, and armpits (something many consultants I met did not do); use deodorant, "but not as a way of masking bad body odor resulting from lack of hygiene"; care for their nails;[6] and always wear stockings, "even in hot climates." The text also advised consultants to use Yanbal perfumes and fragrances.

A handout used by Ligia and other directors in trainings for new consultants featured a cartoonish drawing of the ideal "Yanbal woman." Her hair was cut in a bobbed style, she wore makeup and earrings, and she was dressed in a suit jacket (with Yanbal logo) and skirt, with low heels. The page argued that Yanbal women must "look impeccable at all hours of the day because we are developing ourselves in the business of beauty, and a relation should exist between what we offer [for sale] and what we put into practice." Three areas were given special attention: hair, makeup, and accessories. Sellers' hair should be "clean and orderly." Women with long hair were counseled to wear their hair "especially well-combed or pinned back with a barrette or clip." Those who dyed their hair were warned, "You should be aware of when your hair grows so that you don't show roots of a different color." Makeup should also be "impeccable . . . natural for daytime and more accentuated at night." Jewelry should be in accordance with the occasion, "always avoiding exaggeration." Shoes and pocketbooks should be from the same color palette.

Official messages from Yanbal about how to create an acceptable physical appearance are reinforced and transmitted by sales directors. Ligia always passes on Yanbal's advice about pulling long hair back, and she herself almost never attends any meeting or event without pulling her hair away from her face, usually pinning it back with a sparkly clip. In the first orientation session for new consultants that I attended, held in a long, narrow conference room in Ligia's office building, the topic of sellers' appearance was at the top of the agenda. Ligia asked the group of about twenty women, "What does it mean to sell cosmetics?" People seated behind me said, "Beauty," and Ligia repeated, "Beauty, image . . . ," and then said that besides being called *consultoras de belleza* (beauty consultants) they were also *ejecutivas de venta* (sales executives).

As she began to pass out the handout described above, she said, "We have to pay attention to our image." Although low-rise pants and belly-revealing shirts might be in style,[7] she told new consultants, this clothing is not appropriate for going out to sell and representing Yanbal. According to Ligia, new consultants only had a few responsibilities: to attend meetings, to "go around well dressed [*bien vestidita*], representing Yanbal," and "to place orders." As among the teenage girls I had studied previously, the emphasis was on being well groomed and well dressed, *arreglada*, rather than on being beautiful. Ligia encouraged the women to scrutinize the successful directors whose testimonies were featured in the Yanbal video, saying, "They are not prettier [*más guapas*] than you. They are just like you." She congratulated the meeting attendees for arriving "super-handsome, super-put-together [*súper-guapas, súper-arregladitas*]." When phoning women to invite them to meetings, trainings, or other events, she routinely reminded them to come dressed nicely (*bien guapas*).

Indeed, most women who attend events at the Yanbal headquarters or directors' offices come with their hair and nails done, with at least some makeup on, and wearing modest slacks and stylish tops or blouses. Those who don't fit this model often turn out to be new consultants or guests rather than consultants who have been working with Yanbal for some time. Director Betty Brigss advises her consultants that they have to dress well, not in jeans, when going to Yanbal group meetings. She herself sets the example: "I go well put-together [*arregladita*]. I go as if to a party. . . . I have to go with a jacket . . . because that is what I sell: through me, the image is sold."

Sales directors tend to differ from their consultants, especially those who are new to Yanbal, in their style of dress and self-presentation. This makes sense, as directors are more steeped in the Yanbal image-conscious corporate culture than consultants are.[8] To meetings, most directors wear suits or similar business apparel, nearly all wear makeup, and quite a few apply a liberal dose of Yanbal fragrance. At the national convention attended by successful directors, I found the combined aroma of hundreds of women wearing Yanbal perfumes dizzying.

Directors also wear symbols of success, status, and corporate belonging on their bodies, such as small rectangular "Yanbal" logo lapel pins. When I first began observing the directors, some who had secured their participation in prize trips to Jamaica or Colombia (by meeting sales and recruitment goals) wore colorful rubber bracelets with the name of their destination. During my fieldwork, Ligia offered fabric for uniforms as a prize to daughter directors who "formed" new directors. Other incentives for her directors to meet specific goals included custom-made blouses and evening gowns brought from the United States. The message that directors receive from the company and from each other is that appearance is of utmost importance.

A director's status within the company depends on the success and the reputations of her daughter and granddaughter directors. One afternoon, while ordering cappuccinos for four of her directors during a meeting, Ligia told three of them that they would have to have theirs without cream, as they were a bit fat. On another day, I accompanied Tía Ligia and Tía Fátima, her daughter consultant and director-in-training as well as my husband's paternal aunt, on a *barrido de manzana* (neighborhood sweep) to recruit new clients and sellers in Fátima's neighborhood. Ligia asked Fátima, who was then in the months-long process of advancing to director status, to change out of the capri pants and flip-flops she was wearing and to put on her uniform, saying, "You are image. You have to go around well-dressed."

The audience for this self-presentation as Yanbal director is often the company itself, and Ligia counsels those who are attending trainings at the Yanbal office to go especially nicely dressed. Before one such meeting, she advised Fátima to make sure that her nails were looking good, either with fresh polish or clean with no polish; no peeling nail polish allowed. This may seem like a small detail, but *guayaquileñas* of middle- and upper-class status are almost never seen with fingernails and toenails in disarray or unpolished. Many of those with lower class status emulate this custom by painting and caring for their own nails rather than paying someone to do it.[9] Even I succumbed to this social pressure while in Guayaquil, keeping my usually ragged nails presentable through regular manicures and pedicures.

At meetings, directors advised consultants who had recruited others to make sure that those daughter consultants were "taking care of their image." A young woman from one of Ligia's granddaughter director's groups came into the office one afternoon, and Ligia asked her, "Why don't you use makeup?" The woman, to my surprise, asked her, "Why don't *you* use makeup?" Ligia was dressed rather casually and appeared not to be wearing makeup, although she told the consultant, 'I am wearing foundation and eyebrow pencil, and if I just put on lipstick, I would be made up.' She advised the woman that she could use the same look if she didn't like to wear much makeup. I found it interesting that Ligia thought the woman was not made up, given that she appeared to be wearing eye shadow and mascara. Ligia went on to explain to the young woman that she would sell more products if she used them herself. Interestingly, she never justified her comments to directors (or directors-in-training) by using this logic of looking good to sell more. With those women, appearance was seen as a sign of professionalism and commitment to a career with Yanbal, not simply a way to sell more. For directors' self-presentations, the audience was different, and thus the reasons for looking good had become different as well. There was still, of course, a focus on appearance for both consultants and directors.

Some women so fully embody the image of the Yanbal woman that I had no trouble picking them out in line at the bank, in their neighborhoods, or in rural towns. When a woman was especially *arreglada* or had carefully applied makeup in colors that matched her clothes, I always found myself looking for that Yanbal pin, catalog, or tote bag, which more often than not I found. I was surprised to find out that many of the Yanbal consultants and directors who looked put-together and middle-class lived in humble or unfinished homes in marginal, or at least not luxurious, neighborhoods. Thus, through the fashioning of a socially acceptable, middle-class, professional appearance, Yanbalistas can obscure their socioeconomic origins and give the impression that they have already climbed the company's "ladder of success."

Even a man associated with Yanbal got the message that image is important. When I met male seller "Carlos Zambrano"[10] in December 2007,

Director Ligia García de Proaño (*right*) with her sister Cecilia (*left*) in 2009, at the annual Christmas party Ligia organizes for her "daughter" and "granddaughter" directors. Cecilia is Ligia's "daughter" in the direct sales organization. (Photo by the author)

Consultants Daniela Solís (*left*) and María Bustamante (*right*) in the living room of Daniela's home in southern Guayaquil. (Photo by the author)

he was preparing for his group's Christmas party in Guayaquil. Living and working in a small town just outside the city, Carlos had never attended a meeting of the group with which he was affiliated; he was to be honored that night for having the highest sales in the group. He had decided that he needed to go into the city a few hours before the party to buy a new outfit. "I dress casually," he told me, "and for these things, you have to go well put-together [*bien arregladito*]." He confessed that he thought he should work on his image, because doing so, in his opinion, would allow him to sell more.[11]

Not everyone agrees that Yanbal sellers must focus heavily on image because all women have access to this work, regardless of their appearance. María Litardo Santos, a new consultant, appreciated that, in her opinion, women didn't have to fit a certain physical ideal in order to join Yanbal. She said that she had been discriminated against in the formal labor market for being overweight, but that, in Yanbal, importance was not placed on looks and consultants could be "fat, ugly, or old" without penalty.[12] It is true that while Yanbal consultants are encouraged to care about their appearance, there are no set rules about how they should dress or make themselves up.

SELLERS OF LOWER STATUS

The symbolic foil for the put-together Yanbal "sales executive" is the woman who sells in the market.[13] This symbol has a visual element, as many market women in Ecuador wear variations of indigenous dress, which is associated with low class status and a stigmatized ethnicity (Pequeño Bueno 2007). The racialized image associated with market vendors is incompatible with the white-mestiza and professional image of the idealized Yanbalista.[14] In a meeting with some of her daughter and granddaughter directors, Ligia used an example of a woman in a market selling vegetables, saying that her business is not well organized, because she simply sells all day and then goes home and dumps the money out of her "little bag" to count it. This woman had a business system (*control de negocio*), Ligia noted, but it was "very rustic." Yanbal directors, on the other hand, had tools to organize their business and keep track of important information. Ligia pointed out that, instead of a "little bag," they carried a briefcase or a Yanbal tote bag. By denigrating the "rustic" organization of a market seller, Ligia symbolically associated Yanbalistas with a more middle-class or professional set of practices and accessories.

During another meeting, while encouraging consultants to look for potential clients or recruits in unlikely places, Ligia said that she used to sell Yanbal products to a woman who worked at a stall in the downtown market: "The lady sold me chicken, and I sold her perfume." This anecdote provoked laughter, as if there were something inherently funny about a market woman buying Yanbal beauty products. Ligia, herself chuckling, said, "It sounds like a lie [*parece mentira*], but everyone buys Yanbal." Another day, when I was visiting a consultant who lives in El Guasmo, she began to sing to herself as she cleaned up the kitchen. Her friend and neighbor, also a Yanbal consultant, commented that she had a beautiful voice. "For selling potatoes?" joked the first consultant, pretending to be offended. People who sell on the street commonly call out their offerings in a singsong voice, and in this instance the consultant was jokingly accusing her friend of comparing her to these low-status sellers.

People affiliated with Yanbal do not usually use the word "seller" (*vendedora*) to refer to its direct sellers, and the image of the executive is preferred. Director Betty Brigss said that many people join Yanbal not understanding that being a beauty consultant is different from being "a common seller" (*una común vendedora*). These people are not concerned with their appearance when they first enroll as consultants. As consultant Gioconda Ibarra put it, "We are not sellers. A seller tells you, 'Just put this on.' We are sales executives, and we have to take care of our appearance when others are around in order to sell to them." Indeed, the creation of a professional image, similar to that of women who are formally employed in offices, helps Yanbalistas to symbolically separate themselves from other kinds of working women.[15] Although selling Yanbal products often involves physical labor, with plenty of walking and sometimes lugging around heavy products and catalogs, women are encouraged by the company and its directors to present a professional image. Dressing nicely visually separates this work from other paid and unpaid jobs that women do, which may involve getting dirty and thus prevent women from looking *arreglada*. As Freeman put it in her discussion of Barbadian women's performance of middle-class working femininity, "The fashion statement they make through their 'professional' appearance is a mode of distinction as much proclaiming who they *are not* as proclaiming who they *are*" (2000, 226; emphasis in original; cf. Nencel 2008, 79–80).

WHEN IMAGE AND SOCIAL CLASS DON'T MATCH

Since the image of the Yanbal woman is associated with middle-class standards of appearance and professionalized work settings connoting middle-class status, it is worth examining instances in which image and social class do not map onto each other. What is portrayed in Yanbal rhetoric and the group's folklore as upward social mobility may instead be a form of disguising low-class origins through the fashioning of an "appropriate" appearance. A change in appearance is much easier to manage than a change in living conditions, and women may think that presenting a middle-class appearance will open doors for them in direct sales and help them to achieve that status. In this way, women may appear to be well-to-do professionals while living in marginal neighborhoods or scraping to make ends meet.

On the other hand, some women do not work as hard to disguise their class standing, and their casual appearance may belie their high earnings and success within the corporation. These women often adapt or reject elements of the prescribed Yanbalista appearance, making concessions to the conditions and location of their work by dressing practically rather than to match an idealized image of professional femininity. There are many successful sellers and directors for whom the Yanbal image does not come naturally, and for some, it may actually go against their preferred style of self-presentation. Directors to whom this appearance seems unnatural or uncomfortable are still likely to tell their consultants and daughter directors to follow the company guidelines regarding dress, accessories, and makeup. Looking at the cracks in the chain linking class to appearance can allow us to see how complex the issue of self-presentation can become when women attempt to reconcile the professional, middle-class image promoted by the DSO with their individual financial situations and preferences.

SOCIAL/ECONOMIC MOBILITY OR A MAKEOVER?

A physical transformation can be seen by others as indicating a transformation in class status and economic situation as women move up the ranks as Yanbal consultants and directors. A sales director once pointed to a photo of a well-dressed director receiving an award and told me, 'She wasn't always so regal. When I met her, she was *bien cholita.*' The expression "*bien cholita*" implies not only racial impurity but also a lack of sophistication in dress and behavior associated with those from the countryside. Another director, Carmen Díaz, told me about a "country girl" from a small town two hours outside Guayaquil, whom Carmen's sister had recruited into her group: "She has become so polished that it has left me with my mouth hanging open [in surprise]." The body is a form of capital, and both rich and poor people perceive it as an "important vehicle for social ascent" (Goldenberg 2007, 13). The body is one of the few resources that women from the lower classes have at their disposal.

Narcisa Zambrano Valdez, a director originally from the coastal province of Manabí who now lives and works in Ecuador's capital city, Quito, described the physical transformation that she had witnessed in some members of her group who have low socioeconomic status and work in a stigmatized occupation:

> I can tell you that I have some four or five ladies [in my group] who are domestic employees. . . . When I met the ladies, their skin was dry, they had very low self-esteem, they were people who didn't fix themselves up. I even think they bathed [only] every four days or so. . . . I would like for you to see them now. They are people who bathe every day before going out, their faces look better, their appearance. Now they fix themselves up; now they use a bit of makeup. They don't exaggerate, but they do use a bit of makeup, and now they go out of the house well groomed. . . . And they tell me, "Believe me, Nachita. Believe that my life changed."

This narrative of domestic employees' changed lives reinforces the idea that the material conditions of lower-class people's lives lead to an unattractive appearance, but that this appearance can be improved through skin care and cosmetic products—that is, by striving to achieve certain norms of femininity. Narcisa credited this change in part to the free products that Yanbal sends as prizes to sellers who reach minimum sales amounts. Although some consultants sell these prizes to bring in extra money or increase the capital available for growing their business, Narcisa believed that her consultants had kept some prizes and used them. If the products come to them free, she said, "then of course they are going to fix themselves up."

The equation of a change in appearance with a change in a person's financial situation and self-perception was a commonly held assumption among many women associated with Yanbal. A shift in appearance, toward a more middle-class norm, can represent a real rise in socioeconomic status, or—more likely—it can substitute for a significant change in material conditions.[16] In this way, the appearance-class connection is often more imagined than real. Director Betty Brigss is a statuesque woman in her mid-thirties who is usually seen in Yanbal meetings wearing a pantsuit and pointy-toed pumps, her face impeccably made up and her long black hair often held back by a pair of black sunglasses. After seeing her around Ligia's office with such a professional appearance, I was somewhat surprised to visit her home and find that it was unfinished and located on an unpaved road. Based on her style of self-presentation, I had imagined her living a comfortable life in a well-to-do neighborhood.

Directors see a need for lower-class consultants to work to disguise their social origins in order to be accepted in professional settings. In January 2008, Ligia booked a meeting room in a luxurious office tower in northern Guayaquil for a joint campaign launch event with some of her daughter directors' groups. Like many members in Ligia's own group, many consultants in these groups come from marginal neighborhoods and have low socioeconomic status. She warned her directors that they needed to make sure that their consultants were well dressed and well behaved (two of the primary social/cultural demands placed on Ecuadorian women) when they were in the building for the meeting. The directors agreed, adding that their consultants would need to wear makeup and dress like executives, with no skimpy shirts; they would also have to keep their voices down. Loud talking is stereotypically associated with the street life of Guayaquil's urban poor neighborhoods; and in racist sayings and jokes commonly heard in the city, it is also associated with blackness. People from certain class situations are not expected to be seen in certain spaces, so they must disguise their socioeconomic status by working to create an acceptable (middle-class) appearance, including dress and manners. What I would like to highlight is that these outward, temporary changes did not represent any alteration in the women's material conditions.

ADJUSTING IDEALS TO REALITY

Despite all the talk about image and the importance placed on appearance, the women most closely matching the Yanbal ideal for consultants and directors were often not the ones who had the highest sales. This fact presents a paradox that consultants and directors sometimes had difficulty explaining. If this style of self-presentation is recommended because it will lead to more sales, then how can Yanbalistas explain the selling success of some women who did not present a middle-class appearance? For example, one of the top five sellers in one group that I studied dresses in clothes that appear to be hand-me-downs, and she is missing a couple of her front teeth.[17] In another group, the highest-grossing consultant is overweight and has a pronounced underbite and frizzy hair. These are not women who fit the middle-class prototype of acceptable or attractive feminine appearance. Ana María Briones, a director who has a middle-class background and is a college graduate, complained to me, "I don't understand how those ladies who go around so poorly groomed [*mal arregladas*] do so well. I have asked myself that question many times: who would buy beauty products from that lady?" These are the points at which the emphasis on appearance seems to be challenged by the experiences of real women on the ground, showing cracks in the tablet of Yanbal commandments. Based on my observations, these women do well in direct sales because they are hard workers, motivated by real economic needs, who are able to create and cultivate a myriad of social networks in order to sell and recruit; appearance doesn't enter into the equation.

There are times and situations in which women do not or cannot fix themselves up in accordance with the middle-class, professional ideal emphasized by Yanbal and the directors. Consultant Narcisa Pazmiño, an ambitious and friendly seller, often works in downtown Guayaquil for an entire afternoon, going from client to client to take orders and collect money, or visiting her daughter consultant who sells in the bargain shopping district known as La Bahía. Although she is often going to ask them for money, her clients seem genuinely happy to see her as she strides into a shop, calling out in a cheerful voice, "¡Hola, amores!" (Hello, dears!) Wearing a suit and high heels would be impractical given the amount of walking she does, the heavy bag she carries, and the uneven conditions of downtown sidewalks and streets. So Narcisa, a stout, short woman with a cloud of curly black hair, chooses a more practical wardrobe of jeans, a knit top or T-shirt, and one of two pairs of comfortable sandals that she uses for walking. She always makes sure to wear an "Ask Me About Yanbal" button so that she can be identified as a representative of the company, which stimulates conversations with potential customers or recruits.

Accompanying sellers and directors as they worked in marginal neighborhoods showed me an image quite different from the official recommendations of the DSO. When director Cecilia García goes out to prospect (recruit new sellers), she dresses casually, in a Yanbal polo-style shirt, jeans, and sneakers. Director Maryuri Palma, who usually works in low-income neighborhoods at the southern end of the city, said that she favors more casual clothing for going out to work in the streets; the climate is hot, during certain times of year there is heavy rain and flooding, and the roads are unpaved or full of potholes. Given these conditions, she advises her consultants to wear a Yanbal T-shirt, jeans, and comfortable shoes. Her opinions on work clothing point out the inappropriateness or impracticality of "professional" dress in some socioeconomic and geographical settings. Other sellers agreed that they chose clothes according to the situation, rather than always being dressed to the nines.

Another consideration when it comes to clothing is cost. Many Yanbal consultants survive on small incomes, and clothing tends to be expensive in Guayaquil, even in discount stores. Some directors and consultants deal with limited money for clothing by having a uniform made and using it when they are working. Acknowledging the financial realities of many consultants, some directors advise them to get uniforms made,[18] which they can wear more than once and in this way not "wear out their Sunday clothes," as Ligia put it. Consultant Diana Hurel told me that she had bought the material for a uniform over a year ago and just had not gotten around to getting it sewn. She said the advantage of a uniform is that "I don't wear out the few clothes I have for going out"; a uniform also resolves the question of what to wear when going out to work or to a meeting. As has been pointed out in public debates over school uniforms in the United States, another benefit of a uniform is that it can conceal the socioeconomic status of its wearer. Once she had her uniform, said Diana, she wouldn't have to worry about others criticizing her by saying, "Ugh, there she goes again in the same outfit." As other working women in the developing world have expressed, "The uniform is a symbol of professional status just as it is for airline workers and bank tellers [who wear uniforms in many parts of Latin America and the Caribbean] . . . and presents an economical way of adhering to the style protocol" of employers, or in this case, the DSO (Freeman 2000, 220–221). While some scholars might interpret self-fashioned uniforms as a form of "false consciousness," in which women acquiesce enthusiastically to the demands of the capitalist firm (Freeman 2000, 221), a uniform, like a professional appearance more generally, is desirable because it separates direct sellers from low-status informal workers and unemployed housewives.

DEPRIORITIZING APPEARANCE

Not all women are convinced by the company's discourse on appearance. For example, some people resisted the idea that the seller's appearance was correlated with sales. Consultant Carolina Cevallos Plaza, a high school student and former domestic employee when I met her in 2007,[19] told me that appearance was less important than the consultant's personality. She believed that consultants should treat people well and be friendly, attempting to make friends with the people to whom they are trying to sell. Érika Martínez does not like to wear makeup, and upon joining Yanbal as a beauty consultant, she asked her director if that would be a problem. The director told her that it was up to her, but Érika felt a bit pressured. She resisted the Yanbal version of being *arreglada*, which includes using at least a little makeup. Érika disputed the maxim that you have to use the products in order to sell them, saying that "people who wear makeup know what they like, so it's not necessary for me to wear it." I found Érika's story ironic, since her director had confided in me that she herself doesn't like to wear makeup, but "I have to do it for my job." This woman had serious allergies to eye makeup, and at Yanbal events to which she wore makeup, I frequently saw her with red, runny eyes, as if she had been crying. Nevertheless, she advised her consultants to wear makeup and use Yanbal products.

Around her house or working in the office, Tía Ligia was likely to wear a knit top, capri pants or jeans, and sandals. However, before any meeting with directors, Yanbal corporate staff, or consultants, she usually changed clothes (into a suit or other office attire), pulled back her hair, put on makeup, and selected a matching earring and necklace set from one of the many silver Yanbal boxes she kept on a shelf in her office. One afternoon in December as I accompanied her downtown to finalize the arrangements for her group's Christmas party, Ligia received an urgent telephone call. She had to make an unexpected trip to the Yanbal office in northern Guayaquil to advocate for one of her daughter directors who was in danger of losing a car she had been told that she had won through her work with the DSO. Ligia seemed more concerned with not being well dressed or made up than with the situation itself, asking me if she looked ugly as she examined herself in her SUV's rearview mirror. We laughed as we repeated in unison the Ecuadorian saying, "There are no ugly women, just poorly groomed ones."

The idea that there were two styles of dress (one for home and one for going out to work) was common among many consultants and directors. I observed that people dressed and groomed themselves differently to go to a meeting than when I visited them at home. When I went to interview successful consultant Marjorie González in her home in southern Guayaquil, she was dressed casually in a T-shirt, stretch pants, and house shoes. When I brought up the topic of appearance and work, she said, "I couldn't go out like this, never, . . . [But] I complain when I have to go out, 'Oh my God, I have to go out—I'm going to bathe, I'm going to put on makeup, I have to do my hair!'" There is pressure for women working in direct sales to fix themselves up according to social and cultural norms of feminine appearance and to approximate the idealized image of the seller as it is presented by the DSO. Many consultants and directors believe that they must use Yanbal products in order to recommend and sell them to clients, and that they must fix themselves up in certain ways, regardless of whether they enjoy these beauty practices.

MY APPEARANCE

During my nearly six months of fieldwork in Ecuador, and during subsequent visits, I often found myself "passing" for an Ecuadorian in daily life. This was due to my Spanish, which grew more Ecuadorian by the day; my association with people known to be Ecuadorian, as niece, cousin, or friend; and the fact that few foreign tourists (especially Europeans or North Americans) visit Guayaquil. Although I never claimed to be Ecuadorian, many people simply assumed this to be true and were often surprised when I told them that I was a *gringa* from the United States. Of course, there were many Ecuadorians, from taxi drivers and shopkeepers to Yanbal consultants, who immediately identified me as a foreigner and asked me where I was from. Once I was classified as a foreigner, I stood somewhere outside the status-appearance matrix within which urban Ecuadorians are enmeshed. That which is North American or European is positioned as superior in mainstream Ecuadorian culture, as in many postcolonial societies. When people knew I was a *gringa*, my whiteness and status became undebatable. My dress was not scrutinized in the way it would have been had I been Ecuadorian, since foreigners are expected to dress more casually. In fact, I dress more formally and perhaps more modestly when in Ecuador than when in the United States, in an effort not to stand out. Despite this personal exemption from scrutiny according to Ecuadorian standards, I still became engaged in social interactions regarding appearance: I was the recipient of beauty and skin care tips (and quite a few free Yanbal products, given to me as gifts by sellers and directors) and was complimented on my clothing from time to time.

Several Yanbal directors and consultants whom I met asked me if I wore makeup. I usually answered the question according to whether I was wearing any cosmetics that day, so that I would either say no or say that I was wearing just a bit. It is true that I rarely wear much makeup, mostly because I don't care to invest the time necessary to apply it. I consider myself made up if I have on concealer to hide the dark circles under my eyes, mascara, and lip gloss or light-colored lipstick. To my surprise, the Yanbalistas did not criticize me for not wearing makeup; nor did they try to sell me the tools of their trade. In fact, some of them openly approved of my "simple" appearance. When I confessed to Érika, the consultant who resisted the pressure to wear makeup, that I also wasn't big on makeup, she told me, "That looks good on you." I think that my whiteness may have acted as a protective factor, shielding me from criticism for not wearing makeup.[20] People were so used to seeing me without obvious makeup that when I showed up at holiday parties in full makeup, they were a bit taken aback. After the yearly Christmas party Ligia holds for her consultants, Tía Fátima told me that all of her daughter consultants had commented on how good I looked with makeup on; they had had trouble recognizing me. Fátima told me that I looked much younger with makeup on, which seemed somewhat counterintuitive.

Two conclusions can be drawn from reflecting upon my appearance and its effects during my field research. First, once I was outed as a foreigner, my status within the social circles in which I moved seemed to result from place-based identification as a North American rather than from my appearance as an indicator of (racialized) social class. It would not have mattered that I am not a wealthy American, for most Ecuadorians see all Americans as being relatively wealthy, which is true in a sense. Of course, it is difficult to separate status from appearance and ideas about the superiority of Caucasian looks, and my white skin and blue eyes were seen as desirable traits whether people assumed I was Ecuadorian or knew that I was not. (For example, when I took my baby daughter to Guayaquil in December 2009, several strangers came up to us on the street to admire her gray-blue eyes and predict that she would grow up to be Miss Ecuador.)

Second, despite my nationality, Guayaquilean women engaged me in the same types of positive, complimentary interactions that regularly take place between and among them. This pattern of reassuring friends and acquaintances that they are looking good is something I had observed and discussed in relation to the adolescent women I had studied in Guayaquil in 2001 (Casanova 2004). Such positive interactions were thus not predicated on equal social status or shared national identification, which I find interesting. These types of routinized interactions can be viewed as an everyday form of solidarity between and among women who are subjected to strict regimes of appearance.

CONCLUSION

In Guayaquil's urban society, what part of town you come from has inherent meaning: it indicates your class position. Similarly, men's and women's physical appearance, including dress, serves as a marker of socioeconomic status, and an appropriate appearance is culturally and socially valued. In a context in which appearance is seen to stand in for class, how you look is how you are treated (a uno como lo ven, lo tratan), and looking good becomes a priority for poor and rich alike. As many scholars have noted, appearance has greater social and economic consequences for women than for men. This is true even—or perhaps, especially—in a "feminine" organization like Yanbal.

Within this social world or subculture, the emphasis on appearance and image as key to success in direct selling was constant, beginning the moment a woman was recruited. As women move up the Yanbal "stairway of success" (the hierarchical ranking of sales directors by level) and their responsibilities change from primarily selling to primarily recruiting, image becomes more important. In part, directors' focus on appearance is based on who is watching the performance of embodied gender. The consultant's audience is her diverse group of clients and her fellow sellers, while the director's audience is the DSO itself and other directors with whom she is in competition. Consultants receive instruction on appearance from their directors, while directors experience pressure from their peers to conform to a middle-class, "professional" standard of appearance, the embodiment of financial success. Ultimately, a professional image (in body, makeup, and dress) "has everything to do with the public persona they [working women] wish to cultivate in their own communities" (Freeman 2000, 221). Strategies for conforming to this culturally approved model of appearance go against the women's own preferences in some cases, leading them to engage in beauty practices that are uncomfortable for them. For other women, experimenting with cosmetics and dressing up are enjoyable and seem to suit their personality (cf. Sutton 2010).

The narrative of upward social mobility, with which many Yanbal directors strongly identify, is seen to be represented by a change in physical appearance. This change may include beginning to use makeup and refined makeup techniques, wearing modest professional clothing of good quality, and wearing jewelry. However, in many cases, the degree of actual economic mobility is minimal, and the outward changes serve only to disguise rather than change the material conditions of the women's lives and their class origins. In the absence of financial change, some women work on changing their physical appearance in order to embody their desired socioeconomic status. This is especially the case for new directors, who need to look successful in order to recruit new consultants, but who may not be financially stable or have high incomes.

I have discussed women's (and men's) decisions about family, work, and direct sales using the language of gendered economic strategies in previous chapters. Gendered economic strategies, understood as plans of action based on consideration of both cultural norms of gender and material conditions, also come into play in how women go about performing their selling work and constructing work identities through image. A variety of such strategies emerge from the accounts of women direct sellers. Some women with few resources join the DSO so that they can afford to meet cultural expectations of femininity by lowering the costs of becoming consumers of Yanbal products. Some sellers downplay the need for a certain (gendered) look or "professional" dress because of its impracticality in the urban selling terrain: high heels and mud puddles on dirt roads do not mix, for example. Others may decide not to use makeup (emphasizing instead the cultivation of internal qualities of "appropriate" femininity), while still seeing cosmetics sales through Yanbal as a good way to make money. Each approach represents a reconciling of cultural demands, individual preferences, and material/economic realities.

The irony of all the hype about image and appearance, coming from Yanbal and its directors and consultants, is that the prototypical image of the successful Yanbalista is not necessarily accurate. Direct selling is open to all women (unlike many other professions) and favors women who are outgoing, ambitious, and hardworking, not those who are good-looking or have fabulous wardrobes. This means that sometimes the biggest sellers are those who are most motivated by financial need; these are also the women most likely to be out of sync with the idealized middle-class look. This fact, while noticed by some, has not altered the organizational and interpersonal focus on looks as having paramount importance, which resonates with existing discourses of socially acceptable feminine appearance in Guayaquil.

NOTES

1. The term "mestizo" as used in this book refers to Ecuadorians of mixed indigenous and European ancestry. Mestizos are the majority ethnic group in the country and in Guayaquil. Economic and political power in the country has traditionally been held by the most European-looking members of this group, whom some social scientists refer to as white-mestizos.

2. One of the Peruvian women in Seligmann's study claimed that women in Lima tried to hide their *chola* (mixed-race) and rural origins with "different clothes and makeup" (2004, 154). This assertion shows the links between race and class and the role of the body in displaying status in hierarchical urban Andean societies.

3. In Freeman's study of data entry workers in Barbados, the women also aspired to an "executive" style of dress, despite the low-wage nature of their jobs (2000, 219).

4. In Peter Cahn's work (2007) on a Mexican DSO focused on health products, he quotes a female distributor as telling him, "If you don't look good, your clients won't believe you." This woman claimed to buy well-fitting clothing and keep her nails clean and her face made up in order to help with her sales.

5. Coordinators are Yanbal staff members (formal employees of the DSO) whose job is to support sales directors and those on track to become directors.

6. Nails are an important aspect of embodying femininity and middle-class status. Having one's nails done implies not only an acceptance of normative femininity but also the ability to avoid the types of manual labor that are associated with poor women (Sutton 2010).

7. See Cerbino, Chiriboga, and Tutivén (2000) for an interesting discussion of how lower-class Guayaquilean youth appropriate new fashion trends, rendering these styles off-limits for well-off people, who "need" to differentiate themselves visually from the masses.

8. Among the informatics workers she studied, Freeman noted that the managers felt pressure to dress better than those under them in the office hierarchy. Managers were aware of being "watched not only from above [by corporate management] but also from below" (2000, 219).

9. Although anyone can paint her nails, thus achieving this symbol of status, those who work with their hands have a more difficult time keeping the paint intact. The association of "fixed-up" nails with middle-class standards of embodied femininity was also found by Sutton (2010) in Argentina.

10. This is a pseudonym.

11. Carlos's story and the phenomenon of men in direct selling are discussed in detail in chapter 2.

12. For more about how labor market discrimination influences women's decisions to become direct sellers, see chapter 6.

13. Social scientists have examined the complex image and everyday lives of Andean market women, who are ubiquitous features of urban centers in Ecuador and Peru, especially in the highland regions (Babb 1998 [1989]; Seligmann 2004). In her study of direct selling in Thailand, Ara Wilson also found the direct seller—whose selling was associated with a "cosmopolitan, Western model"—placed in a superior position to low-status sellers (2004, 183). Another foil for the put-together direct seller is the housewife, whose frumpiness is associated with an idle, unproductive femininity oriented toward the home; for more on the negative connotations associated with unemployed housewives, see chapter 6.

14. The market woman is an example of appearance and social class not necessarily matching up. Even though market women's appearance may be associated with low class status, unattractiveness, and (sometimes) indigenous background, some of these entrepreneurs earn a good living selling their wares.

15. In a similar way, the data processors in Freeman's study separated themselves from factory workers, although both groups of women were employed by multinational corporations and were paid similar wages (2000, 220, 236).

16. As Freeman puts it, drawing parallels between her work on Barbados and Elsie LeFranc's research on Jamaican women: "Status through appearance becomes a replacement for economic prosperity in a ritualized process whereby structural constraints . . . prevent individuals from reaching those goals and values held most highly by society" (2000, 233).

17. Missing teeth are a good example of what Adair calls the "not-so hidden injuries of class," an embodiment of low-class status in the United States, where her research was based, and elsewhere (2001, 454).

18. Having a uniform made would usually involve buying the material, choosing a style or pattern, and having a woman working as an informal seamstress make the garment. Direct sellers who are adept at sewing can make their own uniforms.

19. Carolina has since stopped selling Yanbal, after obtaining a more prestigious office job in Quito.

20. In Bank Muñoz's ethnography (2008) of a Mexican factory, the darker-skinned women employees were seen as "needing" makeup, and they engaged in competitive displays of cosmetic creativity, whereas lighter-skinned women were thought of as attractive without makeup.

CHAPTER 5

THE PICTURE OF SUCCESS: PRIZES AND STATUS
IN THE DIRECT SALES ORGANIZATION

Aquí nadie regala nada; todo se gana con esfuerzo, con cariño, con dedicación.
[Here no one gives anything away; everything is earned with effort, with love, with dedication.]
YANBAL ECUADOR'S GENERAL MANAGER ROBERT WATSON, SPEAKING AT
THE GALA AWARDS CEREMONY AT THE 2008 NATIONAL CONVENTION

LEARNING THE LANGUAGE OF PRIZES

At the 2008 Yanbal national convention in Guayaquil, in the large hall filled with nearly five hundred of the company's top-selling directors, it takes a few moments for the chatter to die down as a pantomimed skit begins on the platform at the front of the room. Three women in pageboy wigs, skirt suits, and large sunglasses are talking and laughing, each holding shopping bags. An enthusiastic Yanbalista, recognizable by her gray Yanbal tote, approaches and tries to interest the women in joining Yanbal, showing them the benefits as portrayed in her *álbum de incorporación* (a notebook that serves as a recruitment tool). One woman rejects this offer, miming "no" and waving her index finger from side to side emphatically as soon as she realizes what is happening, gesturing as if to say, "I know all about this, and I am not interested." The Yanbalista is able to persuade one woman to join, who in turn recruits one of the other women—not the one who had objected so strongly. Before we know it, the first recruit appears in an elegant black dress, wearing a sparkly necklace, and the original director places a sash and tiara on her, mimicking the Yanbal awards ceremonies held at each annual convention. After a dramatic pause, the Yanbal representative hands the newly crowned director a key to her new Yanbal car, along with some sprigs of dried flowers to suggest a bouquet. Upon seeing this, the woman who originally turned down the Yanbal "opportunity" (as the company and its sales force call it) begins to cry, thinking about what might have been. She immediately finds one of the Yanbalistas and signs up on the spot.

This comic sketch was performed by Yanbal Ecuador corporate staff members during the company's national convention, an annual event that aims to recognize and motivate directors. The presentation's happy ending was followed by laughter and applause. Two aspects of the skit are key to understanding the organizational culture and structure of Yanbal and similar direct selling organizations. The first of these is the focus within the organization's culture on prizes as the culmination of work well done and as motivation for new people to join. Prizes are strongly associated with DSOs in the popular imagination and are the most visible material symbols of success both within the sales force and among outsiders. Second, the way to achieve these prizes, in the case of directors such as those viewing the sketch, is to recruit more consultants and directors, resulting in increased sales and a rise in status.

Even Ecuadorians who know virtually nothing about Yanbal products or the structure of the DSO may see Yanbal-emblazoned vehicles on the street and recognize these cars as rewards offered to top performers. In promotional and recruiting materials, the company prominently features the silver cars, with orange Yanbal stickers on both front doors and above the windshield, as a visible icon of success. After a Sunday morning ceremony on the final day of the 2008 national convention, fifty-one brand-new Yanbal automobiles, ranging from compact cars to sport-utility vehicles and a Mercedes sedan, snaked through the streets of Guayaquil en route to the most luxurious hotel in the city. It is this association with upward mobility and visible status that motivates some people to join Yanbal and move up the ranks of the sales force. The convention itself is a prize, word of which reaches even the newest consultant through videos and directors' testimonies. The language of prizes infuses official and interpersonal discourse throughout the various levels of Yanbal Ecuador, and thus this feature of the DSO deserves attention and analysis.

Previous studies of direct selling have emphasized the important symbolic and material role of prizes within DSOs, the construction of images of model sellers to be emulated by others, and the salience of meetings and conventions for furthering interest in selling and recruiting (Biggart 1989; Cahn 2006; A. Wilson 2004). In ethnographic descriptions of direct selling events, the marketing of ideology has often been highlighted in

Awards displayed in Ligia's office include tiaras, sashes, certificates, trophies, and medals. (Photo by the author)

a way that leaves the materiality of the prizes and their inclusion in individual narratives of success largely unexamined. For example, there has been no scholarly examination of the use of unofficial prizes within direct selling groups (that is, prizes that do not come directly from the DSO but are given to sellers by their mother directors), nor of the ways that sellers talk about, think about, and use prizes in their everyday lives.

This chapter discusses prizes in three contexts: the hypervisibility of prizes during the annual convention; the importance of role models or exemplars of success within the official (corporate) and grassroots cultures of the direct selling organization; and the meanings sellers and directors attribute to prizes in everyday life. Data for this section are drawn from participant observation at the 2008 national convention and other meetings and events in 2007, 2008, and 2009 and from conversations, observations, and interviews with Yanbal consultants and directors in Guayaquil between 2006 and 2009. The language of prizes is so ubiquitous in the world of direct sales that it could almost be overlooked as straightforward and superficial. However, the ways in which prizes connect to social class, family dynamics, and ideas of success show that this language is more complex than it appears at first glance.

THE NATIONAL CONVENTION AND CONSPICUOUS PRIZE GIVING

In order to be able to attend the national convention held by Yanbal Ecuador each May or June, directors must meet target sales totals and recruitment numbers. At the time of the study, there were seven ranks of directors (depending on a woman's number of daughter and granddaughter directors), with sales and recruitment goals gradually increasing with each rank. Directors must meet the goals for their rank during nine of twelve months to be eligible for the convention. As the sales force grows each year, the number of convention attendees increases, and in 2008 a total of 481 directors were eligible to attend the convention in Guayaquil. The directors hail from all regions of Ecuador, and in recent years the conventions have been held in Quito or Guayaquil because few other cities have hotels that can handle events of this size. In fact, in 2008 the directors and about one hundred corporate staff members were divided among three hotels because no single hotel could provide a sufficiently large block of rooms to house all the participants. The common perception among convention attendees and other Yanbalistas is that the convention is a prize or a reward for hard work and that, in exchange for their efforts, top directors are treated "like queens" by Yanbal Ecuador.

Having been invited to attend the convention by the corporation's general manager in Ecuador, I did not know quite what to expect. When I arrived at the mezzanine level of the Hilton Colón in northern Guayaquil on the first morning of the convention, the excitement was palpable. Women of all ages, shapes, and sizes were clustered around several stations, playing or waiting to play games, and many were clapping and cheering. Most had already checked in and received their name badges, polo shirts, and baseball caps, as well as notebooks and other materials in a logo-bearing leather tote bag. Whenever a photographer appeared, squealing women came running from all directions to squeeze into the photo, in what resembled a modest parody of the infamous *Girls Gone Wild* videos sold in the United States. Some of the games were related to prizes, such as the dart game where women aimed for their desired destination in the upcoming year's trip competition. Each year, directors can earn invitations to international trips, with all expenses paid by Yanbal. For the upcoming year, the destinations included Medellín, Colombia; Buenos Aires, Argentina; and, the highest-level trip, known as the Galaxia, to Germany and Austria (attended by directors from all countries where Yanbal International operates). As discussed in chapter 3, international travel is associated with the wealthy elite in Ecuador. Thus the vacations won by Yanbal sales directors contribute to their being perceived as having high socioeconomic status and help support their claims to that status.

Another game being played on the first morning of the convention was a version of "pin the tail on the donkey," in which blindfolded women had to place a sticker with the Yanbal name in the correct location on a photograph of a silver sport-utility vehicle like the ones given away by the company. The car is the icon of success within Yanbal, as is the pink Cadillac for Mary Kay distributors in the United States, and many directors claim that winning the car is one of their major career goals. Once convention attendees had completed at least one of the four games, they lined up to receive prizes based on how many games they had completed. Those who had played all four games were given a tablecloth. This seemingly trivial prize was the source of much excitement among the directors I spoke with during the morning. Providing a musical backdrop to the giveaways and prize-themed games, the speakers were blaring songs by Colombian pop singer Carlos Vives. This choice of music was not coincidental and was also linked to a prize contest: all consultants and directors who met prescribed sales targets between Campaigns 7 and 9 of that year would receive tickets to one of two special concerts by Vives in Quito or Guayaquil that were closed to the public.

At the opening-night dinner, first-time convention attendees were recognized. As each name was read aloud, the woman walked up to the stage to receive a small lit candle. When I complained the next day to one of Ligia's daughter directors (a first-time convention winner) about the nearly hour-long duration of this ceremony, her eyes lit up as she disagreed, saying that it made her feel happy to hear her name called and receive the candle. Although the candles were not prizes per se, the women were flattered to be recognized for their hard work.

The same night, directors attending the convention in the company of four, six, or eight daughter directors (who had also won the right to attend) were recognized. Ligia was one of the three directors who had eight daughter directors win the convention. When she was brought onstage and one of Yanbal's managers asked her how she did it, she explained her simple, prize-based strategy: she had promised to buy all of her daughter directors who won the convention a *vestido de gala*, an evening dress to be worn on the last night of the event. For those who had also "formed" at least one daughter director during the year, she had promised the matching shoes and pocketbook to complete their outfit. The promised dresses highlight the importance of image for Yanbal directors and Ligia's interest in reinforcing this priority with her "daughters." The dresses were certainly not the sole motivation for the high convention attendance rate among the directors in this "family,"[1] but the unofficial contest did provide some additional incentive. Directors often spend their own money on prizes that go beyond those offered by the company; these expenses grow more considerable as the women move up in rank on what Yanbal calls "the stairway of success."

The second day and evening of the convention were devoted to treating the directors to the rewards of their labor. Three training sessions were held, in which motivational speeches were given by a prominent psychologist, by Yanbal International's most successful director for that year, and by Iván Hurtado, the first Ecuadorian to climb Mount Everest. During the evening's activities, hosted by a national celebrity, the women were treated to dance performances and were given a bottle of Yanbal's newest perfume (which would cost clients $54). The evening culminated with a surprise concert by Ecuadorian pop star Fausto Miño, whose presence excited some directors to the point that they jumped onstage to kiss him, before being escorted back to the audience by security personnel. Five ecstatic women won an extra prize through a random drawing: breakfast with Miño the next day.

The final day of the 2008 convention was dedicated to recognizing Yanbal's top directors through the presentation of the company's top awards and prizes. The morning began with the *entrega de autos*, in which directors who have reached sales and recruitment goals receive free new cars from Yanbal. Before the event began, the theater of the Centro de Arte in western Guayaquil began to fill up with directors attending the convention and guests of the winners, often family members and daughter directors. Upbeat Yanbal songs played as some directors clapped along. The theme of the event was "Grand Prix," and a national race car driver cohosted the event with the sales managers for the Andean and coastal regions. The company's managers wore white jumpsuits of the type used by race car drivers and pit crews, and red ball caps with the Yanbal logo.

The ceremony kicked off with a small four-door Chevrolet sedan rising out of the front part of the stage as uniformed dancers playing a pit crew danced around pretending to change tires. Meanwhile, two large screens on either side of the stage played a video montage of race cars and drivers popping champagne to celebrate wins, accompanied by intense rock and techno music. During the event, a total of fifty-one cars were given out, roughly half to directors at the lower ranks and half at the upper ranks. Two master directors (the highest possible rank for directors) received cars, including Ligia, who accepted her sixth car from Yanbal. At one point during the event, the company's strategic sales manager tried to get the directors in the crowd excited by asking who would win a car at the next convention. After the women finally shouted "Me!" loud enough to satisfy her, she had them hold up invisible keys and show them to their neighbor. Then they were instructed to hug their neighbor in congratulation.

The presentation of cars is the only Yanbal gathering at which husbands and male family members are welcomed and are part of the target audience. After watching video clips of husbands congratulating their wives on their achievement, family members were admonished by the strategic sales manager: "Be proud of your wives and mothers." She said that she wanted husbands to leave the event transformed, ready to support their Yanbalista wives more wholeheartedly. It is significant that this ceremony honors the work of the directors in the presence of their husbands, who may be unsupportive or skeptical (as discussed in chapters 1 and 2). After the keys were handed over, and the cars blessed with holy water by a priest, family members climbed in and were driven caravan-style by Yanbal staff to an elegant luncheon at the Hilton.

The convention ended typically, with a gala evening during which the nation's top-selling consultants (six attended the 2008 convention) were presented with awards, including the crowning of a *princesa*, who was given a sash, a tiara, and a bouquet of the type seen in beauty pageants. Then the three top-selling directors in each rank were brought onstage and given custom-designed jewelry sets and sashes. Finally, the top three directors in the country's sales force were given sashes, tiaras, and bouquets. Once the *reina*, or queen, of the convention was crowned, she was escorted by the general manager to a throne attached to the backdrop of the stage as confetti rained down. While a photographer snapped pictures, the seated winner was handed a microphone and gave an emotional, tear-punctuated speech reminiscent of those delivered by beauty queens. After

Each year at the national convention, one director is crowned queen for her achievement in group sales and recruiting. (Photo by the author)

the speech, her daughter directors were invited onstage to help celebrate her achievement and to pose for photographs. The gala awards ceremony, along with the car presentation, is the prototypical recognition of directors' success and is featured in advertising and recruitment materials throughout the year. The use of symbols associated with beauty pageants—such as tiaras and sashes—highlights the company's beauty focus (and sponsorship of high-profile pageants such as Miss Ecuador), while rewarding women for revenue generation rather than appearance.

Although fewer than five hundred Ecuadorian Yanbalistas qualified to attend the 2008 national convention, and numbers had been smaller in past years, the event's symbolism and impact are far-reaching. I witnessed directors who had attended the convention going back to their groups and using stories of the event to attempt to motivate their consultants. Ligia showed the video montage of the convention in the next campaign launch meeting, highlighting the moment when she received her new Yanbal sport-utility vehicle and thanking her consultants for helping her achieve this goal. Director Maryuri Palma also shared her convention experience with sellers in public and private settings, while discussing other prizes she had won in an effort to impress consultants with the possibilities in Yanbal. "I am going to Jamaica," she told consultant María Bustamante as the three of us sat in Maryuri's home office, "and I've never even left the country before."

Although the most prestigious prizes, such as cars and international vacations, are only offered to directors meeting certain requirements and are thus out of reach for the average consultant, they are highly visible symbols of the potential for success within the sales force. These prizes embody success, equating it with the consumption of luxury goods and services. The only difference between the conspicuous consumption of these directors and other well-off Ecuadorians is that, in this case, Yanbal is picking up the tab, freeing up the directors' earnings to buy other status-conferring commodities. Despite the high visibility of these top-level prizes, most consultants are more preoccupied with the weekly prizes offered by the company and the monthly or bimonthly prizes, all of which are made available to both consultants and directors based on sales totals.

MODELING SUCCESS: THE ROLE OF "STAR" DIRECTORS

At the convention, in Yanbal recruitment materials, and in interpersonal interactions among Yanbalistas, references are often made to the elite members of the sales force, the consistent top performers whom I call "star" directors. These directors' testimonies and achievements are featured in the videos shown to prospective and new recruits, in the magazine for consultants and directors (called *EntreNos*), and on the Yanbal website. Directors frequently share their stories and accomplishments in meetings and at events. In all these ways, sellers become aware of their directors' visibility and position within the social world of Yanbal Ecuador. Members of Ligia's group, for example, marvel at her upward mobility in her twenty-one years with the company. They are familiar with elements of her backstory: her small-town roots and previous home, a humble rented apartment in the Sauces neighborhood of Guayaquil, the young age of her children when she began with Yanbal, and the fact that, in the early years, she and others worked without the full-color catalog seen as indispensable to the DSO today. When I asked consultants and directors whom they admired as a role model within Yanbal, they often named Ligia; of course, it is possible that this choice was motivated by my association with her as her niece-in-law. Ligia's message is, "If I can do it, so can you." Because of her career trajectory and her high standing in the sales force, her words and advice carry weight with her consultants and those from other groups. Sometimes this advice is not taken at face value, however; several consultants told me, "You know, it's not as easy as Ligia makes it sound."

Star directors have influence not only on sellers and junior directors but also on the decisions of the company and even, in the case of the ICE debate, at the level of national politics. Yanbal Ecuador's managers and corporate staff are in constant contact with these directors and often hold special meetings for them, both one-on-one and in small groups. When these directors have complaints, the company listens and often responds. For example, in late 2007, the lists distributed to directors by the company, which enable directors to track activity within their group and family, changed format. The matrix became more difficult to read and eliminated information that high-level directors perceived as crucial to their work planning and to the monitoring of their families' activities. For months, Ligia called, e-mailed, and wrote letters to various staff members in the Quito-based corporate headquarters, explaining why the "new lists" were unusable and how they would hurt business. She encouraged other directors to do the same. Despite the pleas of coordinators (Yanbal staff who support and monitor directors) that the women give the new lists a chance and try to use them, the more experienced directors stood firm. By the time I made a follow-up trip to the field in May 2008, the old list format was back, and Ligia, for one, was thrilled. Since Yanbal corporate staff members and management often claim that the company listens to directors' feedback, they can be pressured to live up to this claim, as they did in this case.

The handful of directors who have reached the highest levels in Yanbal are women whose words and actions matter to a variety of audiences. Consultants and lower-level directors value their advice, even if they do not always act upon it. Their stories become legendary within their groups and beyond. The Yanbal corporation, which is at least partially responsible for these women's development into confident and self-assured businesspeople, both promotes the idealization of star directors and responds to their questions and complaints, while being able to count on their loyalty in times of economic or political need. With their reputation as hardworking mothers (*madres de familia*), respected Yanbal sales directors were even able to bend the ear of the president of the republic when their livelihoods were threatened.

THE EVERYDAY LIFE OF PRIZES

Most women who sell Yanbal products, and even most who become sales directors, never win a Yanbal car or an international vacation. They never have their photo taken with the Yanbal executives while wearing a tiara and a sash, never walk into a national convention. But despite the exclusivity of such iconic rewards, prizes do matter to these women. The structure of this DSO is such that there are a range of prize sizes and values, and just about everyone can win something or other if she works consistently. These prizes complement monetary earnings and, in some cases, eclipse cash as the most important motivating factors behind women's direct selling work.[2] Unlike cash, prizes can be seen by others, making the rewards of work with Yanbal conspicuous and helping to recruit new members into the sales force. As Biggart puts it, cash awards are less effective, as they "are invisible and can be spent by spouses" (1989, 154). Consultants and directors I know often claim that the prizes were the reason they originally joined Yanbal.

There are several different levels of prizes for Yanbal consultants and directors. Each week, when women place their orders, they can earn prizes according to the *monto*, or total amount sold, which is calculated according to the price paid by the client and not the discounted price paid by the consultant/director. For example, in the first week of Campaign 7 of 2008 (in June), women placing any order (the minimum order was $80) would receive a makeup remover worth $9. For an order of $185 or more, they would receive a blush compact worth $22. And for a *monto* over $330, they would receive a bottle of the popular perfume Osadía, worth $47. These prizes were cumulative, meaning that the consultants and directors would win not only the prize of the top level they reached but also all the prizes for the lower levels.

Products won as prizes are generally sold to clients, resulting in a profit of 100 percent for sellers on those items.[3] When consultants call in to place orders, directors often encourage them to increase their order enough to reach the next prize level: "Did you know, Señora So-and-So, that if you order just ten dollars more, you will get this perfume for free?" Product prizes are seen as allowing Yanbalistas to increase their earnings or build capital for future orders. In some cases, a woman will keep a prize for herself so that she can try out the product, rather than buying it with her hard-earned money. Consultant María Bustamante told me that she only kept small prizes, such as eyeliners or lipsticks, for herself; any items of higher value went into her "stock"[4] to be sold to clients.

In addition to the weekly prizes, Yanbal offers bigger prizes to be earned over the period of one or two campaigns (roughly one or two months). These prizes are seen as a major source of motivation to increase sales. Prizes of this level are often items used in the home, whether functional or decorative, highlighting women's traditional domestic role. In Campaigns 4 and 5 of 2008, for example, prizes included a pressure cooker, a hand mixer, a set of pots, a cabinet for dishes, and a dining room table with four chairs. To reach the highest level of prizes and win a dining room set, a cabinet, and a set of pots, consultants and directors had to sell a total of $5,000 over the two campaigns.

Because of some issues with suppliers, Yanbal had been late in delivering prizes during the time I was in the field; the most-awaited prize was the sofa-bed that many of the women I knew had earned but not yet received. By the time of my follow-up trip in May–June 2008, the furniture had arrived, and the women were excited to show it off. At consultant Narcisa Pazmiño's home, the sofa still had the plastic wrapping on it, although it had arrived months earlier. When I joked that it looked as if they were never going to use the sofa, she told me that she was waiting for Christmas to remove the plastic and that no one was allowed to sit on it until then. When I asked her about it more than a year later, she still had not removed the plastic cover from the sofa. Prizes are often cared for in this painstaking way, especially by consultants with fewer economic resources; smaller prizes are often kept stored in their original boxes.

Some husbands made fun of their Yanbalista wives because of the importance the women placed on prizes. Consultant Elizabeth Contreras told me that she can't wait to open packages from Yanbal and see what prize might be inside. Her husband makes fun of her for this, but, she said, "I tell him, 'My dear, it's that this is something that I have earned with my effort. Selling bit by bit,' I tell him, 'I have arrived at this sum.' Then he laughs at me and says to me, 'The smallest things make you happy.'" Elizabeth makes a habit of showing her husband Yanbal's *EntreNos* magazine and telling him which prizes she is planning to win. She claimed that when she showed him a set of Pyrex baking dishes that she wanted to earn, he said she should just "go out and buy them!" But that wouldn't be the same, as Ana María Briones explained: "It's like when they give you a trophy, how much does that trophy cost? Maybe not even ten dollars . . . but the recognition that they gave me, that I earned, that I deserved, I have it here, I use it, and I tell everyone that I won it."[5] Long after cash earnings are spent, either reinvested or used to pay expenses, said Ana María, the prizes remain as a lasting reward for the women's work.

When visiting consultants in their homes, if the talk turned to prizes, I could be sure of being treated to a show-and-tell presentation of the items that they had won. On one of my visits to the home of Vanessa Paredes in the southern neighborhood of El Guasmo Central, she showed off her prizes to her mother-in-law and sister-in-law, who were not enrolled in Yanbal; these included an iron and a combination ironing board/cabinet, and the coveted sofa-bed. When I asked Jacinta Menoscal if she had won any prizes, she made a list, pointing out the items around her home: "That television, [and] in the room there is another television, [and there was] another television that I sold. . . . I have suitcases, microwaves—I've earned two microwaves—the stove, I'm telling you, a lot of things." After giving me a similar rundown of the items he had won, a male seller told me, "And you can go on like that, furnishing your house [with Yanbal prizes]."

Perhaps exaggerating slightly, consultant Marjorie González, who sold for other DSOs besides Yanbal, told me that it had been years since she had had to buy a household appliance—she won them all through her selling. Maryuri Palma, who had also won an impressive collection of prizes, put it this way: "The pots that I use are the ones I won in Yanbal, the dishes are from Yanbal, the spoons are from Yanbal, the glasses are from Yanbal, practically everything, and that is what I say the husbands don't see, that the woman is helping them avoid that expense." Even with the remote control of the Yanbal prize television in his hand, Maryuri said, her husband didn't see these nonmonetary rewards for her work with Yanbal.

Scholars and people affiliated with direct sales organizations see the use of prizes as a major difference between this type of work and what might be called traditional jobs (Biggart 1989; A. Wilson 2004). A postal worker or a bank teller works for a salary or a wage, not for a new stove. Of course, contemporary management methods increasingly place importance on rewarding performance with bonuses or prizes, but the emphasis on prizes is still weaker in the typical formal corporate workplace than in the direct sales sector. Within the social world of Yanbal, however, there is one prize that symbolically denotes direct selling as "real" work and gives sellers the sense of respectability that comes with belonging to the formal workforce. This prize is the Christmas turkey, which is traditionally eaten on Christmas Eve in the homes of Ecuadorians who can afford to do so. People with formal-sector jobs of a certain level, such as university professors, corporate managers, and government researchers, receive a turkey and a basket of provisions every Christmas from their employer.

Each holiday season, Yanbal gives consultants and directors a chance to win a large turkey and a bottle of wine for their holiday celebrations.[6] More than any other single prize throughout the year, the turkey motivates women to sell. The turkey is connected to local ideas about the foods eaten by different social classes and is a marker of sought-after inclusion in the formal labor market. Maryuri, marveling at the number of consultants who won the turkey in 2007, told me:

> Many had never eaten turkey, I'm telling you, and it's not because the turkey is expensive but because sometimes right around those dates [Christmas and New Year's] there wasn't even enough money to buy a turkey, or they think the turkey is expensive, that it is out of reach or for people with money—there are people who think that way. . . . Sometimes [there's money] not even for a chicken, so imagine, in this case, to be able to win the turkey with your work, and the bottle of wine. . . . It's been five years that we have been eating turkey in my house [at Christmas].

Maryuri's description and the association of this food item with the formal workforce helps us understand why the turkey is so important to the Yanbal consultants and directors. Earning the turkey prize shows that they have "real" jobs and that they are associated with a company that recognizes them as real employees (although they are officially self-employed), as long as they meet certain goals. Also, since more men than women have access to the kinds of white-collar jobs that confer these types of benefits, Yanbal is providing access to this symbolic capital to people who do not have many other avenues for obtaining it.[7]

Directors recognize the importance of the turkey to their consultants, and they monitor the women's progress toward winning this symbolic prize, making phone calls to those who are in danger of missing out and encouraging those who are on their way to winning it. Ligia provides an extra incentive for members of her group, by promising all the consultants who win the turkey a "basket" (actually, a large plastic shopping bag) of food products. This includes ingredients typically found in holiday meals, such as raisins and nuts, as well as everyday staples such as rice and cooking oil. In December 2007 approximately eighty of Ligia's consultants had earned the turkey and received a basket.[8] Ligia spent about $1,000 of her own money to add this extra recognition of the consultants' work and motivate them to sell.

This reward was in addition to the Christmas party, complete with lunch and disc jockey, that Ligia holds each year for the turkey winners. (A separate party was held for all of her daughter and granddaughter directors.) It is common for directors to promise and deliver additional prizes, or to reward prizes unexpectedly, to consultants who are top performers or meet certain goals or milestones. This represents an out-of-pocket expense that is also an investment in their business. Yanbal International's top sales director, a fifty-something woman from Colombia, claimed in a speech at the 2008 convention to spend around 10 percent of her earnings on prizes for her consultants and the directors in her family network. These supplementary prizes are often advocated by the company and individual sales directors as a key strategy for improving sales and recruitment numbers within the group, although the prizes provided by Yanbal are also seen as indispensable.

CONCLUSION

Prizes are an important ingredient in the organizational culture of direct selling organizations, as prior research has shown (Biggart 1989; Cahn 2006; A. Wilson 2004). Yanbal also follows this pattern, recognizing distributors' achievements through small weekly prizes (generally products), more substantial monthly or bimonthly prizes (usually home-related goods), and luxury prizes (cars, trips, etc.). The luxury prizes are highly visible in the company's advertising and recruitment materials and are often portrayed as the culmination of star directors' career trajectories, both in official and micro-level discourse. Yet the lower- and middle-level prizes are accessible to the average seller, and these sellers often see the prizes as a major source of motivation and satisfaction in their work lives. Products can either be kept for personal use by those who cannot afford to buy Yanbal goods even at the consultant discount, or they can be sold to increase earnings and build capital. Goods for the home, such as sheets, furniture, and household appliances, save women extra expenditures, are useful, and impress friends and family members. Such prizes derive their value from, and reinforce, cultural norms that assign care of the home to women. The prizes also help women with low incomes to perform this domestic role, potentially improving their material conditions by freeing up cash earnings for other uses.

It seems that, despite the women's appreciation of these prizes, some husbands see the value of cash earnings but not the utility of blenders and silverware. Many sellers are undeterred by their spouses' lack of enthusiasm for prizes won through the DSO. A Yanbalista's home (or office, in the case of some directors), filled with prizes, is an archive of her work with Yanbal over the years; she proudly points to the items she has won, whereas the money is more ephemeral or temporary.

Certain prizes hold a special place in the organizational culture of Yanbal. The premier icon of success within this DSO is still the automobile, but in the daily lives of most women who sell, smaller prizes symbolize the women's efforts and the recognition of these efforts. One annual prize symbolically marks Yanbalistas as "real" workers and members of a formal enterprise: the Christmas turkey. Earning the turkey helps differentiate direct selling from other, less socially valued types of selling, showing it to be "a distinct, and superior, mode of work and business, one that is middle-class or upwardly mobile and cosmopolitan" (A. Wilson 2004, 182). Associated with the middle and upper classes because it is a benefit commonly extended to white-collar and professional workers, the turkey is sought after by consultants. Like wearing a business suit or carrying the Yanbal tote bag, earning a turkey shows that their work is respectable and professional and that they belong to an established corporation. This symbol is important because most Ecuadorian women do not have access to the types of jobs that traditionally include a Christmas turkey as one of their perks. Having partaken of a couple of Yanbal turkeys myself and seen the pride and care with which they were prepared and served, I recognize the full impact of this seemingly trivial gesture.

Prizes are a key element in the recruitment process of DSOs, which in Ecuador are characterized by several degrees of informality. By "degrees of informality," I mean that people who are not registered consultants help those official distributors sell products, so that there are many more sellers than the number officially registered.[9] It is up to the registered consultants, who receive prizes, whether and how much to share their winnings with their unofficial sales assistants.

In the case of Yanbal Ecuador, prizes are a major reason that women who help enrolled consultants sell decide to officially join the DSO. When you help a friend or neighbor sell, you may receive the earnings provided by the consultant's discount while helping that Yanbalista achieve a higher total sale, but the official distributor generally keeps all the prizes generated by this combined effort. For this reason, many women who start out helping others sell decide to join the DSO once they have collected sufficient capital to begin placing their own orders. The power of prizes is sometimes irresistible.

NOTES

1. The term "family" refers to the entire genealogy or network of a high-level director's daughter and granddaughter (and great-granddaughter, etc.) directors' groups.

2. See Biggart (1989, 154) for a discussion of this extramonetary value of prizes in U.S. DSOs.

3. The Mexican Tupperware distributor profiled by Ariel de Vidas (2008) also sold prizes she won, as a means of increasing her income.

4. Sellers used the English word "stock," usually pronouncing it "es-tock." Depending on the level of capital a seller or director works with, her stock may be just a few products or may include a wide range of items.

5. As one of Biggart's informants said, expressing a similar sentiment, "It's not what you get, it's the idea of accomplishment" (1989, 154).

6. The free holiday turkey was also a perk typically associated with formal employment in the United States, a tradition that has largely disappeared except in a handful of unionized industries (Barron 2008).

7. According to consultants who also sell for Avon in Ecuador, that DSO also rewarded sellers with turkeys up until 2006. During the 2007 holiday season, however, Avon gave a roasting chicken instead of a turkey, which certainly disappointed many of that company's distributors. In general, those familiar with other DSOs operating in Ecuador agree that Yanbal's prizes are "better," meaning more valuable, although the waiting period for prize delivery is sometimes longer than with other DSOs.

8. In December 2009, for the first time, Ligia decided to give consultants a $25 gift card to a supermarket, rather than physically giving them food items. She reasoned that this was not only easier for her but would also save the women money on taxi fare to lug the heavy bags back home.

9. For another way of thinking about "degrees of informality," see Benería and Floro (2006), who use this term to characterize women's jobs according to the amount of protections and stability they provide. Of course, women who are less formally connected to the DSO in this case are also likely involved in what Benería and Floro would call "highly informal" work.

PART III

DIRECT SELLING IN CONTEXT:
CAREERS AND CONSUMPTION

WHAT WOULD THEY BE DOING IF THEY WEREN'T SELLING BEAUTY PRODUCTS?: WOMEN'S WORK EXPERIENCES IN CONTEXT

UNDERSTANDING THE ALTERNATIVES

From the time I decided to study the women who work with Yanbal and began turning over the topic in my mind, I consistently returned to the question, "What would they be doing if they weren't selling beauty products?" Of course, this is a hypothetical question that is impossible to answer, but it points to a necessary area of inquiry. Although we cannot know what these women would be doing if Yanbal did not exist, we can examine the context of women's employment in Guayaquil—that is, women's material living conditions and the range of job options open to them in a city where 87 percent of residents live in poverty (Floro and Messier 2006, 234). It is worth noting that in contemporary Ecuador, both "women *and* men are becoming more limited in their options regarding employment" in a climate of increasing unemployment and disappearing formal work (Pitkin and Bedoya 1997, 46).

Both experts and the women in my study agree that employment discrimination plays a significant role in Ecuador's labor markets "in terms of access and wages" (Pitkin and Bedoya 1997, 40), a situation that makes easy-entry and self-chosen careers such as direct selling more attractive. We can also look at what types of work people did before joining the Yanbal sales force, what types of work they engage in alongside their selling, and what their future career goals are. I found that information about previous work histories, concurrent income-earning activities, and future plans was readily available by talking to women informally, observing their daily lives, and interviewing them about their work activities and decisions. Constructing an accurate profile of the employment options for women of various educational and class backgrounds proved more difficult, principally because of the general lack of social scientific or economic studies on Guayaquil.

The purpose of this chapter is to place women's (and men's) work with Yanbal in context by examining the labor market in Guayaquil and how it intersects with existing material conditions as well as micro-level decisions about education, work, and money. The chapter paints a portrait of the employment context in which Yanbal distributors and directors go about doing their work, primarily using the women's own perspectives and accounts. I first summarize the findings of a recent survey of economic conditions in Guayaquil neighborhoods, to give an idea of the overall employment picture. I then move on to women's work histories, the issue of employment discrimination, work that they do in conjunction with their direct selling of Yanbal products, and their work-related goals for the future.

Based on the women's accounts, I argue that Yanbal presents an attractive source of income and employment and that, while direct selling becomes a full-time career for some women, for others it represents "one potential component of the economic bricolage necessary in a changing, cash-based world" (A. Wilson 2004, 165). Scholars of women and work in developing countries have remarked on the multiplicity of income-earning strategies, which change over time depending on both macro- and micro-level conditions. It is common for women in poor countries to combine a variety of informal jobs with formal jobs and to engage in ongoing as well as temporary income-earning activities (Ariel de Vidas 2008; Freeman 2000; Seligmann 2004; Weiss 1997; A. Wilson 2004). This combination of informal and formal work extends even to women who are incorporated into the export processing operations of multinational corporations: in her groundbreaking ethnographic work on Mexican maquiladoras, Fernández-Kelly noted that women employed as factory workers engaged in direct selling of cosmetics on the side (1983, 159).

As Benería puts it, "household survival strategies include very unstable links to the labor market, combining, often within short time periods, wage labor and self-employment as well as temporary migration (domestic and international)" (2003, 112). Although Benería is generalizing about employment patterns throughout the developing world, among the women in my sample I found that very few had been involved in formal employment after becoming mothers, and those who did continue working after giving birth tended to be highly educated, middle-class women. As for migration, most of the women I knew had not left the country, though many had engaged in (permanent) internal migration to urban centers either as children or as adults. The narratives of Yanbalistas often included a formal to informal labor trajectory or a complete bypassing of the formal labor market (due to barriers discussed below) in favor of a multipronged informal income-earning approach.

It is important to note that women's "shifts between different jobs and tasks are highly associated with their involvement in domestic work and care responsibilities" (Benería 2008, 7); that is, the burden of their reproductive work affects their work trajectories and leads to frequent changes in income-earning strategies. In addition, "domestic responsibilities penalize women in the labor market and are a key factor in women's weak position in terms of earnings and occupations" (Elson 1999, 612). It is significant that the women in this study reformulated or stretched ideals of motherhood to include paid work, as has been shown in studies of Latin American immigrant women who redefine motherhood to incorporate their new roles as breadwinners (Hondagneu-Sotelo and Ávila 1997; cf. Medved 2009 for a U.S. example). Among women direct sellers, a common gendered economic strategy involved challenging traditional ideals of gender that assigned women to the home[1] and reworking gender norms to include paid work outside the home, a practice that was necessitated by the material conditions of women's daily lives. This redefinition of ideal motherhood differs from other Ecuadorian mothers' view of their work outside the home as a "sacrifice" (Pitkin and Bedoya 1997, 41); in general the women in the present study were proud of their contributions to the family and felt that bringing in an income was part of being a good mother.

ECONOMIC AND EMPLOYMENT CONDITIONS IN THE YANBALISTAS' NEIGHBORHOODS

Women's work with Yanbal should be examined in the context of employment alternatives in the city and, more specifically, in their neighborhoods. The *Encuesta del Sistema de Información Social* (*ESIS*),[2] a survey conducted by the Ecuadorian Instituto Nacional de Estadística y Censos (National Institute of Statistics and the Census, or INEC) in December 2006, shows marked differences between the economic conditions of "consolidated" and "unconsolidated" areas of Guayaquil.[3] Although the survey data yield little information on gendered patterns of employment and socioeconomic status, the aggregate results can help provide a window into the lives of women living in these areas. Although some Yanbalistas I know, especially directors, live in the consolidated areas of the city, many more are living in the unconsolidated areas.

The portrait that emerges of the wide swath of the city considered "consolidated" is one of high levels of education, high levels of employment (including among women), and high levels of informal sector employment. In unconsolidated neighborhoods, the *ESIS* found lower levels of education, higher rates of unemployment (well over 10 percent among people aged eighteen to twenty-nine in some neighborhoods), and greater participation in informal employment, as high as 55 percent in one area (INEC 2007). The stark contrast between economic indicators for consolidated versus unconsolidated areas shows the gap between the well-off and the poor in Guayaquil. People living in consolidated areas have more years of schooling on average, and fewer people in these neighborhoods have incomes below the monthly minimum wage. Women from better-off neighborhoods are more likely to work, and this higher rate of female employment may be related to the fact that families with higher incomes are able to hire domestic workers to help with housework and child care. Greater numbers of women working for pay may be correlated with the higher levels of education in these areas, which is not broken out by sex in the *ESIS*.

On several measures of economic conditions, however, consolidated and unconsolidated areas look similar. These include the percentage of households headed by women (generally less than 30 percent), total unemployment rates, and self-employment rates (between one-quarter and one-third of workers in all neighborhoods). The first set of statistics tells us that family composition does not differ greatly across social classes, despite popular stereotypes to the contrary. The second set of figures shows that *guayaquileñas* and *guayaquileños* of all socioeconomic levels are affected by high unemployment rates at the national level, which in late 2009 hovered around 9 percent (and 14 percent in Guayaquil). The final similarity, in self-employment rates, shows that entrepreneurialism also cuts across class lines, perhaps as a common response to the lack of formal sector jobs.

It is safe to assume that there is more formal sector self-employment (e.g., small stores, restaurants) in consolidated areas and more informal sector self-employment (e.g., itinerant vending, home-based food selling) in unconsolidated areas. Across the neighborhoods in which my study participants tended to live, there was variation in the percentage of workers in the informal sector, with a high of 55 percent in El Guasmo and Bastión Popular, 46 percent in Los Vergeles, 42.5 percent in Mapasingue, and a low of 40 percent in consolidated areas (INEC 2007). It is probable that the greater informal economic activity in El Guasmo and Bastión has to do with the geographic isolation of these two neighborhoods. If poor people live in areas like these, cut off from shopping and other services, there is a greater probability that local people will jump in to fill the void, offering food and other necessities to their neighbors. Because these marginal neighborhoods lack adequate public transportation, it is also more difficult for Guasmo and Bastión residents to obtain and commute to jobs in other parts of the city, where more formal employment is available.

The *ESIS* provides a snapshot of employment and economic conditions in Guayaquil neighborhoods with differing patterns of employment, education, and infrastructure or resources. The findings of the survey that are most relevant to women's direct selling work have to do with formal and informal employment. In the areas in which many of this study's participants live and work, formal employment is scarce. Throughout the city, an average of around 30 percent of workers use self-employment as an income-earning strategy, so it is no surprise that informal entrepreneurs abound in poor neighborhoods. Yanbalistas fall within this category, and considering the relatively low levels of education and high rates of unemployment in the marginal neighborhoods of many of this study's subjects, it is understandable why direct selling might be an attractive option. It does not take much capital to get started, there are no rigid entry requirements, and the provision of products in areas that are cut off from the city's formal network of retailers guarantees sellers at least some clients. Yet rather than simply assuming that formal employment is difficult to obtain, I explore the formal labor market a bit further, since many sellers and directors I met claimed that rampant discrimination was a real factor in their employment decisions.

DISCRIMINATION IN THE FORMAL LABOR MARKET

In interviews and casual conversations with Yanbalistas, I did not bring up the issue of employment discrimination based on gender, age, or appearance. Yet the topic was raised by the women so frequently that I had to consider it seriously, as an important piece of the overall labor puzzle in Guayaquil and Ecuador. Women working with Yanbal had experiences of and opinions about the difficulty of entering the formal labor market, and they identified discrimination based on age and appearance as the most prevalent barriers. Perhaps they did not identify gender-based discrimination as important because of the large number of sex-segregated jobs, meaning that, except at the highest education levels, men and women were not often in direct competition for positions.[4]

Age discrimination was taken for granted by the Yanbalistas as an ugly yet unchangeable aspect of the formal labor market. In fact, many consultants, directors, and Yanbal corporate staff espoused and promoted the idea that one advantage of working with the company was that "no one will kick you out because you get too old," a well-known practice among local employers. Getting and keeping a job apparently becomes more difficult as a worker ages. Favorably comparing her new work with her old job as a corporate accountant, Yanbal director Ana María Briones explained, "For example, one of the most beautiful things about Yanbal . . . [is that] there is no age limit. A woman my age [forty years old], it is considered practically impossible to get a formal job."[5] A little over twenty years ago, Nancy Torres worked in an office before becoming a Yanbal consultant. When the company went bankrupt and its owners moved to Quito, Nancy was already too old to find another job—"*mayorcita*" (a bit old), as she put it. "No one hires anyone" at that age, she told me; at the time, she was twenty-seven years old. Consultant Ramona Delgado also claimed that age discrimination was rampant and affected even younger women. When I asked Ramona if she thought there were many job options for women, she told me:

> No. Listen, now they are not giving many options—for example, for office work or things like that—not anymore. Now they look at your age, and if you are already older, you can't get in anymore. Now from [age] twenty, twenty-five, and up they won't take you in any job. Unless you go in as a domestic in a house, doing just household chores.

Yanbal is seen as more welcoming and is presented as the alternative to prevailing prejudice against older workers in public and private employment. Ana María provided a detailed comparison:

> Yanbal doesn't close the door on you. In fact, it tells you, "Over there they don't want to give you a job. Come here and I will give you the opportunity. It doesn't matter to me that you are fifty or sixty, that maybe you feel that your life is over. In the company where you went you presented your employment application, and they told you that your life was over." Because when they deny you a position, what are they saying? The message they are giving you is that you are finished—go and die at home.[6]

Another aspect of employment discrimination is a vaguely defined emphasis on appearance. Many job advertisements restrict applicants to those with "*buena presencia*," a loaded term that not only implies a "presentable" (i.e., middle-class) appearance but also excludes people with certain undesirable features or darker skin tones.[7] Further evidence for the importance of appearance in applying for a job is the customary requirement that an applicant submit a passport-size photograph along with his or her résumé. This handy device can be used to screen applicants by age, race, sex, and appearance, all at once. Consultant María Litardo told me that because of age discrimination and appearance-based prejudice, she had not been working a stable job before joining Yanbal. She said, "Every time I go to drop off a résumé, they tell me no, because of my age. . . . Or if not, that it's because I'm fat [*gordita*]." María, who was not a very heavy woman in my opinion and who was only twenty-nine years old when I met her in 2007, had had enough experiences of age and appearance discrimination that she no longer tried to enter the formal labor market, choosing instead direct selling because of its minimal access requirements.

Oscar García, an independent employment expert who runs a job-placement/recruiting agency in Guayaquil, agreed with the women in my study that employment discrimination was common in Ecuador. In an interview, when discussing employment options for women, he reminded me that there were no legal part-time jobs in Ecuador. According to laws passed by the current government, all formal employees were guaranteed an eight-hour day and had to work eight hours. This was another reason that women might not find formal employment: with their domestic responsibilities, a part-time job might be more feasible than a full-time position. But at least officially, part-time jobs did not exist. Rather than viewing flexibility as a euphemism for unstable work and for employers' shedding obligations to their workers, Oscar saw it as being something that workers need and from which they can benefit. This need to organize one's time, he told me, explains the growth of informal selling and direct selling, as well as the variety of part-time arrangements between formal employers and informal workers hired off the books. Because of the needs of workers, especially women workers, such informal arrangements are common in Ecuador. García also believed that there was a greater degree of informal economic activity in the coastal region than in other parts of the country. Given the challenges of obtaining formal employment and workers' need or desire for flexibility and greater earnings, he saw Yanbal and other direct selling "formulas" as an appealing alternative. Being associated with a reputable brand name helped open doors to sellers despite the informal aspects of their work; in this way, Yanbal provided "credibility" for sellers.

WHY YANBAL IS AN ATTRACTIVE OPTION

Working for Yanbal is different from other types of jobs because the entry requirements are minimal: to enroll as a consultant, a person must be female, eighteen years or older, and an Ecuadorian citizen or resident legally permitted to work. Priscilla Molina, the corporate sales manager for the coastal region, provided the official position on why Yanbal appeals to many women from the popular classes:

Can you imagine a place where they don't require you to have studied, to have a profession, to have a degree, where they don't ask you to have studied English, nor French, nor computers? Simply look, with fifteen dollars,[8] enroll and have your business. . . . Of course they are interested.

As Ana María bluntly put it, showing a bit of class prejudice, "The majority are uncultured women [*mujeres sin cultura*], without a university degree, without any degree of financial knowledge. . . . Those women are surely not the most well-bred [*cultas*], the most educated [*estudiadas*]." Director Betty Brigss, many of whose consultants are drawn from marginal areas of the city, said much the same thing: "Many consultants who join Yanbal are people who are not trained, because they don't [Yanbal doesn't] ask for a certain level of education. That is, someone can join who hasn't studied at all."

Things that matter in other employment situations in urban Ecuador, such as age, "social condition" or status, and a worker's last name (connected to status and social origin) are unimportant to Yanbal, according to Ana María; what matters is, "Do you want to do the work?" Ligia always tells me that the people who have the greatest success in Yanbal are those who have the greatest economic need; that is, those whose lack of education, low class status, and lack of prestigious social connections lock them out of the formal labor market. As in other countries, the educational requirements of many office and other formal positions are increasing in urban Ecuador. Nancy Torres, a consultant who is forty-nine, remembers a time when she was able to get a good clerical office job with just a high school diploma, but she told me that now such jobs require college degrees. As mentioned above, age discrimination is another reason why many Yanbalistas say their work is preferable to more formal employment. Carmen Díaz, a director who is fifty-eight, exclaimed, "How beautiful that we don't have a limit for how long we can be in Yanbal. . . . I tell my young consultants, 'You can work here for a long time. Here no one will kick you out.'"

Several people with whom I spoke about employment options for Guayaquilean women described two main types of relatively stable work: one for educated women, and one for less educated women. Women who had gone to college could find work in their profession, and women who had a high school education or less (the majority in most neighborhoods in the city, according to the *ESIS*) could work as domestic employees. Consultant Érica de la A explained it to me this way: "In companies, if a woman doesn't have a profession [college degree], they won't take her. So if you haven't studied, then what they do is go as [domestic] employees to people's homes. And then there are women who don't want that." Érica recognized that people could not freely choose whether to go to college, but that this access was restricted by income and socioeconomic status: "Sometimes it's also not possible to study, so what's left for a person to do?" The answer that she had chosen for herself was selling.

A few participants defined migration as an alternative strategy to increase their incomes, and some had seriously considered leaving Ecuador as so many of their compatriots have done. When weighed against the difficulties of having to travel to another country and adapt to a new culture, direct selling seemed like a better option for these people. One male seller's sister lives in Germany and had urged him to move to that country a couple years back. He told me that he decided not to go because of the degree of uncertainty involved in international migration, concluding, "If I really dedicate myself one hundred percent to Yanbal, I am going to earn more than [by] going to any other country."

Because of the sheer numbers of Ecuadorian emigrants, especially in recent years, it is not uncommon to hear of Yanbalistas who moved to Spain or Italy. Some return and rejoin the DSO, and others remain abroad. Yanbal Ecuador has actually followed Ecuadorians in their mass exodus to Spain, starting up two years ago in that country and serving immigrant communities and Spaniards.

Although there is a growing body of social scientific work on Ecuadorian migration (Herrera, Carrillo, and Torres 2005; Jokisch and Pribilsky 2002; Kyle 2003; Meisch 2002), this topic is not my primary focus here. However, it is worth noting that migration is for many women a real alternative to scarce formal employment, informal selling, or work with a DSO like Yanbal. In 2008, Betty was planning to move to Spain with her children to reunite with her husband, who had emigrated five years before. (In the end, she decided against making the move.) Many consultants and directors introduced in this book belong to families touched by migration in some way. Migration is thus an important component of the overall employment context and household strategy options in contemporary Ecuador. At the 2008 national convention, in the ceremony during which high-achieving directors were awarded their Yanbal cars, two car winners explicitly mentioned Yanbal as an alternative to migration. In a taped piece played as she walked to the stage to receive the keys to her new car, one director said, "We don't have to leave [the country], but rather move forward here in our Ecuador." Another director said that her achievement represented

an invitation to all those women who might be thinking of, at some time, leaving their homes, leaving their children, and dismantling their marriages, dismantling everything because then they could bring a bit of

money from abroad, at the price of working day and night, sleeping very
few hours . . . that don't do anything for them [the women] because they
[return to] find their family destroyed.

For these women, at least, direct selling with Yanbal is preferable to leaving
Ecuador to seek work in Europe or the United States.

The consultants and directors, even those whose incomes were not substantial or who did not dedicate many hours per week to their work with
Yanbal, made convincing arguments that direct selling was preferable to
the alternatives in the labor market. They saw Yanbal as a type of work with
the respectability of formal employment—made possible by the backing of
a respected corporation—and the advantages of informal employment (e.g.,
customized schedules, no bosses). Successful seller Narcisa Pazmiño told
me, "Yanbal is definitely giving a lot of permanent work to women, and
if anyone doesn't work, it's because they don't want to." It is interesting
that she defined this informal-type work as "permanent," since direct selling could be seen as just the opposite, as a form of employment whose flexibility is associated with fluctuating economic gains rather than a consistent income.

YANBALISTAS' WORK HISTORIES: PREVIOUS JOBS

The stories of the women I came to know during my research on Yanbal
ring true with the neighborhood-level employment statistics summed up at
the beginning of this chapter. Of the thirty-four directors and consultants
I interviewed,[9] fourteen had previously held formal sector jobs. Eleven had
worked in the informal sector, mostly in some type of selling. Four women
(and one male seller) had engaged in both formal and informal employment
at various times; this crossing over shows that the choice between informal
and formal work is often shifting and situational rather than being deter-
mined by skills or education level. Three had not worked prior to joining
Yanbal: two had been housewives and one a student.

Thus, the majority of Yanbalistas had worked for pay before enrolling
as consultants, even if there had been a gap in some cases between previous income-earning activities and direct selling work with Yanbal. That
women had been making money before joining the DSO contradicts stereotypes outsiders might hold about Ecuadorian women's concentration in
traditional domestic roles or about direct sales as bringing housewives into
the labor force for the first time. For some time in Ecuador, families at all
economic levels have been unable to survive on one income alone.

I will highlight one caveat to these findings. The people I was able to meet, and who were willing to speak with me, may represent a segment of the Yanbal sales force that is more active or more engaged with the company. For this reason, it is possible that those with a history of formal employment are slightly overrepresented in my sample. Those with lower educational levels or less formal work experience might choose to "go it alone" more than the people I met—that is, sell using the catalog but without being in continuous contact with other sellers and directors or without attending meetings or events. I cannot speculate, but this may be the background of many of the large number of women who help official consultants sell, a common practice that adds another level of informality to a type of work that is already teetering on the formal/informal divide.[10]

Going beyond the informal-versus-formal nature of consultants' and directors' previous employment, further patterns emerge. Three women interviewed had college degrees and had worked as professionals before joining Yanbal: an accountant, a dentist, and a nurse (the dentist was still practicing). Nearly half of the women had been engaged in selling before turning to Yanbal; of these, the majority had sold informally or through other direct selling organizations. This makes sense: if you already know how to sell and what the work entails, you may be more willing to try selling beauty products than someone who has never sold anything.

Two women had been domestic workers, one as a live-in and one as a live-out. These women's connections to well-off Guayaquileans helped them develop their business with Yanbal. In one case, a domestic worker asked her employers to loan her the capital to place her first order. In the other, a woman who had worked doing housework, laundry, and ironing in private homes turned her former employers into her client base; she explained to me that she started selling to them first, because she knew they had the money to pay up front.

Seven women had worked in offices prior to joining Yanbal; these women tended to describe their old jobs as too structured and confining, and they appreciated not having to deal with bosses or rigid schedules as direct sellers. Five women had been entrepreneurs (defined here as having a wholesale or retail business in a fixed location), some as business partners with husbands or ex-husbands. Women who owned small stores (*despensas*) talked about the higher profit margins in Yanbal relative to profits from the goods sold in their shops.[11] These female entrepreneurs were already convinced of the advantages of self-employment over what Yanbalistas call "dependent" employment; they used their business acumen to determine that Yanbal products were a good investment.

Three groups of women, or three types of work histories, are worth examining in greater detail because of what they can tell us about the labor market and women's income-earning strategies and decisions. I call these women the sellers, the housewives, and the refugees. This last term was coined by Brodie, Stanworth, and Wotruba in 2002 to describe people who fled the formal labor force in favor of direct selling.

BORN TO SELL

It has been said that in Guayaquil 70 percent of small-scale informal sellers (*microcomerciantes*) are women (T. D. Wilson 1998, 108). Selling becomes an important source of income in the context of limited employment options, as one of Seligmann's participants put it, referring to the situation in Cuzco, Peru: "With such high unemployment, everyone's become a *comerciante* [seller]. . . . There's no other way to make a living" (2004, 112). Some consultants I spoke with described themselves as die-hard sellers throughout their lives; these people typically told me that they had *always* been selling something or other, as far back as they could remember. Consultant Narcisa Pazmiño told me about accompanying her father to sell in Guayaquil's markets from the time she was a young girl. She said she learned how to sell and how to work hard from his example. Narcisa was still immersed in the world of selling: many of her customers worked in either retail stores or stands in the bargain market district of La Bahía. It was not uncommon when she was selling or collecting money in La Bahía for her to buy items to sell in the small store that she owned with her husband. Buying from her Yanbal clients, even in small dollar amounts, helped maintain rapport between individuals who were both sellers and consumers.

Director Maryuri Palma also cited her father's involvement in selling as a major reason that she sells today. "I have always known how to sell," she said. "I have worked since I was five years old." Consultant Marjorie González tells a similar story of continuous selling, crediting her mother with getting her hooked on sales. "My mom inculcated it in me, instructed me," she remembered, smiling. "She sent me to sell lollipops, bread, and candies in school, although it was prohibited. . . . And later, when I was in high school, I sold other things." Marjorie's mother "made" her study accounting in college, because she told her daughter that she needed to make her own money and that business sense was useful in sales or any kind of other business activity.

Carlos Zambrano, the male consultant I interviewed, also described a long and varied sales history. As he put it, "Since I have had the use of reason, I have been a merchant [*comerciante*]. . . . I believe in microenterprise."

When I asked him what he had sold before turning to Yanbal, the list was varied, including gold jewelry, Barbie dolls and toys "during Christmastime," underwear, clothing, and shoes. He had also worked for two years in one of Guayaquil's most prestigious department stores, and although his job was in the warehouse, he said he would often wander over to the sales floor and end up selling something, since "not all sellers have the ability or the aptitude to sell, . . . not everyone is born to be a seller."

HOUSEWIVES: JUST "WATCHING SOAPS"?

Among the women in this study, the phrase "watching soap operas" (*viendo novelas*) was a favorite euphemism for the inactivity stereotypically associated with housewives who are not earning an income. As one Yanbal coordinator told women in a recruitment meeting, even husbands do not want their wives just sitting around the house "watching soaps"; they prefer them to be economically productive.[12] Of course, the housework and child care performed by wives and mothers is time-consuming and labor-intensive work, despite not being remunerated (see discussion in chapter 1). Despite this reality, the myth of "watching soaps" lives on. When I asked María Bustamante, a consultant in Maryuri's group, what attracted her to Yanbal, she told me, "I decided to join because I wasn't doing anything at home, so I was idle [*ociosa*]." Of course this was not exactly true, as María prepared three meals a day for her family, often including grown children no longer living at home, as well as cleaning, doing laundry, and sometimes caring for her eighteen-month-old grandson. Then she revealed a more convincing reason for wanting to become a consultant: "I was staying alone here in the house." Housework leads to isolation rather than inactivity, and this seems to be one reason that housewives seek work opportunities.

In my interview sample, only two women had been housewives with no work history prior to joining Yanbal. It is common for women of all socioeconomic levels to generate income in some way or another. The stereotype of housewives as lazy, reclining to watch television, despite its inapplicability to most real-life women, may be part of the ethic that spurs women to work and earn money or a justification for their work outside the home. One director, Marjorie López, swears by this image's veracity, saying that she was practically "vegetating" as a housewife before joining Yanbal; in the afternoon, after cooking, washing, and ironing, she told me that she sat on her sofa and watched "eleven *novelas* a day." Marjorie might have been exaggerating for effect, or she may have been multitasking—say, folding clothes while watching television. In any case, she favors her work with Yanbal over the supposed laziness of domestic life.

The myth of the lazy housewife shows how Ecuadorian women, including those portrayed here, are redefining ideal motherhood and wifehood to include paid work. They derive self-worth from their work and feel that they are helping their families by earning an income. One high-ranking Yanbal director, upon receiving a new Yanbal car during the 2008 convention, put this sentiment into words:

> Yanbal has given me that . . . the love for the work, the ability to progress, to not be a parasite, to not stretch out my hand and say [to my husband], "Can you loan me some money so I can eat a fried egg?" Rather, to know that I can, by my own means, help out, support the family unit.

Whereas traditional demands on wives and mothers dictate that they remain in the home, contemporary women defend their decision to become economically contributing members of the household, thus helping to rewrite this script and devising new gendered economic strategies. In this formulation, it is the straw woman of the economically inactive, soap-watching housewife who is ridiculed, and the prototypical working woman who is idealized.

REFUGEES FROM THE PROFESSIONAL WORLD

In their 2002 study of direct selling, Brodie, Stanworth, and Wotruba defined the category of "refugees" as people who are pushed out of the formal labor market and toward direct sales. These people have either lost formal jobs or have been turned off to formal employment because of bad experiences at work. Doubting whether they fit in the formal labor market, they attempt direct selling to see if it can provide a living wage.

In my sample, two professional women fit this profile, as did some other women who had worked in office or clerical positions. Ana María Briones was fed up with her work as a corporate accountant in Guayaquil, a high-pressure job with long hours and strict deadlines. She did not like the way employees were treated, and she hated having to pull all-nighters when big projects or reports were due. Narcisa Zambrano, now a Yanbal sales director in Quito, was working as a nurse in a hospital until a year and a half before this study. Then the hospital changed ownership, cutting salaries and benefits. She felt that this shift pushed her to look for other options to help support her family. Nancy Torres turned to direct selling when the company where she worked as a secretary went bankrupt and she felt that she was too old to find formal employment elsewhere. In a sense, these refugees are silently protesting poor working conditions, low wages, or eco-

nomic changes by opting out of the formal labor market and pursuing direct selling as an alternative income-earning strategy.

COMBINING STRATEGIES: YANBALISTAS' OTHER JOBS

Given the high percentage of Yanbalistas who had worked before, and the
disparities between incomes and expenses in many of Guayaquil's neighborhoods, it is not surprising that some women would have other jobs aside
from their work for Yanbal. These women participate in a time-honored
tradition among many women in the developing world: cobbling together a
household income from a variety of sources. These multiple income sources
are often present whether or not a male partner is working. In my sample of thirty-four consultants and directors, eleven of them—nearly one-
third—had incomes in addition to the money earned through Yanbal (not
including spouse's incomes). Four more were students, who all planned to
continue with Yanbal while practicing their new profession. Most commonly, selling Yanbal products was combined with other types of selling,
including selling for other DSOs (e.g., Avon), whether officially or unoffi-
cially;[13] selling in a fixed retail location, or *despensa*;[14] or selling food prepared at home.[15]

Érica, a consultant for three years, had a common-law husband who
worked on weekends as a clown for children's birthday parties. She sometimes accompanied him and painted the young party guests' faces. In addition, she prepared food and sold it out of her home on the northern pe-
riphery of the city. Marjorie González, who had been selling since she was a
schoolgirl, sold three other beauty product lines (for three other DSOs) in
addition to Yanbal, as well as occasionally selling jewelry and clothing that
she thought would interest her regular clients. Although her mother director Ligia has been trying for years to talk her into beginning the path toward a directorship in Yanbal, Marjorie consistently refuses, because she in-
sists that she will lose clients if she commits to just one DSO. (Exclusivity is
required for Yanbal directors, but no restrictions are placed on what other
DSOs' products consultants may sell.)

Jessie Apolinario, who has been a director for nearly a decade, runs her
Yanbal business out of her *bazar*, a little shop that sells everything from
clothing to small kitchen appliances and decorative housewares. Jessie em-
ploys an assistant to help with the store, which is especially necessary on
Wednesdays, when consultants are constantly stopping by or calling with
their orders. Jessie, whose husband has a relatively high position at a local
utility company, might not really need two income sources, but she is com-

Vanessa Paredes sells Yanbal products and other items from a storefront in the first floor of her home in El Guasmo Central. (Photo by the author)

mitted to running her store and her Yanbal business. And as she told me one afternoon, laughing while pointing at the television mounted high on the wall, "I also watch *novelas*."

One sunny late morning in the final week of December 2007, I took my husband and son to consultant Ramona Delgado's house, located across the street from a mammoth high school in the northern outskirts of Guayaquil. Ramona had mentioned to me on a previous visit that she sold food out of her home on weekend mornings and afternoons, the typical home-cooked specialties that *guayaquileños* often seek out after a night of drinking. Her patio, which had been bare cement when I saw it last, now held four small tables with colorful tablecloths and small wooden benches on either side. A window in the cement-block structure served as the place where customers placed orders and received their steaming plates of *encebollado* (a fish soup that is probably the city's most famous dish), *caldo de salchicha* (blood sausage soup), or *cazuela* (a thick fish stew). These are the only menu options, aside from a variety of sodas.

Ramona told me that she needed the revenue from her food sales to supplement her earnings from selling Yanbal. Her family helps her in her efforts: her aunt and mother often pitch in with cooking, serving, and cleaning up on the weekends, and a brother-in-law who works as a taxi driver was conveniently hanging around when we needed a ride home. Each weekend she usually sells between $30 and $40 worth of food, which she says at least helps cover some of her monthly bills. Another reason that she prepares and sells food in addition to selling Yanbal products is to keep herself busy and occupy her mind. When she is sitting around the house, she told me, she gets to missing her two children, who have migrated to the United States and cannot return to visit her because of their illegal immigration status. When I returned to Ecuador in the spring of 2008, Ramona told me that the rising cost of food was cutting into the already small profits of her food business and that she was thinking of closing up the weekend restaurant to dedicate her time to Yanbal, which she saw as allowing her to earn more. Thus, women with multiple income-earning activities make adjustments based on their analyses of how much they are earning and in response to macro-level economic shifts such as rising food prices. Visiting Ramona in December 2009, I found that she was still making and selling food to supplement her income.

CAREER GOALS

What's next for these enterprising women? Do they intend to stick with Yanbal or move into other types of work? Most of the women I interviewed claimed that they wanted to continue as Yanbal consultants and/or directors. Thirteen of the consultants I interviewed, and many others with whom I spoke informally, had the goal of becoming Yanbal directors. For these women, becoming a director was an explicit career goal. Many more said it would be great to be a director, but it seemed like a lot of work; in Diana Hurel's words, "It's not as easy as they [the directors and Yanbal] make it sound." Those who were in school, most studying law, planned to continue selling Yanbal products as they built their new careers.

The women who were already directors had more concrete goals, such as reaching a certain rank, winning a car through Yanbal, or buying a house. These types of consumerist goals are highly visible in Yanbal's promotional materials and seem to provide motivation beyond just increasing incomes, allowing successful directors to engage in conspicuous consumption and make symbolic acquisitions that enhance their status both within the DSO and in the wider society.

Career goals, including those within the context of Yanbal, are conditioned by the perceived economic situation of the direct sales sector and the country as a whole. For example, when Yanbal directors' earnings dropped suddenly and drastically in early 2008 because the new luxury-item tax known as ICE caused perfume prices to soar, even some of the most gung-ho directors were thinking of jumping ship. Once a woman has been a Yanbal director, however, she tends to think of career options not in terms of formal waged or salaried employment but in terms of starting a business.

CONCLUSION

The hypothetical question of what women would be doing if they weren't working with Yanbal is impossible to answer. However, by examining the contemporary labor market, we can get an idea of what women's employment options are, given a relatively gender-segregated employment picture, high unemployment and underemployment and poverty rates, and how Yanbalistas have decided to go about earning an income within the context of those options. This labor market, while affected by global and national economic trends and conditions, is ultimately a local one. The employment context of Yanbalistas in Guayaquil will necessarily look different from that of Quito or Ecuadorian migrants in Spain.

Recent data on Guayaquil show that many women are working for pay and that there is a high level of employment in what is known as the informal sector. Not surprisingly, residents of poor neighborhoods have lower levels of education and are more likely to work at informal jobs such as selling. It is within this generalized culture of small-scale selling that joining a DSO, with its low entry requirements, may look particularly appealing. Ara Wilson argues that, in Thailand, choosing direct sales is a form of "resistance to frustrations with low wages, bureaucracy, and exploitations as well as with limits of local social hierarchies" (2004, 187). While I do agree that these are also sources of frustration in the Ecuadorian context, I see direct selling not as resistance but as one of several survival strategies that women employ at any one time. In fact, rather than challenging these structural constraints, direct selling allows them to stand and upholds models of economic development that require women to bear the brunt of economic crisis by "multiplying themselves."

Women direct sellers in this study, nearly all of whom were mothers, defined being a good mother as involving financial contributions to the household, in contrast to more traditional ideals of domestic femininity. In fact, they indirectly disparaged unemployed women through the evocative image of reclining housewives "watching soaps" and "vegetating." Despite their commitment to earning money for themselves and their families, Yanbalistas from all educational levels felt that the formal labor market was difficult for many women to enter.

Barriers to entering the formal labor market included a lack of available positions and what the women perceived as rampant discrimination. An independent employment expert agreed with the women's claim that discrimination based on age and appearance does take place. In his view, this discrimination exists because of the lack of sufficient positions. The lack of legal part-time employment, due to the government's rigid position on workers' rights to a full workday, disproportionately affected women, who would benefit most from work that is both stable and flexible in terms of schedule.

Women, aware of the constraints placed on them by both material conditions (e.g., inability of households to survive on one income, lack of formal employment) and cultural norms of gender (limiting women to "feminine" jobs or to unpaid work in the home), construct gendered economic strategies such as combining direct sales of cosmetics with other types of informal work. The variety of gendered economic strategies represented by the women in this study is based on differences among women in terms of their willingness to challenge accepted ideas about gender and on differences in the availability of alternatives to direct selling, depending on their class status and education level (which are linked).

While there was a great deal of diversity in the work histories of the Yanbal sellers in my interview sample, a few patterns became clear. First, most people had had some experience with the informal labor market, primarily through informal selling.[16] Second, nearly all of the women had worked for pay before joining Yanbal, a fact that contradicts some academic and popular assumptions that direct selling organizations recruit housewives who are not already economically active. Third, about half of the consultants and directors had worked in some type of sales prior to joining the DSO.

This shows that sales is seen as a viable income-earning strategy for women living in Guayaquil, and also implies that Yanbal may seem more attractive to people who have already tried their hand at selling.

Yanbal's promotional materials often emphasize the "career" path, encouraging women to dedicate themselves to the DSO rather than to other types of work. In at least one-third of the cases examined here, however, people were combining sales of Yanbal products with other income-earning activities. The reasons for this are complex and diverse, ranging from a perceived need to keep clients happy by offering them a variety of product lines to a desire or obligation to participate in an existing family business. Whatever the motivations, Ecuadorian women from all walks of life are experts in attempting to make ends meet by combining a patchwork of incomes from different sources, whether or not a spouse or other earners are contributing to the household.

After examining the context of women's work options in Guayaquil and Ecuador, it is easy to see why Yanbal is an attractive alternative. Entry into this type of employment does not require the education, skills, or personal connections increasingly needed to find work in the formal sector. There is no overt discrimination based on women's age, appearance, or class background (although individual directors certainly may engage in favoritism or bias). Selling with the backing and respectability implied by association with a well-known company is generally viewed as an acceptable line of work for women, except by certain ornery husbands discussed earlier. And, as chapter 5 showed, the highly publicized success stories promoted by the company inspire women to pursue a career with seemingly unlimited earnings and to aspire to a particular style of consumption.

NOTES

1. The ideal of domestic femininity, "that a married woman is considered of higher status if she does not have to work and can stay at home," is propagated by the middle and upper classes, as Seligmann shows for Peru (2004, 56).

2. For the story of how I came to find out about the *ESIS*, a useful yet little-known source of statistical information on Guayaquil broken out by neighborhood, see the appendix.

3. Consolidated areas are parts of the city where nearly all inhabitants' basic survival needs are fulfilled, with reliable infrastructure such as running water and electricity. Unconsolidated areas are neighborhoods or sectors where infrastructure is not reliable and the struggle for survival is at a more basic level. From what I can tell, there are no equivalent terms in U.S. popular or social science lexicon.

4. One consultant, Érica de la A, did claim that men had an easier time finding work than women, saying that she knew men who had studied only through high school and

were able to find decent jobs, whereas women with similar education levels had fewer opportunities.

5. The phrase Ana María used here was "un trabajo en relación de dependencia," literally, "a job based on dependent relations." This term, which originates from Yanbal corporate-speak and is commonly used by directors, signifies any job in which a worker is employed for wages or salary and is therefore "dependent" on the employer or the company for her income. Direct selling is seen as the opposite, a type of work that is independent and in which a person is her own boss. In Seligmann's study of Peruvian market women, participants also described the undesirability of having to depend on an employer for wages (2004, 52). This image of independence is occasionally criticized by sellers: during a period in which many Yanbal products were back-ordered or unavailable due to issues with suppliers, one sales director complained that in the end she was not independent, since her only access to products was through the company. In her study of women's work in Mexico, Chant cautioned against overestimating women's "autonomy" when they had to obtain supplies from companies who employed them informally (1991, 17).

6. Ana María linked a preference for younger workers to the perception that young people will be satisfied with lower wages, an opinion shared by the employment expert I spoke with. In Ana María's words, "Today there is too much competition: intelligent, recently graduated girls with few economic aspirations who can fill quite well any open job."

7. Job advertisements, such as those in the classified section of the newspaper, also routinely delimit applications by sex. For a discussion of how the qualification of *buena presencia* also operates as job discrimination in Argentina, see Sutton (2010, chap. 3).

8. By the time of one of my return trips in December 2009, the enrollment fee had risen to $16.

9. All of the consultants lived and worked in or near Guayaquil; three of the directors worked in Quito, and the rest in Guayaquil.

10. Distance from the formal DSO in terms of participation in events may affect women's perceptions of themselves as workers and direct sellers. Ariel de Vidas (2008) noted that the rural women in her study of Tupperware in Mexico were largely disconnected from organized DSO events and, perhaps as a result, seemed not to identify with the "'self-help' and 'entrepreneurship' rhetoric that is part of the recruiting and training strategies" of DSOs.

11. Consultants and directors keep between 25 and 35 percent of the retail price of each Yanbal product, depending on sales volume and promotional prices. Ligia often told prospective or new sellers that profits for a retail operation such as selling produce tended to be in the 1–3 percent range.

12. As we saw in chapters 2 and 3, this is not always the case, and men often place conflicting demands on wives regarding their productive and reproductive work.

13. The number of DSOs with which a person is involved can change over time and is often based on an assessment of clients' needs and desires as well as on changes in the economy. In response to the difficulties created by a new tax on perfumes, known as the ICE (discussed in more detail in the introduction and in chapter 7), several consultants I knew decided to join a Colombian-based clothing DSO called Leonisa in the early months of 2008. According to one Yanbal director, increased taxes on certain imports in late 2008 and 2009 led to a decrease in selling for this DSO.

14. Moser claims that such "front-room selling" is "probably the most involuntary part of the informal sector given its capacity to absorb additional labour without increased productivity" (1993, 182).

15. In Cahn's study of direct selling in Mexico, most direct sellers "engage[d] in petty commerce, selling food in their homes or from street carts" (2006, 136).

16. This finding is consistent with Weiss's study of households in Quito, in which 73 percent of women had worked in "commerce" (1997, 22).

CHAPTER 7

BUYING BEAUTY: FLEXIBLE PAYMENT AND EXPANDING CONSUMPTION

"THE PRICE GAME" AND FLEXIBLE CONSUMPTION

A recent *New York Times* article encouraged American consumers to bargain for lower prices on a range of retail items in large chain stores, such as televisions at Best Buy and grills at Home Depot (Richtel 2008; cf. Tugend 2008). Despite most shoppers' assumption that price tags in retail outlets are not negotiable (unlike more flexible prices at garage sales or flea markets), the economic downturn in the United States has apparently caused stores to respond more favorably to customers' efforts to nudge prices downward. While flexible pricing in retail and other sales settings may be the exception rather than the rule in the United States, it is ubiquitous in developing countries such as Ecuador. Bargaining and the idea that no price is fixed are things I learned in Ecuador, although even there, in most established or chain stores, prices cannot usually be questioned. But everywhere else, from mom-and-pop shops to street stalls, the informal market rules, and prices are made to be lowered.

In many of Guayaquil's urban shopping venues, a cheaper price is often expected by those paying 100 percent of the value up front in cash (called paying *al contado*). People paying on credit tend to pay more, whether or not the additional cost is called interest.[1] Credit, especially that offered in small neighborhood stores, is one of the household survival strategies of many urban Ecuadorians, especially those who are poor (Moser 1993; Pitkin and Bedoya 1997, 37).

In Yanbal director Jessie Apolinario's small shop, or *bazar*, in Guayaquil's northeastern neighborhood of Los Sauces, I noticed that items costing more than $20 were marked with two prices. There was a lower price for those who could pay *al contado* and a higher one for those paying on *crédito* (credit). Many Yanbal distributors use similar formulas when dealing with clients, allowing only *al contado* customers to buy items at the temporary sale price, for example. Although Yanbal puts out the monthly catalog that is used to sell, the company has no real way of enforcing prices, and many consultants engage in what veteran sales director Ligia García calls "*el juego de los precios*"—the price game. As long as sellers are paying the required price to Yanbal for the products they buy (at a discount of between 25 and 40 percent off the retail price) and as long as they are comfortable with their profit margin, they can sell products to clients at whatever price they wish. Many employ some version of the credit/cash differential, and others adjust prices in a more idiosyncratic manner.

At no time was the price game more clearly visible than after the infamous tax known as the ICE was imposed in the final days of 2007. It added 20 percent to the final retail price of perfumes and also applied to other "luxury" goods and services such as automobiles and cable television.[2] Since the tax literally went into effect overnight, consultants and directors had to scramble to adjust. Many opted not to tell clients about the new tax and its implications just yet, covering with their own money the sometimes significant difference on orders already placed and waiting until the next order to explain the new prices. Others met clients somewhere in the middle, between what customers were willing to pay and the new retail prices of the products.

This situation allowed clients a considerable degree of leeway in negotiating for lower prices on fragrances, since the new tax was not reflected in the catalog prices for four months. In the Yanbal catalog, as in so many other local shopping situations, the prices were open to debate and interpretation, even in the context of rising costs and declining earnings for sellers. But the ICE did not introduce what I call "flexible consumption" to the direct sales world;[3] it merely made more visible the negotiations between buyers and sellers that were already common practice. The wiggle room in terms of prices can help explain how it was possible to sell a $60 bottle of perfume to someone who earned the minimum wage of $200 a month.

This chapter aims to answer a complex question—how does Yanbal Ecuador succeed in a difficult economic climate?—by delving into the details of how sellers and directors on the ground actually do business with customers.[4] These interactions are predicated on cultural understandings of buying and selling and on the social and economic standing of each participant in the exchange. Information about buying and selling practices is drawn from my observations in the field; accounts of sellers in interviews, trainings, and other settings; and a brief survey conducted with clients of the DSO. I found that, in a situation of low wages and a high degree of economic informality, Yanbal products (which are not cheap) become affordable through a practice that I have chosen to call flexible consumption.

"Flexible consumption" refers to the existence of individually negotiated payment arrangements between buyers and sellers that usually allow clients to pay for items in multiple installments over time.[5] Only two studies of direct selling, both published while I was conducting fieldwork, highlight this practice. In studying direct sales of nutritional supplements on the U.S.-Mexico border, anthropologist Peter S. Cahn found that sellers allowed customers to pay in installments "without charging interest" (2009, 344). In analyzing the social and economic significance of Tupperware sales in a rural Mexican village, anthropologist Anath Ariel de Vidas describes a seller who, "to encourage her customers and facilitate economic access to Tupperware, . . . sells them [the products] in installments" (2008, 269). Ariel de Vidas notes that this "facilitation" (a word used by the Yanbalistas I studied) involves "repeat visits to her clients: here to collect the equivalent of a dollar, there 50 cents, until the total debt had been paid" (2008, 269). I found a similar practice among direct sellers in Guayaquil, though generally payments were in somewhat larger amounts than what Ariel de Vidas describes. She notes that visits for collecting money often followed the protocols of hospitality for social visits, with money being mentioned only at the end of the visit; I have also witnessed this type of collecting in Guayaquil. While these ethnographies of direct selling note that installment payments are common, they do not examine how sellers determine who can pay when. That is, they do not discuss in detail the way that flexible consumption is practiced at the interpersonal level.

My surprise at discovering flexible consumption in direct sales interactions led me to examine more closely how payment arrangements are established, how they vary from person to person and over time, and how they compare with the company's prescriptions for the selling process. When economic and social relations mix, as in the case of clients who are also sellers' friends and family, what does this mean for the price game? How do cultural ideas about family and gender combine with people's understandings of each other's status and material conditions in selling-buying interactions? These are important questions for understanding the success of Yanbal in Ecuador. As Ara Wilson stated in her study of Avon in Thailand, "the power of direct selling lies in its ability to tap individuals' social worlds and so enter extremely local markets" (2004, 171). Thinking of consumer markets and social/familial networks as overlapping helps us understand how women go about selling in Guayaquil.

Beginning Yanbalistas and women recalling their start in the business describe collecting money as a dreaded activity. Some sellers get past this and are able to make a decent living for themselves. Those who cannot overcome the fear of collecting usually do not last in the DSO and can end up losing money they have invested in products. How does social etiquette concerning money affect the money-product exchange (the payment phase) in the sales process? Why is collecting money the most hated, most varied, and most consequential part of the direct seller's job? Once these questions are considered, we can begin thinking about how the consumption of Yanbal products fits with other types of consumption in contemporary urban Ecuador and how it reflects larger trends in consumption. Flexible consumption can be a key to business success in developing countries such as Ecuador, and, as the *New York Times* report shows, may become more common in rich countries like the United States as well (Richtel 2008).

THE SALES PROCESS AND PAYMENT ARRANGEMENTS

The official portrayal of the direct sales process, as seen in Yanbal's training videos and materials, encourages consultants to collect half of the total amount due when the client places the order. The seller should then find out when the client will have the remainder of the money and plan to deliver the products and collect the remaining cash due at that time. Directors advise consultants to collect this deposit as a means of ensuring that the client will be able to cover the order, although not all directors push sellers to get half the money up front. If a client wants to order a large amount but cannot come up with a sizable deposit, sellers are taught to split the order up into smaller orders so that they do not get stuck paying for an order that a client cannot afford. For example, if a client wants $100 in products but can come up with a deposit of only $5, the consultant may suggest that the customer first order $30 worth of the desired products and then request the rest of the products in subsequent orders, once the first order is paid.

In reality, most distributors require either no down payment or less than half of the amount due prior to delivering the product to the client. Also, while training videos promote the idea of two payments, many consultants allow some of their clients to split the amount owed into more payments. In addition, there can be different payment arrangements for different clients, and these arrangements may change over time. It is this flexibility of payment terms that allows even those with very low incomes to afford Yanbal products. When I asked Yanbal Ecuador's general manager, Robert Watson, how the company sold so much product in a country with such low wages, he pointed to flexible consumption as a primary reason. "We scrape the floor," he told me with a smile. "This is a process of collection, but it's like picking a grain of corn at a time from your field." Although Watson claimed that the company did not extend credit (which is not exactly accurate, as will be seen later), he said that the sellers "in many cases give credit so that [clients] can pay them in three or four parts." This comment shows that although Yanbal recommends a particular selling protocol that includes payment in two equal parts, the corporation is aware that a variety of payment arrangements exist and that this diversity of consumption patterns ultimately allows the company to make a profit.

Collecting money is often seen as the most difficult and most intimidating part of direct selling work. The anxiety with which sellers approach collection confirms Hochschild's claim (1983) that debt collection involves emotional labor on the part of the collector. Not wanting to ask people for money is one of the main reasons for women not wanting to become Yanbal beauty consultants, and it is frequently mentioned by ex-sellers as a reason for not earning well and for eventually dropping out of the DSO. Consultant Carolina Cevallos, then a high school student, told me in 2008 that she was uncomfortable with collecting when she first joined Yanbal, until she told herself: "If I'm going to have that embarrassment, I am never going to get ahead." This gave her "strength," she said, to get over her fear of collecting money and to earn more.

Director Maryuri Palma told me that "there are no bad payers, just bad collectors." She tells her daughter consultants that they need to show up on the agreed-upon day to collect the money they are owed, because if they don't, clients will use that as an excuse, telling consultants, "Why didn't you come yesterday? I already spent the money." Because collecting is sometimes a dreaded activity, some consultants postpone it as long as possible and do not insist that clients pay them when promised. Many Ecuadorians consider direct discussions of money to be unseemly, which makes collecting promised payments difficult for sellers. As new consultant Daniela Solís told me, "We have people spoiled [*mal acostumbrada*], taking them the product and [saying,] 'Pay me when you have [the money].'" This stance toward collecting money can of course prevent consultants from placing new orders and maximizing their earnings and can lead to them having to ask family, friends, or husbands (often the last resort) for cash to cover orders.

Most consultants and directors admit that the ideal situation would be to receive cash up front for products at the time they are ordered or when they are delivered to the client. However, most people realize that this scenario is sheer fantasy, given the economic realities of life in contemporary Ecuador. As endearingly straightforward consultant Ramona Delgado put it, as we chatted at her dining room table one sunny afternoon, "Right now things are a little bit sort of screwed up [*un poco medio fregadas*] for people, you know?" What this economic mess meant for buyers, according to Ramona, was that "they don't have [money] to pay all at once in cash for things." Male seller Carlos Zambrano agreed that basically no one could afford to pay cash up front for products like those Yanbal offered: "At least in an economy that is not that good, like the Ecuadorian one, you can't do *al contado* sales." Instead, sellers were "obligated" to give clients time to pay, in his view. The sellers and directors thus believe that flexibility and patience in collecting money from clients are a necessity due to the difficult economic conditions in which Ecuadorians are living. Of course, those with more capital can turn orders around more quickly (Ariel de Vidas 2008, 270) and can afford to be more lenient with clients than those who are scraping and saving to cover the cost of their orders.

CULTURAL NORMS AND MATERIAL CONDITIONS IN THE SALES INTERACTION

Before I explore further the Yanbalistas' accounts of how they go about getting money from clients, two cultural dynamics at play in the sales and collection process are worth examining. The first is the idea that people feel pressure to *quedar bien*, a hard-to-translate idea that is akin to saving face or maintaining a good reputation. In theory, because Ecuadorians want to *quedar bien*, they will feel obligated to pay their debts, including money owed to Yanbal consultants. This face-saving also takes place at another level; people who buy Yanbal products from a friend or neighbor not only want to maintain their own social reputation but also feel somewhat responsible to help their friend *quedar bien* by paying Yanbal for products ordered. Clients do not want to lose face with sellers, and sellers do not want to lose face with their directors, fellow sellers, or the DSO. Sellers are often embarrassed when they have to borrow money from friends or relatives to cover orders because a client failed to make a promised payment.

The importance of this cultural ideal seems to motivate both men and women of varying socioeconomic backgrounds. The opposite of *quedar bien* is *quedar mal*, an expression that is commonly used by Yanbalistas to describe clients who do not pay (e.g., "A veces los clientes nos quedan mal," or "Sometimes clients don't live up to their commitment"). Consultants I spoke with especially dreaded having to ask their husbands for money to pay for Yanbal orders, although some had husbands who routinely and willingly helped out in this regard. Elizabeth Contreras told me she sometimes gets customers to commit to paying the amount due on time by asking them to not make her look bad by having to ask her husband for money to cover her order. She said her clients respond by saying, "No, no, no . . . I will make you look good [*Te hago quedar bien*]." Consultants are sensitive to failures to *quedar bien*; if a client does not satisfy a debt, the seller will generally protect her own image by not selling to that person in the future. In a way, this decision not to offer more products also helps the indebted client to save face by not being put in a position to have past payment failures pointed out.

Another cultural underpinning of sales and money-collecting interactions is the fear of being tricked or swindled, which I would argue is of special concern in a large city like Guayaquil, where stories of scams and outright robbery are traded enthusiastically at friendly lunches and family gatherings. Although *guayacos* and *guayacas* (as natives of Guayaquil sometimes refer to themselves) often seem to enjoy telling lurid stories about the outlandish ways in which dishonest people tricked them out of their money, it is always preferable not to fall for such schemes in the first place. In colloquial coastal Ecuadorian Spanish, the two cultural archetypes at work in these stories are the *sabido* (literally, "knowing one," but more easily understood as "swindler") and the *cojudo* (the "sucker," or person who gets tricked).[6] The *sabido* is the one who "gets over" on the *cojudo* because of the latter's lack of sophistication or street smarts. This cultural dynamic injects suspicion into direct selling exchanges, as neither the buyer nor the seller wants to be the victim of a scam. The buyer wants to make sure that he or she gets the desired product for a fair price, and the seller wants to make sure that she (or he) gets paid and makes a profit.

Thus, a certain level of trust must exist or be established in order for both parties to be satisfied. The buyer who pays money up front and never receives the products has allowed herself to be tricked; so has the seller who pays for ordered products in advance and cannot recoup their cost or collect her commission from a client. In the buyer-seller interaction, the clients have the advantage because of the hope that they will eventually pay for the product; the seller will be inclined to express deference and exercise patience if necessary to get her money. For this reason, most consultants will (against directors' and the company's advice) order products without taking any money up front and will collect some portion of the agreed-upon price when they deliver the product to the client, collecting the rest afterward in one or more payments.

In deciding what payment terms to give each client, consultants consider the socioeconomic status of each individual, including where they live and the type of paid work, if any, that they do. Elizabeth, who lived in Los Vergeles, a poor and working-class neighborhood at the northern edge of the city, told me, "The majority of people in the sector where I am working—I don't consider myself a millionaire or anything, but their resources are less than mine . . . and when someone has lived that need, that lacking, they understand the person." In this comment, Elizabeth shows that she determines the payment arrangements with her neighbors based on their low socioeconomic status and that her treatment of them is informed by empathy for their situation based on a shared experience of poverty.

In addition to giving sellers clues as to the clients' ability to pay, the city's geography also affects how beauty consultants conduct their selling and collecting. For example, consultant Martha Bermeo gives her neighbors in the northern neighborhood of Colinas de la Alborada up to a month to pay for a product that she has already turned over to them. If the client lives farther away, she gives them only two weeks to pay, since it is impractical for her to make multiple trips to collect money, given the time and expense of traveling to other neighborhoods. She knows she will be seeing her neighbors regularly and that collecting from them will be easier since they are nearby, so she allows them a longer grace period.

The frustration of traveling long distances across the city to collect money that the client then claimed not to have was common among consultants. As seen in an earlier chapter, husbands could get especially grumpy when sent by wives to collect money from clients who did not have it. When I asked Elizabeth's husband how he felt about her work with Yanbal, this was his main complaint. Consultant Érika Martínez found a way to make these wasted trips less costly: if the client did not have the money by the agreed-upon date, Érika asked the client to reimburse the round-trip bus fare she had paid to visit her. Although the fifty-cent fare is probably not a great cost to the indebted client, collecting this small amount means that Érika is not spending her money needlessly. It also pressures the client to have the money ready for her the next time she comes so that the client does not lose face.

Consultants consider other factors when crafting payment arrangements for their various clients. Daniela sets different terms for those who hold salaried positions and those who perform unpaid work in the home: "When I see that they are also housewives and that they pay me from what they can get together [from a spouse's income or other sources], then I give them more flexibility [*facilidad*]." From salaried employees, most of whom get paid on the fifteenth and at the end of each month, Daniela collects payments on or shortly after payday. Daniela's mother consultant, Belén Vera,[7] has clients who pay a small amount weekly, others who are salaried and pay at the middle and end of the month, and some wealthy clients (for whom she used to do domestic work) who pay up front in cash when they order. She told me that she looked at the "economic situation" of her various clients and inferred their ability to pay from this knowledge.

Yanbalistas agreed that, over time, they got to know the payment history of their clients and therefore knew whom to keep on a short leash and whom to allow more time to pay. Marjorie González told me that she was flexible with longtime, responsible clients but strict with new clients. "With time," she told me, "one goes along learning, acquiring knowledge through experience. . . . It's like my eye has become clinical, my bionic eye [*laughs*]. . . . Really, now I can detect [who will pay]." Other consultants employed a similar double standard, with one set of rules for established, trusted clients and another set for new clients. Of course, the only way to find out that a client is not responsible is to get burned, and many consultants had stories of clients who wouldn't pay.

Diana Hurel told me of three sisters who were clients of hers, none of whom had stuck to the agreed-upon payment terms. She blamed herself for losing the money, saying, "I gave them too many items without knowing them well." One of the clients returned the products, meaning that Diana had to find new buyers, since Yanbal does not accept returns except in the case of defective products. A second sister "paid, but not even half" of the amount owed. The third sister worked in informal sales and had convinced Diana to accept some of her merchandise to reduce her debt. This third client still had a hefty balance—as Diana put it, "Imagine! Eighty-seven dollars!" It is through experiences such as these that consultants learn which clients to trust and which to be suspicious of. As Martha Bermeo told me, "You'll fall for it once, but then not again." Some consultants stop selling to these clients, whereas others will sell to them only if they pay 100 percent of the price up front.

SELLING TO FAMILY MEMBERS

Mitigating the importance of these socioeconomic and behavioral considerations is the closeness of the relationship between buyer and seller. Many sellers said that they allowed their friends and family more time to pay, whereas acquaintances or people whom they knew only as clients were given stricter payment terms. There was considerable debate among the Yanbalistas as to whether family members were better or worse payers than other clients. Elizabeth told me with a laugh, "Sometimes our family also tries to sink us, because we give them the product, and since they are family, they forgot to pay."[8] María Litardo said she gave her family members more time to pay and allowed them to pay smaller amounts according to what they had on hand, but, she added, they were good clients because "I have the certainty that they will pay me."

For some sellers, there are limits to this goodwill toward family members who are also clients. Micaela Vera said that extra-flexible payment arrangements were only for "very close family, like a sister, or my mother. . . . If it's a niece, no—same [terms] as the neighbors." By only allowing very close family members to pay in many small installments, consultants can maximize their earnings and train their other clients to pay in a few timely installments. Extending easy payment terms to extended family would be a losing proposition, since Ecuadorian family networks can be quite large. Having family members as clients is thus viewed in two different and contradictory ways by sellers: these clients might be less likely to pay in a timely manner or at all, or they may be seen as a sure bet, clients who will always pay.

GENDERED PERCEPTIONS OF CLIENTS

After my interview with Robert Watson, who told me that a slight majority of Yanbal Ecuador's customers were men, I was curious about the gendered composition of the sellers' customer base and about whether sellers had different perceptions of male and female clients. Most consultants told me either that they had equal proportions of men and women clients or that they had more women than men as clients. A few women told me that they had more male than female clients and that the men bought products both for themselves and for their families. Daniela was one of the consultants who sold mostly to men, and she implied that the sales process was simpler with men. Many times, they already knew which cologne or deodorant they used and ordered it by name, without having to see the catalog.

Consultant Sara Murillo agreed, saying that men were not interested in flipping through the catalog. One disadvantage with male clients, according to Sara, was that they did not order frequently. On the other hand, she said, "With men, the sale is fast. . . . They don't beat around the bush. They want something and they buy that, and when they have the money, they pay right then and there." Sara connected the ease of selling to men to their greater access to cash; this is especially the case when we compare working men with housewives, who generally must get money from their husbands to make purchases. One problem Sara encountered with male clients was that they "betrayed" her; that is, if she wasn't around when they wanted to buy something and another Yanbalista offered to sell it to them, then they bought it from the other consultant. She saw women as being more loyal clients. Interestingly, this perception of female clients' greater loyalty jibes with stereotypes about men and women in Ecuadorian society, in terms of marriage or heterosexual relationships. It is somewhat expected that men will cheat on their romantic partners, whereas such behavior is considered shocking in a woman.

Another advantage of selling to men, which was mentioned by consultants and directors in meetings, was that, because of Ecuadorian gender relations that stereotype men as economically productive and providers, men would pay for products more quickly because they were embarrassed to owe money to women. Of course, consultants had to be somewhat cautious about seeking out male clients if their husbands were the jealous type. It is one thing to be out selling or attending meetings when a husband assumes that his wife is moving in an all-female environment, and quite another to be seen as approaching strange men to sell to them.

CLIENTS' ACCOUNTS OF SELLING AND COLLECTION

Every act of consumption in direct sales involves at least two people: a buyer and a seller. Most studies of direct sales focus on sellers rather than buyers, with an emphasis on the distribution of products and the organizational structure of DSOs rather than buyers' relationships to sellers or buyers' motivations. Many studies of consumption look at consumers but do not pay attention to sellers or the selling interaction or to people's dual roles as both producers/sellers and consumers. I felt it was important to include buyers' perspectives and to learn more about the consumption of Yanbal products from the consumers' point of view. Because of the nature of ethnographic work, and the size and diversity of Guayaquil's population, obtaining a random sample of Yanbal customers was impossible. But since I did not plan to perform advanced statistical analyses on these data, a random sample was not necessary. What I wanted was a general impression of the patterns in consumption of Yanbal products and the relationships between sellers and buyers, as well as confirmation of the information I was receiving from consultants and directors.

Initially I planned to gain access to clients through sellers, but this proved difficult because of the day-to-day organization of direct selling work[9] and because of the issue of bias. If the client met me through the seller and associated me with that person, he or she might be less inclined to be honest with me about the sales and collection process and/or to share impressions of the Yanbal consultant. For this reason, I decided to look for clients outside of my research with an ever-expanding circle of Yanbal consultants and directors. I decided to create a written survey that I could administer and that key informants could distribute within their social networks and return to me.

I was able to survey forty-three individuals, drawn from five sources. In speaking to a secretary at the Universidad Espíritu Santo (UEES) in December 2007, I learned that most of the administrative staff members were Yanbal consumers. She offered to complete and pass out the brief one-page written survey to her co-workers during their lunch hour. She also had some of her friends, neighbors, and family members fill out surveys. In total, this first round of survey research yielded fifteen respondents, all women, who bought Yanbal products at least once per year. During a return trip to Guayaquil in May and June 2008, I contacted a friend of mine who worked in a private English-language institute and had helped with my previous research. She filled out a survey and then had people she knew as co-workers, friends, and relatives complete the survey, for a total of six more respondents. With her help, I was able to gain access to the English school during the period between classes, which yielded eighteen respondents who filled out the survey on the spot. I used my local contacts to complete four more surveys: one was a business owner in the northern neighborhood in which I stayed, and three were participants in a home-based Bible study group to which I was invited. All but one of the forty-three participants were women, and all had purchased a Yanbal product in the past year.

Not surprisingly, most clients bought products from a friend, a neighbor, a co-worker, or a relative (e.g., aunt, cousin, sister-in-law). In terms of the frequency with which they bought products, 35 percent purchased at least once per month; 12 percent bought every two to three months; 28 percent bought every four to six months; and 25 percent purchased at least once per year. Although clients represented a range of occupations and neighborhoods, all but one agreed that Yanbal products were either "expensive" or "very expensive." All but six of the clients had also purchased from other direct selling organizations—including Yanbal's competitors Avon, Ebel/L'Bel, and Oriflame—at least once in the past year. This finding is important, as it points to one motivation for many of the Yanbal consultants who also sell other DSOs' products; if their customers are buying all of these brands simultaneously, selling more than one brand may lead not only to greater earnings for the seller but also to greater customer loyalty. The purchasing of cosmetic and personal care products from different direct sales lines also shows that direct selling is a common way for people to obtain these products. Consumption through direct sales is a socially accepted and, because of flexible payment arrangements, an economical means of obtaining products that are seen as necessary to present a socially acceptable appearance.

I already knew about the existence of flexible consumption from the sellers' point of view, including the calculation of how they set payments for each client depending on the individual's socioeconomic status and relationship to the seller. The responses to the client surveys confirmed the existence of various extended payment arrangements. All but two respondents claimed that their consultant gave them flexible payment options. The most common arrangements (which are not mutually exclusive) were payments in two parts, payments every two weeks or fifteen days, a lump sum payment at the end of the month, and weekly payments. Many of the people with biweekly or two-part payment arrangements were salaried office workers or professionals, meaning that they received a paycheck every two weeks. This makes sense in light of what sellers told me about collecting money; they generally visited salaried workers twice a month around payday to collect. Only three respondents had payment arrangements that were more flexible than those listed here, and in all three of those cases the clients were buying from consultants who were family members. Three respondents said that the payment arrangement depended on the amount owed, a practice that was confirmed by data from consultants.

Many consultants I knew had been clients before joining the Yanbal sales force. This led me to include a question on the survey as to whether respondents had ever sold Yanbal products in the past.[10] I did not ask whether they had been enrolled consultants, because of the large number of women who sell Yanbal in more informal ways, such as reselling or helping consultants sell. The question was simply designed to investigate people's involvement with the DSO as both sellers and buyers. One quarter of the respondents had sold Yanbal products in the past, including two ex-consultants who were buying products directly from their former Yanbal directors. These intriguing findings help us think concretely about individuals' engagement with the direct selling corporation. The common narrative among consultants (and some academic studies of direct sales) portrays a trajectory from consumer to seller, but an opposite or more fragmented path is shown in the surveys.

This path could include a move from being a seller back to being a consumer or an on-and-off relationship with Yanbal, in which women are sometimes selling and sometimes just consuming. For example, the company recognizes that many women join Yanbal toward the end of the calendar year to earn a little extra money for Christmas gifts and/or to obtain products at a discount for gifts; there tends to be a drop in most groups' sales after the start of the new year as these workers drop back out of the sales force. Of course, all consultants are simultaneously consumers, since (by their own accounts) they tend to buy more products because of their consultant discount and their desire to use and become familiar with the products they sell. These patterns show the blurriness of the artificial line separating buyer and seller in direct selling consumption; sellers are also buyers, many buyers become sellers, and people can move back and forth between these categories due to the flexible, informal nature of direct selling.

It is worth noting that the diversity of payment arrangements and the varying ad hoc policies of different consultants are connected to the availability of credit extended to consultants by the corporation. Despite Yanbal Ecuador staff's assertions that the company does not extend credit, credit does exist to some extent. Yanbal's credit policies are less generous than those of other transnational DSOs operating in Ecuador, such as Avon. New consultants must pay in cash at the time of ordering, making bank deposits directly into Yanbal Ecuador's account. Once they have established themselves through consistent payments and order history, they are eligible for the first level of credit—the *pagaré*, or IOU. This gives the consultant an eight-day grace period within which to collect and deposit the money needed to cover an order. In Guayaquil, orders are placed on Wednesday, and they are usually delivered to consultants' homes on the following Friday or Saturday (different parts of the country order on different days of the week). The *pagaré* ideally gives sellers the time to deliver the products to the clients who ordered them and collect money from them before the consultant has to pay Yanbal.

The second level of credit is available to women who have checking accounts (husband's accounts can also be used); this credit takes the form of a fifteen-day waiting period before Yanbal cashes the consultants' check to cover the order. Many clients are not aware of these policies. Whether a consultant purchases products from Yanbal *al contado* (cash on the day of the order), uses the *pagaré* to pay within eight days, or works with checks with a fifteen-day grace period helps her determine how and when to collect money from clients. Sellers with more capital can give more flexible payment terms than those without the money to cover orders.

EXPANDING CONSUMPTION AND
THE ROLE OF FLEXIBLE PAYMENT

As a result of the rapidly increasing connections between economic actors in different parts of the world, the expansion of consumption makes more goods available to more people, despite the relatively low wages of two-thirds of the planet's population.[11] Although some social scientists claim that consumption is contracting, with only the richest being able to purchase nonessential items (Chossudovsky 2003), others have argued convincingly that globalization expands the realm of consumption, thus creating third-world consumers as well as workers (Appadurai 1996; Freeman 2000). Direct selling structures and facilitates consumption practices in ways that differ both from the retail sales model and from types of informal selling such as street vending, based on the unique arrangement of flexible consumption.

In the nearly ten years that I have been visiting and conducting research in Ecuador, consumption has grown tremendously, both in terms of the diversity and quantity of goods consumed by people of all socioeconomic levels and in terms of retail outlets. One large upscale mall in Guayaquil, Mall del Sol, was opened in the northern part of the city in the late 1990s, dwarfing the more modest and older Policentro, a nearby shopping center that had previously occupied this niche. In the past few years, a third mall with Mediterranean-themed décor, San Marino, opened across the street from the Policentro, tangling traffic in that part of town to the dismay of drivers and bus riders. San Marino includes a number of designer and luxury stores, as well as a branch of the restaurant chain T.G.I. Friday's, which is more prestigious and more expensive in Guayaquil than in the United States. Since the 1990s, higher-end retail shopping has also been available in the wealthy suburb of Vía a Samborondón, among other places.

Between 2001 and 2006, mall-type shopping popped up in less-affluent neighborhoods, with the construction of the Mall del Sur and Riocentro Sur at the southern end of the city, an area typically seen as poor and working-class. Guayaquil's new central bus terminal, the Terminal Terrestre, which began operation in 2007, serves a double function, as terminal and shopping center, with a range of shops that includes some large chain stores. Despite the competition, the still-standing stalls of the temporary terminal next door, which offered a variety of goods (clothing, food, shoes, etc.) to travelers using that facility, are still open, providing consumers with a more economical shopping option.[12] The neighborhood of La Alborada, at the northern edge of Guayaquil, has also undergone growth, with an increasing number of strip-mall-type retail offerings that cater to the needs of middle- and working-class residents of the area.

These retail districts and malls increase the number of places that people of all income levels can buy goods and services and can take part in the ever-popular practice of conspicuous consumption or in simply seeing and being seen in a shopping environment. During this time of expanding formal consumption, the informal economy, which also ensures consumers' access to a variety of goods, has continuously grown. Access to relatively cheap goods (especially clothing) imported from China has not only edged out domestically produced goods but has changed the face of La Bahía, Guayaquil's bargain shopping district, with many Chinese-born merchants setting up shop. It will be interesting to see how new, stronger tariffs and taxes on imports affect the China-Ecuador pipeline of goods.

This explosion in consumption sites and opportunities has gone hand in hand with the latest ongoing economic crisis (beginning in 1999) and the country's slow and incomplete journey out of this crisis.[13] The rise in emigration may also be seen as fueling this expansion, allowing people more access to cash in the form of remittances and encouraging the consumption of certain types of imported or status items (Binford 2005; Jokisch and Kyle 2008, 351; Martin 1991). Previously rare items, such as disposable diapers and cellular phones, are now commonly used in even poor households of Guayaquil, indicating an expansion in the categories and quantity of goods consumed across the socioeconomic spectrum.

Expanding consumption is not an indicator of lower prices on consumer goods or higher wages; on the contrary, most Ecuadorians and academics agree that prices have increased (especially after the 2000 adoption of the U.S. dollar as the national currency), and wages have dropped, as has the formal employment rate (Benería and Floro 2006; Herrera 2006b). I see three factors at work in the growth of consumption: in the formal retail sector, these include increasing inequality and increasing access to credit; and in the informal retail sector (including direct sales), flexible consumption. Increasing inequality means that a small handful of wealthy urban Ecuadorians consume ever-larger amounts of goods and services in the rapidly multiplying luxury retail outlets. Increasing access to formal credit mostly helps middle- and upper-class people consume more, since their stable incomes from employment and business ownership qualify them for department store credit cards as well as bank credit cards. Even Yanbal distributors, while not formal employees of the company, can use their order invoices to substantiate their income and obtain formal credit to make large or small purchases.

Flexible consumption, the set of payment and distribution arrangements between direct sellers and their clients, is based upon initial and ongoing negotiations between the two parties as well as the previous or evolving social relationships that connect them. In other types of informal selling, similar arrangements can also exist. In the formal sector, for example, some stores have a layaway system (*plan acumulativo*) that mirrors this practice in a more impersonal way. Flexible payment over time can increase people's consumption of expensive goods by allowing them to pay when they are able.

Interestingly, flexible consumption is not a surreptitious part of the Yanbal direct sales interaction but is openly acknowledged and even encouraged by the DSO, which sees it as a practical solution to the instability of the Ecuadorian economy and the predominance of low incomes. The existence of flexible consumption probably allows the company to charge more for its products, since they are paid for over time, meaning that clients do not have to produce large amounts of money at once. The intricacies of Ecuadorian social etiquette, such as the preoccupation with not losing face and the embarrassment involved in owing money to someone who must be seen socially, help ensure that Yanbal Ecuador gets its cut and that the company's sellers and directors get paid.

CONSUMPTION, SOCIAL CLASS, AND THE NEW TAX

Yanbal products are expensive, and the brand is well respected in Ecuador. Yet Yanbal customers are men and women from all levels of society. Similar socioeconomic diversity can be found among the members of the DSO's sales force, although few consultants and directors achieve wealth through their work. As could be seen in the analysis of Yanbal catalogs in chapter 3, the company strives to create a luxurious image through advertising text and images. Yet, as can be seen from the accounts in this chapter, these seemingly elite products are being made accessible for many Ecuadorians through flexible consumption.

The ambiguous class identity of Yanbal Ecuador was brought to the forefront in early 2008, as the sales force reacted to the passage of the luxury-tax package known as the ICE, which included a hefty tax on perfumes. Prior to his election and throughout his administration, President Correa had set himself up as the enemy of the oligarchy and the traditional elite, specifically criticizing wealthy Ecuadorians' preference for imported goods over domestic products. The ICE can be viewed as an extension of this stance: through it, Correa's government taxed goods and services that he claimed were the province of the wealthiest citizens. Included in this list were cable television and perfumes.

When Yanbal consultants and directors saw their earnings threatened by the additional 20 percent tax on fragrances (perhaps the product most associated with the brand), they reacted to the law's implicit presumption that these products were luxuries, and organized protests in cities across the country. They compared Yanbal perfumes to imported fragrances by multinational corporations like Chanel, saying that Yanbal products were made in Ecuador[14] and were the preference of the masses. The message was that only elites could buy expensive imported perfumes, but that Yanbal was for everyday people. One major difference between, say, a Chanel fragrance and a Yanbal fragrance lies in the ubiquity of flexible consumption in direct sales in Ecuador. To buy Chanel No. 5, you must walk into an upscale department store and pay the total price up front; to buy Yanbal's Osadía, you can work out an acceptable arrangement to pay your beauty consultant smaller amounts over time. For this reason, Yanbal products have wide appeal across the economic spectrum. According to my findings, even salaried professionals prefer to pay sellers over time, allowing themselves more flexibility to manage household expenses with limited resources.

The ICE was unpopular because it affected all participants in the direct selling system: clients, sellers, and the corporation. Of course, its concrete effects differed, depending on one's socioeconomic status and position in this distribution system. Directors were concerned with making enough money to maintain their current lifestyle; for some consultants, the tax actually threatened their ability to put food on the table. Consultants who tended to sell perfumes more than other products were disproportionately affected.

Those of lower social class did not have the capital necessary to weather the effects of the ICE and emerge unscathed; instead, they had to devise tactics to manage the difficulties. Narcisa Pazmiño, for example, showed her clients the price with the ICE added and then took a couple dollars off of that price, so that she was still making a profit on the sale and the client felt like he or she was getting a deal. Many consultants told me that clients thought the sellers were trying to scam them, since the ICE-inflated prices were not those printed inside the catalog but rather were shown in a list tacked onto the inside cover. This case shows the *sabido-cojudo* dynamic in action. To protect themselves from being swindled, many clients chose not to buy perfumes with altered prices. To compensate for their reduced income, some consultants and directors decided to perform more facial cleansings for clients, in order to sell skin care products, which were unaffected by the tax.

All in all, the ICE damaged Yanbal Ecuador's profits in the first quarter of 2008. According to the company's general manager, Robert Watson, the ICE cost the company $8 million in January and February alone. Despite this effect, the sales force bounced back as soon as the tax was lowered. At the 2008 national convention, Watson claimed that the company was fully recovered, setting an all-time sales record in May 2008. Yanbalistas have even reached the point that they can laugh about the ICE. At the convention, one of the company's sales managers referred to the difficult time that the directors had had with the tax, asking the attendees if they remembered that experience. The women laughed and shook their heads, prompting the manager to say facetiously, "No, that must have happened somewhere else. . . . It couldn't have been here."

CONCLUSION

The controversy generated by the tax law known as the ICE, and the government's later reduction of the tax in response to pressure by Yanbal and its sales force, allowed the hidden dynamics of direct selling consumption to be viewed more easily. At the micro level, Yanbal consultants' handling of the new tax brought flexible consumption practices to light, as sellers further tweaked and stretched already malleable pricing and payment arrangements with clients, playing "the price game." The tax caused Yanbal Ecuador's sales to plummet at the outset of 2008, and although sales activity and profits rebounded to some extent (until the next crisis in 2009, caused by government restrictions on imports), many directors and consultants saw their livelihoods threatened and their earnings drop. It also became more difficult for these women to achieve prizes that Yanbal had offered as incentives for meeting sales targets.

At the macro level, the ICE debate brought to the forefront the links between consumption and social class. By singling out perfumes as a luxury good and an indulgence of the wealthy, the Ecuadorian government communicated the assumption that both imported fragrances and Yanbal's products were consumed only by elites and took dollars out of the country. Yanbal countered this stereotype by insisting that its plants employed hundreds of Ecuadorian workers and that, as a direct sales organization, it offered work to many thousands of women. The directors and consultants that make up Yanbal's sales force emphasized the popular appeal of the products they distribute, saying that direct selling provides incomes for average women, whose customers are not elites but hardworking Ecuadorians of all social classes. The objections of people associated with DSOs and the subsequent acquiescent or sympathetic attitude of the nation's president and other lawmakers to the sellers' plight were covered in the press, contributing to a public discussion of the relationships between work, consumption, and social class. As consumption expands and people gain access to more and more goods (through practices such as flexible consumption), ideas tying social and class identities to consumer goods are both questioned and created. As the ICE hubbub showed, these ideas are up for debate and can become a point of contention between government institutions, private companies, and ordinary citizens.

The introduction to this chapter presented questions about the reasons for Yanbal's success in Ecuador's difficult economic conditions and about the ways that social and economic relations mix and mutually shape each other. Flexible consumption is a set of one-on-one arrangements between sellers and buyers that allows more people access to more goods; it is the modus operandi of direct sales in Ecuador and a primary reason for the financial success of direct sales companies. As seen in this chapter, these arrangements are negotiated, sometimes repeatedly, and are affected by a range of independent variables, such as the relationship between buyer and seller, the buyer's socioeconomic status, and cultural mores.

Among the most important cultural underpinnings of flexible consumption and the personalized selling encounter are the desire to avoid being swindled or tricked and the desire to maintain a good reputation within social networks. These cultural understandings, generally shared by buyers and sellers, guarantee (in most cases) that the selling interaction is concluded to both parties' satisfaction. Sellers count on people acting in accordance with these norms, in order to avoid losing money. Given Ecuadorians' low average wages and the economic instability at the micro and macro levels, flexible consumption works surprisingly well. Clients usually get the products they want, and sellers usually get paid, which means Yanbal Ecuador gets paid and remains in business. Having sellers as consumers ensures the widest customer base possible, with profits from products bought by consultants for themselves increasing the company's earnings but not the seller's.

When I began this study, I was convinced that in learning about relationships between sellers and their clients, selling would be of paramount importance. But the moment of selling—the selling interaction—is not characterized by persuasion and sales techniques, nor by emotional appeals of sellers or objections of clients. Selling is more straightforward than I expected. But collecting is another story. Collecting money for ordered products keeps sellers awake at night and keeps them bustling from one part of town to another. Collecting requires sellers to overcome the rules of etiquette that disdain money talk and to be creative in finding ways to get their money. Sometimes it may feel like plucking one grain of corn at a time from a vast field, but collecting through flexible payment arrangements is what allows the whole DSO structure to remain viable in economically uncertain times.

NOTES

1. In this context, "credit" does not refer solely to formal credit cards issued by banks. In fact, other forms of (informal) credit are much more common in Guayaquil.

2. Because of vigorous lobbying by Yanbal Ecuador and protest by directors and consultants, the tax was lowered on many products and eliminated on many others (see discussion in the introduction).

3. Economists use the term "flexible consumption" to describe the change in consumer habits and demand in response to alterations in the supply of a product. I employ it here to mean something different—that is, the way that consumption, in the form of the buying/selling arrangement, can be adapted to the preferences of buyers and sellers, meaning that the delivery of the product, and especially payment arrangements, can be negotiated and renegotiated.

4. Statistics on Yanbal's success appear in the introduction. According to the general manager of Yanbal Ecuador, the company's annual sales are approximately $12 per inhabitant of the country (Robert Watson, interview with author). In 2003 it was estimated that sales of personal care products (e.g., skin treatments, makeup, fragrance) generated $18 per person in Ecuador (*El Comercio* 2003).

5. This type of installment payment arrangement has been associated with poor people's consumption in the United States and elsewhere (Caplovitz 1963) but has not generally been discussed in the context of direct sales, with the recent exceptions of Ariel de Vidas (2008) and Cahn (2009).

6. The word "*cojudo*" is basically a swear word and is not generally acceptable in polite conversation.

7. Belén became a director (and later went back to being a consultant) during the course of this project but was a consultant when she explained these collection practices to me in 2007.

8. Weismantel (2008) reported on an Ecuadorian woman who ran a food stall in an urban market and had the same complaint about family's threat to profitability: "The entire family comes to the market and expects me to feed them for free, but I have to buy all my ingredients . . . [and] pay cash."

9. For example, many direct sellers visit clients when the clients are working, a situation that would make it difficult if not impossible for me to speak with clients at length.

10. One survey from a participant who was currently enrolled as a Yanbal consultant was eliminated from the sample, as the purpose of the client surveys was to learn from clients who were not currently selling Yanbal.

11. For an introduction to "one-third world" and "two-thirds world," terms devised by Esteva and Prakash (1998) and intended to replace the more commonly used "First World" and "Third World," see Mohanty (2003).

12. It seems that this shopping center is here to stay, as on a recent visit the entrance was adorned with an official-looking sign declaring it "Centro Comercial El Provisional," the Temporary [Terminal] Shopping Center.

13. See O'Dougherty (2002) for a fascinating account of consumption and crisis in

Brazil and its effects on middle-class lifestyles. As in Ecuador, Brazilians did not stop consuming in the midst of economic crisis, but they had to cut back and also devise new strategies to obtain the goods and services that supported their lifestyle.

14. Different products are manufactured in the different countries in which Yanbal International does business and shipped to the other countries; however, some fragrances are produced in Yanbal's plants in Ecuador.

Preoccupation has been expressed regarding the extent to which their [women's] labour is infinitely elastic, or whether a breaking point may be reached when women's capacity to reproduce and maintain human resources may collapse.
CAROLINE O. N. MOSER, "ADJUSTMENT FROM BELOW," CITING
RICHARD JOLLY, "WOMEN'S NEEDS AND ADJUSTMENT POLICIES
IN DEVELOPING COUNTRIES"

Direct selling of cosmetics and similar products is a unique type of work that tends to recruit an all-female sales force; mobilizes ideals about race, class, and beauty to sell products; and presents few barriers to entry for most women. In some ways, direct sales exemplifies the kinds of employment that are on the rise in both rich and poor countries: these new jobs tap into female labor, tend to be temporary and/or to offer flexible schedules, straddle the lines between formal and informal employment, and offer little in the way of benefits and guaranteed earnings. The stories of Ecuadorian direct sellers included in this book show that this type of work does not alleviate the pressures on women due to their multiple roles as income earners and unpaid domestic workers.

Direct sales is thus a household survival strategy that sometimes creates or exacerbates conflict and tension in the family over women's competing responsibilities. Over the course of this research, advisers, colleagues, and others who heard about my research often encouraged me to be critical of the corporation whose sales force I was studying, to seek out and reveal exploitation of these women by the capitalist enterprise. It is true that direct selling organizations are more profitable than traditional firms because of the DSOs' highly productive yet cost-effective sales force of pseudo employees, who buy from the company at a discount and sell at full price and who do not receive any benefits such as social security or health care through their work.

Yet I have decided not to write an exposé on Yanbal, for several reasons. First, while the individual success stories used to recruit new distributors are the exception rather than the rule, direct selling does represent a real alternative to other types of informal selling or paid domestic work (in the absence of formal employment options for most women). It is work that anyone can learn to do, regardless of socioeconomic origins or status, although starting out is certainly easier for those with greater access to capital. Second—and this is especially important for those from humble backgrounds—affiliation with a highly respected corporation like the DSO studied here can confer a sense and image of professionalism that is valued by the women in the sales force and often respected by others.

I am generally skeptical of corporate capitalism's incorporation of women in developing countries into paid labor, and of the promotion of microenterprise (in which direct selling is sometimes included) as the answer to women's economic needs and the best path to economic development. I do not think that women's direct selling is a viable economic development strategy for Ecuador in the long run, and I agree with other scholars who see women's survival strategies as necessitated by structural conditions that keep them in poverty or near poverty. We must not romanticize women's ability to "organize themselves" and manage their multiple burdens, or believe that they can bear the weight of economic development or crisis (including the effects of structural adjustment and other policies) indefinitely.

Despite these reservations, I cannot condemn a company in which so many women whom I have come to know and respect truly believe. It may be tempting for casual observers to dismiss their loyalty as "false consciousness," a basic misunderstanding of their place in the capitalist pecking order. Yet women turn to direct sales precisely because they see the limited options for earning money in today's Ecuador; they have assessed the field of possibilities and have chosen to try direct selling, often in combination with other moneymaking strategies. The sense of community created among diverse women within this social world, the self-respect that many have found by contributing economically to their families, and the creation of an accessible means of work when work is disappearing in many third-world urban locales is not so easily brushed aside. People who have put their trust in me have told me their stories, both the good and the bad. I have attempted to communicate their experiences faithfully, which means writing neither a glowing endorsement nor a scathing rant.

The gendered character of direct selling work in Ecuador and elsewhere

deserves attention. Despite traditional ideals of femininity that would con-
fine women to the home, the economic exigencies of everyday life have required women's increasing involvement in paid labor. As employment opportunities for men, especially in the formal sector, are declining,[1] the
growth of global capitalism is expanding job options for women, who
are increasingly entering paid employment. In Guayaquil, some of these
jobs are temporary, low-paid, unpleasant, or in some other way undesirable, such as work at shrimp processing plants. Most income-earning activities exist in the informal sector, where employment is unstable and precarious. Regardless of the type of work women are doing outside the home,
their increased capacity to earn an income, across education levels and social class, has the potential to affect traditional gender roles in the home
(Benería and Roldán 1987; Safa 1995).

I have discussed the importance of domestic partners' stances toward
their wives' direct selling in determining the way the women experience
and carry out their work. Also interesting to scholars of gender and work is
the phenomenon of men becoming attracted to "feminine" work—like direct sales. People's reactions to direct sales as an income-generating activity
both shape and are shaped by their *gendered economic strategies*, behaviors
that represent a reconciling of cultural norms of gender and work with material conditions and financial needs. Individuals, couples, and families are
not completely free to accept or reject traditional gender norms but must
balance their attention to these values with the financial situation in which
they find themselves. For this reason, we find men engaging in the "feminine" occupation of direct selling of cosmetics, couples working as a direct
sales team, and men willing to risk their household's economic survival to
preserve their male privilege by prohibiting their wives from participating
in direct sales.

These new types of flexible, gendered work, with links to both the formal and informal economy, may alter gender relations in the home (and ultimately on the macro level), yet not in predictable ways. For this reason, it
is difficult to answer the commonly asked question of whether direct selling
is empowering for women. Whether or not women experience their work
in the "feminine" world of direct sales as empowering depends on a variety
of factors, including domestic gender relations (which may shift over time),
the financial effects of their selling, and other work experiences. The social
life of this gendered organization is marked by what I call *moments of empowerment*: brief periods of time in which the repression and subordination
associated with women's status are temporarily relaxed, allowing for critiques of gender relations and men's behavior or challenges to restrictions

on women. These critiques and challenges are often couched in humor and do not represent a real, sustained opposition to gender inequality.

The experiences of the women in this study call into question the common assumption that more flexible forms of employment will automatically resolve the difficulties in balancing multiple roles (earner, caregiver, community member) and the paid and unpaid work that these roles require. Although direct sellers largely set their own hours, they feel the demands on their time, energy, and attention acutely. This is especially so for those who pursue the career path and try to ascend the ranks of the sales force. The ways that women deal with these work-family conflicts depend on the resources available to them: middle-class women can afford to pay domestic workers to assist with reproductive tasks, and poorer women often rely on reciprocal relationships embedded in neighborhood and family networks. Despite the strategies used to try to balance work and family responsibilities, women feel the pressure both to be good mothers and to contribute to the family economically, which is only symbolically alleviated by their redefinition of ideal motherhood to include paid work. At the micro level, job flexibility does not erase the potential for conflicts with spouses or *reclamos* (complaints) from children who feel neglected.

One puzzle that this study addresses is how consumer capitalism (and Yanbal's profits) can be expanding in a developing country like Ecuador, where economic indicators, including wages, are remaining stagnant or declining. Part of the answer has to do with economic globalization, in which more trading partners and more goods are available to each other. China is an especially important player in this new drama, particularly in Latin America. Another piece of the puzzle can be seen in the "price game" played by direct sellers. The specialized forms of consumption (including what I call *flexible consumption*) and price setting described here allow customers to pay for their purchases over time, in installments. While this is not necessarily a new phenomenon, it is a place where the junctures between social and economic relations become visible. Sellers create payment plans for their buyers, depending on the buyers' relative socioeconomic status and the social or familial networks in which they are embedded. In this way, macro-level consumption trends and the profits made by large DSOs are ultimately dependent on relationships between individuals on the ground. Consumption and profits are based especially on sellers' combined use of family relations and friendships. In their selling interactions, sellers are influenced by cultural norms, along with shrewd assessments of the material conditions in which they and their clients are situated.

This study is the first to explore in depth the intersection of work and the body in direct selling. Even in gender or feminist scholarship, there is limited overlap between research on the body and research on working women (except in the extreme case of sex workers; Wolkowitz 2006). The qualitative analysis of a DSO's central texts allows us to see how images of embodied social class and race are conveyed through language, image, and organizational discourse.

Examining the experiences of sellers and sales directors through ethnographic study reveals that the power of the ideal image of professionalized womanhood is reaffirmed, even when it is not put into practice. The femininity invoked on the pages of the sales catalogs may harken back to an earlier or more distant ideal of idle, elite women lounging and relaxing, but the focus among sellers and sales directors is on creating a physical appearance that signals activity, ambition, and professionalism. The idealized image of the Yanbalista represents a marriage of the existing social pressures for women to look good, privileging middle-class norms of appearance, with an acceptance of the material conditions that require women to work. From the stories of many direct sellers it appears that makeovers (radical shifts in a seller's image and self-presentation) are more common than concrete upward mobility in terms of income and class status. However, in an urban society where appearance matters and affects how women are treated, a new (middle-class) look may be a valuable asset in everyday social interactions. If we accept feminist scholars' claims that exterior modes of self-presentation can affect our internal attitudes and self-concept (Butler 1993; Freeman 2000; Mahmood 2005) as well as our treatment in society, then we must acknowledge the significance of women's successful embodiment of professionalism.

Through a close look at gender relations, the importance of image, and the context in which women make decisions about selling, I have shown that not only cultural norms of gender (or work or consumption) but also the material conditions of people's everyday lives shape the social world of direct selling. The idealized images in direct selling catalogs, for example, align with a culture that values elites and upper classes over the masses. Yet the individualized payment plans created by sellers for their clients represent a means of affording socially valued products to people who often are in dire economic straits. Cultural norms and material conditions are always present as women and men devise gendered economic strategies that shape their work, relations with partners, and economic activities. Explanations that ascribe too much power to local culture downplay the agency of individuals to accept, reject, or alter these norms. Likewise, strictly materialist analyses overlook the social intricacies of everyday life that sometimes prevent individuals from pursuing certain "rational" income-earning or consumption strategies.

This second type of thinking (a materialist analysis that eschews culture) can give rise to a criticism of Ecuadorians' spending habits that I frequently hear: why are people who are struggling to afford food spending money on expensive deodorants, makeup, and perfume? This attitude represents not only a basic misunderstanding of the importance of physical appearance in a society highly stratified by class and racialized appearance but also an elitist stance that is based on the perception that poor people do not know how to handle money. Criticizing low-income people's consumption patterns cuts off a critique of the economic conditions and social inequality in which they are immersed, and allows for the advancement of a "culture of poverty" argument. Judging women for attempting to embody socially acceptable versions of femininity likewise diverts us from a critical analysis of gender inequality. Instead, people's interactions and decisions must be viewed in the context of a predominant (though by no means unquestioned) set of beliefs and a prevailing, if ever-shifting, set of macro- and microeconomic conditions. The experiences of the direct sellers portrayed here help us see the links between global economic trends and people's everyday (gendered) economic strategies.

In terms of how Ecuadorian women's (and men's) work and family lives could be improved based on the findings of this study, I will highlight a few of the obstacles to economic survival that the participants in this study faced, regardless of their social class position. First, women, and especially older women, experience discrimination in the labor market based on age and appearance, including race. In addition, blatant sex-based discrimination is obvious to anyone who picks up an Ecuadorian newspaper and glances at the classified advertisements. Occupational segregation by sex confines women to the lower-paid positions in the formal sector. Although equal-employment laws are on the books, they are not enforced. Even in countries like the United States, where the governmental and private-sector infrastructure for equal access to employment is in place, such discrimination occurs; since it can be chalked up to subjective preferences on the part of employers, it is difficult to eradicate.

Second, the dearth of formal part-time work is one of the main reasons that direct selling and other informal jobs are so attractive to women who are wives and mothers. The current government champions full-time jobs for all workers, thereby promoting an antiquated (though desirable) model of male industrial labor that (1) does not apply to the new types of jobs that are emerging in contemporary Ecuador and around the world and (2) does not recognize the multiple roles of women workers. For the foreseeable future, Ecuadorian women will bear the burden of caring for the home and family in addition to the need to contribute money to the household. By publicly belittling the economic importance of the Yanbalistas' work, President Correa and his government could be seen as demonstrating a lack of concern for the situation of the great majority of women in Guayaquil and elsewhere. These women are attempting to make up the difference between their income and their expenses, and in many cases they are supporting a household on their own. They turn to informal work, with its lack of benefits and protections, because the formal workplace cannot accommodate their disproportionate share of domestic responsibilities.

There are signs that some Yanbal directors are interested in formalizing their work arrangement with the DSO, and there have been discussions with corporate officials of the company's providing retirement benefits (based on income from sales) and allowing directors to pass their group on to a family member at the end of their career. Such a plan would combine some of the benefits associated with formal salaried employment with the advantages of self-employment. In this way, the company's responsiveness to directors' requests may end up pushing direct selling closer to formal work, at least for the women who have successfully made it to the top of the sales force. In the absence of alternatives, high-earning direct sellers may work to change and formalize their relationship with the DSO. It will be interesting to see how such negotiations develop.

This study highlighted a third area of conflict, difficulty, and possibility: gender politics in the home. Each individual, couple, or family negotiates work-family dilemmas in different ways, based on gendered economic strategies that can shift over time. In many homes, men's opposition to women working exacerbates gender inequality and threatens the family's financial survival. Because of the power of traditional family ideals and the often real threat of domestic violence, Yanbal and most sales directors have opted to stay out of the relational aspect of their sellers' work—that is, women's relationships with their husbands or partners. Whereas Biggart (1989) showed how U.S. direct sales organizations tried to co-opt husbands or build husband-wife sales teams, Yanbal's strategy is best described as one of avoidance. Some sellers and directors expressed their wish that Yanbal would train them on how to negotiate with husbands or would create a sort of orientation program for the men in their lives. Their reasoning was that the men's opposition is born of ignorance about the nature of direct selling work and its potential for profitability. Based on my experience, this type of intervention would be difficult to implement, given men's quickness to assert that they know nothing about Yanbal and their apparent lack of curiosity about work that is so overtly "feminine."

This study examined a rapidly expanding type of work, a formal-informal hybrid that appeals mainly to women and helps promote the expansion of consumer capitalism around the world. This work must be viewed in the context of employment alternatives, gender relations, and organizational discourse. The themes discussed here emerged from the in-depth investigation of one "site," one group of workers. Yet ethnographers must think of other ways to research economic globalization on the ground, perhaps by identifying macro-level trends and then finding sites in which to study them. More empirical, micro-level, qualitative research is needed on the concrete ways in which economic globalization is affecting employment options, gender relations, and cultural ideals. In addition, the substantial literature on work and family conflicts has focused for too long on workers and families in the developed world (the United States and Europe), ignoring the contributions of development scholars and others who study women in poor countries. It is time to turn our attention to these issues in new locations, which are increasingly important as more women are incorporated into the workforce, often in conditions of inequality with male workers or a decline in working conditions for all workers.

NOTES

1. This pattern is now being seen in rich as well as poor countries. For example, the vast majority of workers laid off in the current economic downturn in the United States have been men.

HOW I CAME TO RESEARCH YANBAL

During my first visit to Ecuador in 1999, I stayed in Ecuador's largest city, Guayaquil, with one of my husband's aunts, who had two adult daughters living at home.[1] Recruited by another aunt, Tía Ligia, cousin Karla had begun selling products offered by a direct sales corporation called Yanbal: cosmetics, perfumes, jewelry, and other items. I was in the beginning stages of a research project on beauty and the body in Ecuador, so of course I was intrigued by the images in the glossy, four-color catalog. I was surprised by the relatively high prices of the products, especially in a country that was sliding into a full-scale economic crisis. I observed the equation of beauty with white skin, light eyes, and blonde hair, as evidenced by the models in the catalog. The racialization of beauty ideals and their relationship to young women's body image became the major theme of my master's thesis and subsequent writings (Casanova 2003, 2004). As I was satisfied with my own limited makeup repertoire (two eye shadows, one clear mascara, two lipsticks, and a stick of concealer) but still wanted to support Karla, I opted for a package of six candles in aromatherapy scents, with evocative names like "Balance" and "Sensuality."

Two years later, I was finishing up my thesis research during a trip to Ecuador with my husband, Henry, and Tía Ligia offered to drive us to visit another aunt in the sleepy, scenic highland city of Riobamba. Sitting in the shadow of the inactive volcano Chimborazo, Ecuador's highest point, Riobamba is known for its colonial architecture and is a center of indigenous population and culture. Ligia is a short, curvy woman with light brown hair, light skin, and green eyes. She has a commanding presence and a voice that can become sharp if necessary. Her silver sport-utility vehicle was an incentive she had earned as a sales director for Yanbal, and it bore the company's name and logo in peach-colored letters on each front door. Excited to go sightseeing, my husband and I instead spent an agonizingly boring afternoon trailing along after the two aunts as they went door-to-door in the tiny commercial district of Guano (the next town over), talking to current Yanbal distributors while attempting to sell products and recruit new distributors. Guano is so small that an hour or two was plenty of time to explore its lovely handicraft offerings, yet we stayed for several hours. For Tía Ligia, this family visit was also a business trip; direct sales distributors commonly combine "private" and "public" activities in this way, muddying the supposed dividing line between the economic and the social. Not being terribly interested in direct sales at the time, Henry and I roamed the streets of Guano, which made Riobamba look like a booming metropolis. The exciting highlight of the brief trip was when poor Henry locked Ligia's keys in her company car, which was parked in the small central square.

Tía Ligia got on the phone right away with the young woman who managed her office, and by the next morning the spare keys had arrived via bus from Guayaquil. I observed that Ligia was a woman who got things done, who was comfortable exerting power over people and situations. Since beginning to distribute Yanbal products in the late 1980s, Ligia had experienced tremendous success, allowing her family to graduate from humble living conditions to a comfortable existence in one of the most exclusive gated communities of Guayaquil. Whereas many Ecuadorian women I had known kept their feelings and opinions private, relying in social interactions upon the intricacies of Andean etiquette, Ligia was direct and matter-of-fact, but without being the least bit rude or brusque. She exuded an energy and practicality that I found impressive. According to her, all the women who work with her (in her direct selling network, or "downline") are "positive and enthusiastic." In a conversation we had in November 2006, she told me that selling gives women confidence and self-esteem; women just need someone to tell them that they can do it and to show them how. This was her job as a Yanbal sales director.

Another of my husband's aunts, who grew up in the countryside before moving to Guayaquil and getting married, was recruited by and worked with Ligia as a Yanbal "beauty consultant" (*consultora de belleza*). In 2006, Tía Ligia told us that Tía Fátima was doing well, earning about $300 per month (roughly twice the minimum wage at that time), and that her attitude was becoming more positive. Tía Fátima had been able to buy new flooring for her home; she proudly showed us the rust-colored, diamond-patterned tiles that had been bought and installed "with my work." She sent her North American relatives home with Yanbal products as gifts for each family member. Even in a casual lunch, Tía Ligia mentored and encouraged Tía Fátima, telling her she had to "pull" people in (recruit new sellers) because that was going to help her advance. Listening to Ligia and working hard to sell products and enroll new consultants seemed to pay off. In February 2008, Tía Fátima also became a sales director and began to manage her own group of distributors, while still being mentored by Ligia. Although the two women are not directly related, Ligia is an expert at the strategy of recruiting family members into the beauty business: three of her sisters and two sisters-in-law are or have been Yanbal directors.

Direct selling is not strictly limited to Ecuador's urban centers, which was a misconception I held until visiting some of my in-laws in a rural part of the coastal Manabí province in 2006. In the front room of Henry's aunt's home, just three items were hung as decoration: a color photo of the entire family, taken some ten years earlier; her husband's high school diploma; and a large Yanbal wall calendar. The color calendar included photos of beauty queens from pageants sponsored by the company (including the annual Miss Ecuador contest) and Yanbal's charitable work with the Special Olympics. In an interior room of the house, I noticed stacks of cardboard boxes labeled "Avon." Tía Esterlina (Fátima's sister) had recently become an Avon distributor. A few people dropped by to place orders and pick up items while we were visiting. I later asked Esterlina about her selling. She said she had been recruited by her sister-in-law, who had sold Avon for years with some success, earning cash and winning prizes, including a refrigerator. But Esterlina had defected from her sister-in-law's downline because, she said, the woman did not share or pass on the prizes and incentives as Esterlina felt she was supposed to do. Her new sponsor was apparently more generous. By the time of my fieldwork in Ecuador in 2007 and 2008, Tía Esterlina had been recruited by Tía Fátima into Tía Ligia's group and was selling Yanbal products in addition to Avon's.

As I began searching for a dissertation topic, I wanted to find a concrete way to study the ways in which beauty, femininity, and capitalism play out at the level of everyday life. Soon I realized that the perfect topic had been right in front of my eyes during my time in Ecuador: it was in the Yanbal catalogs, the logo-bearing SUV, the candles I slightly resented buying. Direct selling is an everyday practice that is influenced by local and global ideas about beauty, femininity, race, class, and consumption. In late 2006, I asked Ligia if it would be possible to study her Yanbal group, explaining that I wanted to get to know the women involved in the business. "How many women do you need?" she asked bluntly. Surprised by the directness of the question and the need for no further explanation, I stammered something like "The more, the better." "Well, I have one hundred," Ligia stated confidently, and the project was afoot.

A sophisticated, upwardly mobile urban dweller, a migrant to the city from the coastal countryside, a rural housewife—all engaged in direct sales targeting women as customers and potential sellers. How can the attractive power of this economic activity be explained? What is direct selling, and how does it operate (and succeed) in this setting? How are the sale and consumption of these products preferable to other alternatives? How is this economic activity combined with other remunerated and/or unpaid work? These were all questions I aimed to answer in my study by examining Yanbal distributors, corporate leaders, and customers in Ecuador at the dawn of the twenty-first century.

PRIMARY RESEARCH METHODS

While it is accurate to describe this study as an ethnography, due to its reliance on data collected in the field through participant observation and formal as well as informal interviewing, I have also incorporated other qualitative methodologies in order to answer important questions about the lives and social worlds of the participants. These include content analysis and a survey. I will discuss each component of the study's methodology here, although further information on methods is presented in the relevant chapters.

Participant observation, or spending time with the study's subjects in their environment, is the backbone of any ethnographic project. During my time in the field (September 2007–January 2008 and May–June 2008), spent almost entirely in Guayaquil, Ecuador, I engaged in participant observation in sales directors' offices, in Yanbal's corporate office in Guayaquil, at the annual convention for high-performing sales directors, and in seller's homes, among other places.

In some cases interviews were my first real contact with sellers, sales directors, or company officials, and in other cases interviews came after I had gotten to know someone more informally. Some people with whom I spent time, and whom I came to know quite well, were never formally interviewed. Interviews were often a rich source of information about women's lives and their work. Yet the act of interviewing, especially in someone's home, often became more valuable than the words that were recorded. People who were reserved or shy while the recorder was running were often incredibly chatty outside of the interview situation, and many of the people whose one-word answers I found frustrating became the most helpful in terms of introducing me to other sellers or allowing me to see how they went about their days. This was a lesson to me as a qualitative researcher: interviews were useful in advancing my research, but not always in the ways that I expected. I had to open my eyes to the social environment in which I was immersed, rather than thinking ahead to the transcribed text of the interview and viewing it as the primary, or most authoritative, source of data for analysis.

In other cases, I had to move beyond my original core group of possible interviewees or informants in order to obtain more detailed information about a specific topic. This is how I came to interview Oscar García, the manager of the city's largest staffing firm, about the employment options for Guayaquilean women and men. His perspective proved invaluable to my understanding of the employment context and the formal and informal labor markets. This type of working outward from the original sample, or working inward from unconnected points, also resulted in my meeting with demographer Roberto Sáenz, who provided the statistical data on employment patterns in different Guayaquil neighborhoods that further informed my writing on the topic of employment options for women.

Through a series of chance introductions and e-mail exchanges, I made some productive visits to the Universidad Espíritu Santo (better known as UEES, pronounced "oo-ess") and spent the better part of a December morning chatting with economist Jorge Calderón Salazar. Not only was Jorge interested in questions of employment and unemployment in Guayaquil, but his mother was, coincidentally, a Yanbal director. I explained to Jorge that what I really needed were economic and employment data on the specific neighborhoods in which the women in my study lived. He suggested that I go see sociologist Roberto Sáenz, who works at the Guayaquil office of the National Institute of Statistics and the Census (INEC).

On a sunny Wednesday morning the week before Christmas, I took a taxi down to the INEC office, which is near the sprawling campus of the University of Guayaquil. Roberto's office was kept ice-cold by a blasting window air conditioner, and his desk and bookshelves were crammed with thick reports and bound data on everything from consumer prices to census questionnaires. Starved for concrete information about the city I had been studying for nearly a decade, I had to contain my desire to snatch up and read book after book. Roberto is a pleasant man with a gray beard and glasses, and he was dressed casually in a short-sleeved, button-down shirt. Passionate about his demographic work on Ecuador and Guayaquil, he was willing to share whatever data I needed. I was in luck—INEC's Guayaquil branch had just finished a report based on surveys completed in December 2006. The surveys covered a range of topics and compared an aggregate of "consolidated areas" with "unconsolidated areas," with data for the poor and marginal neighborhoods of the city broken out by neighborhood. Given that the most recent Ecuadorian census was completed in 2000, the data from this new survey, called the ESIS (*Encuesta del Sistema de Información Social*), were much more recent and detailed than the information available through the INEC website or other sources.

It is sad that this information can be obtained only directly through Roberto; he and his colleagues gave a copy to the municipal government of Guayaquil, and that was the extent of the report's distribution. Since there is always tension and sometimes outright conflict between the leadership of INEC in Quito and the branch in Guayaquil (responsible for the entire coastal region), Roberto said the institute's headquarters didn't want to publish the information or put it on the website. If it were not for a series of coincidences, I would never have discovered this treasure trove of statistical information, which provides a valuable quantitative socioeconomic and demographic context for the ethnographic data I have collected. This fact speaks volumes about the regionalism in political and intellectual circles in Ecuador and about the lack of detailed information on Guayaquil and its inhabitants.

TRACING SOCIAL NETWORKS IN SEARCH OF STUDY PARTICIPANTS

My access to the participants in this study and to the social world of Yanbal in Ecuador initially came from three main sources, although later on, the sources of access multiplied as I came to know more women working in direct sales. These three sources were Ligia García de Proaño, a sales director and my husband's aunt; people in Yanbal's corporate headquarters in Quito, principally the company's general manager, Robert Watson (whom I contacted on my own, without an introduction from Ligia); and Fátima Casanova, my husband's paternal aunt, who was a consultant and became a director during the course of the research. These points of access, and my expanding network of informants and participants, allowed me to see, hear, and experience things that are not usually witnessed by those outside the direct sales industry.

As Ligia's daughter directors often participate in her meetings and events, bringing along their consultants, I immediately had access to sellers from every corner of the city and from several different groups.[2] In the early days of my research, I often introduced myself at meetings, explained my project, and asked for volunteers for interviews, who wrote their names and phone numbers on a legal pad that I passed around. This straightforward approach, and following up with the people I met in this way, resulted in interviews with thirty-four consultants and directors in Guayaquil, belonging to at least six different Yanbal groups. I also came to know and spend time with several others who were never formally interviewed.[3]

Through Ligia and the meetings she organized at her office in northern Guayaquil, I met a great number of consultants and directors. This was how I first got to know a boisterous and friendly group of sellers from El Guasmo Sur in southern Guayaquil, from whom I learned a great deal about the multiple strategies for earning an income and the harsh realities of life in this most infamous of poor neighborhoods, realities that the women both accept and resist with tremendous humor and strength. They were all members of director Maryuri Palma Pico's group, though I had not met Maryuri yet. After the meeting, I called up one of the women, María Bustamante, a bubbly and energetic grandmother, to ask if I could interview her. She was quite excited and agreed to meet me at a local shopping center and take me to her house. When I called the next person on my list—a young mother of four, Érika Mártinez García, who had been sitting with María and other consultants from the group when I met them—I told her that I would be visiting María. 'Oh, we all live right next to each other,' she said. 'Just come see me when you finish with María.' I didn't call the rest of the group, deciding instead to play it by ear and see if they really did all live in the same area and if I could just drop in on them.

Érika was right. Six sellers lived within two or three blocks of each other in the neighborhood near the city's naval base. All were recruited either by one young woman, Mary Vera Marín, whom everyone calls Belén, or by one of her daughter consultants, Tania Zambrano Burgos. Most of the women were relatively new to Yanbal, having enrolled within the last eight months (some as recently as one month prior to the meeting where we had first spoken). Throughout my research, María was a source of information about her neighborhood and its residents and about the dynamics of the Yanbal group. This pint-size dynamo is also probably the funniest Yanbalista I know, always ready to crack a joke or make a sassy remark. She is quick to tears as well as laughter, beginning to cry when she talks about her love for her work with Yanbal and her sometimes difficult relationship with her husband.

I had spent time with all of these women before sitting down to talk to their director, Maryuri, which gave me a unique bottom-up perspective on the group and the area in which its members worked. Maryuri was surprised that I had been down to El Guasmo and gone to the ladies' houses. Maryuri Palma is probably the director who most styles herself after Ligia in terms of her work ethic and her approach to the business. She is motivated and no-nonsense when dealing with her consultants, and an enthusiastic teacher in a meeting setting. She claims to want to be Yanbal's best director and works hard to achieve this goal. At a party, Maryuri, a mother of four who could pass for a nineteen-year-old, is always one of the first to start dancing, and she is known for inventing moves and routines that other women imitate on the dance floor.

Betty Brigss Mantilla, an especially chatty director with television-star good looks, struck up a conversation with me about the state of men's and women's employment opportunities in Ecuador one day, as I copied one of Ligia's presentations onto her flash drive after a meeting. I asked if I could go to her office and see how she worked, and did so the following week. This was the beginning of my involvement with her group, which led to more days spent at her home office in northern Guayaquil, connections and interviews with several consultants, and an invitation to the crowded but animated group holiday party. Having a degree in business and experience working in a government office, Betty brought an analytical perspective to her work with Yanbal, keeping detailed statistics on her group's performance that were used to distribute about a dozen prizes and awards at the end of each calendar year. Through Betty, I came to know two of her group's top performers, law student Vanessa Paredes Márquez and Narcisa Pazmiño Beltrán, who, in addition to selling Yanbal products, ran a store out of her home along with her husband. I became close with these two women, visiting their homes and accompanying them as they worked. Both introduced me to their daughter consultants, who provided additional perspectives on the group and the work with Yanbal.

Another director whose group and daughter directors I came to know was Cecilia García Torres, Ligia's sister in real life and daughter in the DSO. Cecilia is younger than Ligia and has been in Yanbal for many years. She has dark hair and bright blue eyes and a jovial disposition. Before I got to know Cecilia, I spoke at length with her daughter director, Ana María Briones, a former corporate accountant and a mother of three young daughters; she talked frankly about the difficulties of working as a Yanbal director. I spent more time with Cecilia during my follow-up trip in May and June 2008, when we hung out together at the national convention, and I spent time at her home office as she worked alongside her newest daughter director.

From these core informants, the study blossomed as I met the "daughters," friends, family, and colleagues of women I already knew. Although I began with the women who were the most connected to the relatively formal structure of the Yanbal group and family—those who attended meetings or came into the directors' offices—this snowball sample allowed me to meet women who had only recently joined, who were considering joining, or consultants who rarely or never interacted with sales directors or the Yanbal corporation. I was also able to meet women who were not enrolled as official consultants but who "helped" consultants sell; this allowed me to see the multiple levels of informality in this direct sales business and the diversity of approaches to selling Yanbal products.

In an effort to acknowledge that hours spent chatting with me were hours not spent selling or collecting money, I made a onetime payment to each interviewee in the amount of $20 (one-tenth of the monthly minimum wage in Ecuador at that time). Although this was a modest amount, the gesture was intended to recognize the disparity between my economic situation and those of the women participating in the project.

The payment was not mentioned prior to the interview, in an effort to counteract possible objections and avoid coercion. In keeping with customs that view the frank discussion of money between acquaintances as distasteful, I passed the interviewees the money in a plain white envelope at the end of the interview. I am certain that some of the most enthusiastic recruiters of interviewees had the financial reward in mind as they pitched the opportunity to others. A handful of women, mostly sales directors, did not accept the money, and a few even seemed slightly hurt by the offer of such a monetary gift (one woman said it would "make her heart hurt" to accept money from me). When I returned for follow-up trips in the summer of 2008 and in December 2009, I took small gifts for my informants. These gifts were a good pretext for getting together with women I had not seen in a while and recognizing their contributions to my work. Interviewees who were interviewed more than once were not paid for follow-up interviews. While most sellers and sales directors received these gifts and money, they were not offered to corporate officials or interviewees outside the DSO.

COMPLEMENTARY RESEARCH METHODS

Even before I made an initial trip in late 2006 to discuss my idea for this project with Ligia García, I knew that I wanted to analyze Yanbal's sales catalogs. I returned to the United States from that trip with permission to begin the research with Ligia's group and with a catalog in hand to begin the work on this part of the study, which took place both in and outside the field. I have always been interested in popular culture and the ways that people and lifestyles are represented, especially in advertising. Having written an article on the representations of feminine beauty in women's magazines in Ecuador, I had some preconceived ideas about what I might find in the catalogs, which resemble fashion magazines, just in a smaller format and with less text. Rather than starting from scratch, I used this previous research to anticipate some of the visual and textual themes that I might encounter in the sales catalogs. I knew, for example, to be on the lookout for references to ideas about class, race, and beauty.

Rather than simply creating categories and tallying up items that fit these categories, I approached content analysis in a more organic way, analyzing the text and images in a sociologically informed variant of literary analysis. I have used a similar method in previous work (Casanova 2003); and it has been successfully employed by other social scientists (Lutz and Collins 1993; Peiss 1998; Pequeño Bueno 2007). Being alert to both the social context for and the subtle nuances of certain images and words/phrases allows researchers to move beyond classifying cultural representations as "good" or "bad" and to instead link them to popular conceptions of gender, race, and class without engaging in value judgments.

As I returned home to the United States after my longest period of fieldwork and began to reflect critically on direct sellers' accounts of their work, I realized that I needed to know more about the customers. I could take sellers at their word, but I preferred finding a way to check the validity of their claims. Every act of buying is also an act of selling, a social fact that studies of consumption often overlook. I was mostly concerned with sellers; however, I needed to take buyers into account. Due to limitations of time and energy and my desire to pursue in-depth ethnographic research with direct sellers, I devised a survey as a way to gauge clients' experiences of direct selling.

As discussed in chapter 7, the bulk of the survey respondents came from two sources:

staff, students, and families at the COPOL English Institute (whose turtle mascot still baffles me); and staff at the Universidad Espíritu Santo, a private university in Guayaquil. In total, forty-three people shared their experiences as direct sales customers.[4] Survey data were used to produce descriptive statistics on the frequency of purchases, payment arrangements between buyers and sellers, buyers' previous experience as direct sellers, and the products purchased. Answers to open-ended questions provided clues about the social networks within which direct selling (and consumption of Yanbal products) took place, and the preexisting relationships between buyers and sellers.

The survey allowed me to confirm that the accounts of direct selling that were emerging from my interviews and participant observation represented the exchange in a way that matched up with buyers' experiences. An unexpected bonus of the surveys was the way they helped me to connect the dots between buyers and sellers embedded in common social networks. For example, on one survey, in a response to the question about whom the client bought Yanbal products from, I was pleasantly surprised to see the name of a seller I knew. The respondent was not only this seller's client but also her cousin. This coincidence highlights the ways that direct sales relationships are simultaneously social, economic, and (sometimes) familial and how they cut across social classes and neighborhoods.

LIMITATIONS AND REFLEXIVE ANALYSIS

All empirical research is subject to certain limitations and methodological challenges. The recognition of those challenges specific to the researchers' ethnic, national, gender, and class location has become somewhat institutionalized in the fields of anthropology and sociological ethnography as reflexive analysis. In the introduction to the book, I address some of the obstacles to objectivity posed by my individual and sociodemographic characteristics and by my access to the direct sales world through a powerful and influential figure. My status as the mother of a young child, an expectant mother when I was pregnant with my second child, and then a mother of two children also proved important for creating rapport with subjects, something I discuss in greater detail in a paper co-written with another ethnographer and mother, Tamara Mose Brown (Mose Brown and Casanova 2009).

As a foreigner in a country where people and things that come from outside are met with a mixture of curiosity and enthusiasm, I was often asked questions about my country and culture. Several people told me that they would like me to teach them English, and some asked me specific questions about vocabulary or pronunciation, since English (or some version of it) is widely taught and studied in Ecuador. In many cases, however, my nativelike Spanish and familiarity with Ecuadorian and Guayaquilean expressions and slang led to a sort of linguistic "passing," in which people assumed I was from Ecuador or Guayaquil until someone told them differently.[5]

Some people were surprised to learn that my connections to the country and city were a result of my marriage to a man who grew up in Guayaquil, and upon further probing, they were shocked to hear that I did not have a Latino background. I told them that I had spent most of my life learning and improving my Spanish and that my family and social circles included many people with diverse Latin American origins. As I have found in my informal interaction and ethnographic research with Latinos in the United States, in Ecuador I was granted a sort of honorary or provisional status of belonging because of this linguistic and cultural fluency and highly personal ties. Being the wife of an Ecuadorian (accepted as niece and cousin by his large family in Ecuador), knowing the country and city relatively well based on many repeat visits since 1999, and having a half-Ecuadorian son who was, for four months, a student in a local school, gave me some measure of legitimacy that lessened—but could not erase—the impact of my outsider status. Of course, people learned facts about my personal life at different times, meaning that my ethnic and national positioning with individuals in the field changed over time. (The significance of my appearance and whiteness, in a highly race-conscious society and a beauty-oriented business, are discussed in chapter 4.)

One final role set me apart, which is connected to my foreign citizenship and my ability to move freely between North and South America. This was the role, familiar to so many emigrants and returning migrants, of transnational courier. Interestingly, I performed this role both as a member of my husband's extended, transnational family and as a member of the social world of Yanbal in Guayaquil. My self-claimed reputation for packing light and my willingness to help out and, in some small way, help repay people in Ecuador for their kindness, led to my shuttling back and forth a variety of items between New York City and Guayaquil. One director's secretary, who was also an enrolled consultant, asked me to take two bags of Yanbal products to her mother and sister in New York; although she said that these items were for her mother's personal use, it is possible that at least some of them were resold. There is a lively suitcase trade in Yanbal products among Ecuadorian migrants, since the company does not officially operate in the United States, and immigrant men and women want the products because of familiarity or nostalgia or some other reason.

For Tía Ligia, I took to Ecuador clothes to be sold, given away, or used as prizes for her Yanbal group. For my husband's parents (now living in Texas), I took down clothes, shoes, and vitamins for relatives in the countryside and in Guayaquil. On one trip, the Guayaquilean woman who cared for my son in her family day care in Queens asked me to deliver a letter and a small amount of money to her sister in Guayaquil. I am sure that this back-and-forth transfer of goods will continue into the future, highlighting my physical/geographical in-betweenness and my U.S. citizenship, which allows me to move freely across borders that are more difficult for others to cross.

A few other dimensions of this research are worth pointing out. First, the matter of how people became incorporated as participants in the research project is significant. I began with one direct selling group and branched out into other groups, but primarily within the same "family"; that is, the directors of these subsequent groups were either daughters, granddaughters, or great-granddaughters of my original informant, Ligia García. Therefore it is difficult to say with certainty how social interactions or perspectives on direct selling might differ in other direct sales genealogies or, indeed, in other cities. To some extent, I worked to reduce this bias, by interviewing sales directors in Quito and conducting participant observation in two other coastal provinces, Santa Elena and Manabí.

Another bias inherent in the study has to do with direct sellers' engagement with the direct sales organization (DSO). Since I tended to meet participants at group or company events, they were often sellers who were more engaged with other sellers and/or their sales director—that is, people who were more in touch with the formal structures of the DSO. They may have been more active in terms of selling than those who did not attend meetings or appear in directors' offices. Of course, I worked to go beyond this group, meeting women (and men) who rarely or never attended group functions or organized meetings. Approximately one-quarter of my interviewees attended such events rarely or never. These were sometimes newer sellers, and perhaps because of their lack of engagement with the DSO's support networks, they also tended to abandon direct selling or have low sales during the time of my fieldwork and afterward.

Finally, there were the logistical constraints of time and money. During the time of this research, I was a graduate student at the City University of New York, a public university in one of the most expensive cities in the world. Since funding for graduate students is far from abundant in this setting, I and all of my fellow students had to work to pay the bills. After entering the program in 2004, I worked at different times (and sometimes simultaneously) as an adjunct instructor of sociology at the college level, a tutor of high school Spanish, a researcher on an ethnographic team, an instructor of English grammar for at-risk high school students, and a grant writer at a nonprofit organization. My original plan had been to land a sizable research grant and go to Ecuador for a year or two to conduct my fieldwork. When those grants did not materialize, I decided to use my family's meager savings to fund as much fieldwork as possible, spread over two extended trips to Ecuador in 2007 and 2008 and a very brief one at the end of 2009.

The ideal situation is for an ethnographer to spend as much continuous time in the field as possible; I attempted to do this within my financial constraints and worked to maximize the productivity of my time in the field by treating fieldwork as a full-time job (with lots of unpaid overtime!). I view this work as an ongoing project; I try to keep in contact with subjects when I am in the United States, and I am always planning the next trip. Each time I communicate with the participants in this research by phone or e-mail or see them in person during follow-up trips, I learn more about the world of direct selling and how this work is integrated into and shapes women's everyday lives. Given my lack of institutional and other resources when I began the research, I decided to do what I could when I could rather than putting off the fieldwork until the conditions met idealized expectations. As with everything else in life, procrastination was a tempting option, but I was reminded of Lennon's musical admonition that "life is what happens to you while you're busy making other plans." I decided to go to the field and experience life in the direct selling world, and this book is an account of that journey and that world from many perspectives.

NOTES

1. The Spanish word "*tía*" means "aunt." It is often used alone to address one's aunt and is combined with a first name when talking about the aunt in the third person.

2. As other scholars have noted, network direct sales organizations, in which women recruit other women, tend to use familial terms to connect recruiters with new members (Biggart 1989; Lan 2002). If I recruit a woman, I become her "mother" consultant or director, and she is my "daughter." As women rise up the ranks of the sales force, they can give birth to many generations; someone like Ligia, who has been with Yanbal for nearly three decades, can have great-granddaughters and even great-great granddaughters who are sales directors.

3. I also interviewed three directors in Quito; three members of Yanbal's corporate leadership (two in Quito and one in Guayaquil); and one employment expert, for a total of forty-one interviews.

4. A forty-fourth survey was completed, but the respondent claimed to be a Yan-bal consultant at the time, and for this reason I did not incorporate that data in the analysis.

5. For an interesting discussion of "passing for a native speaker" in the context of identity and second-language acquisition, see Piller (2002).

REFERENCES

Acker, Joan. 1990. "Hierarchies, Jobs, Bodies: A Theory of Gendered Organizations." *Gender & Society* 4: 139–158.

Adair, Vivyan C. 2001. "Branded with Infamy: Inscriptions of Poverty and Class in the United States." *Signs: Journal of Women in Culture and Society* 27 (2): 451–471.

Agadjanian, Victor. 2002. "Men Doing 'Women's Work': Masculinity and Gender Relations among Street Vendors in Maputo, Mozambique." *Journal of Men's Studies* 10 (3): 329–342.

Appadurai, Arjun. 1996. *Modernity at Large: Cultural Dimensions of Globalization.* Minneapolis: University of Minnesota Press.

Ariel de Vidas, Anath. 2008. "Containing Modernity: The Social Life of Tupperware in a Mexican Indigenous Village." *Ethnography* 9 (2): 257–284.

Babb, Florence. 1998 [1989]. *Between Field and Cooking Pot: The Political Economy of Market Women in Peru.* Austin: University of Texas Press.

Bank Muñoz, Carolina. 2008. *Transnational Tortillas: Race, Gender, and Shop-Floor Politics in Mexico and the United States.* Ithaca, NY: ILR Press.

Barron, James. 2008. "Free Holiday Turkeys, a Ritual in Decline." *New York Times,* November 26, 2008. http://www.nytimes.com/2008/11/26/nyregion/26turkey.html.

Beckerman, Paul, and Andrés Solimano. 2002. *Crisis and Dollarization in Ecuador.* Washington, DC: World Bank.

Benería, Lourdes. 1992. "The Mexican Debt Crisis: Restructuring the Economy and the Household." Pp. 83-104 in *Unequal Burden: Economic Crises, Persistent Poverty, and Women's Work,* ed. L. Benería and S. Feldman. Boulder, CO: Westview Press.

———. 2003. *Gender, Development, and Globalization: Economics as if All People Mattered.* New York: Routledge.

———. 2008. "The Crisis of Care, International Migration, and Public Policy." *Feminist Economics* 14 (3): 1–21.

Benería, Lourdes, and Shelley Feldman, eds. 1992. *Unequal Burden: Economic Crises, Persistent Poverty, and Women's Work.* Boulder, CO: Westview Press.

Benería, Lourdes, and María S. Floro. 2006. "Informalización del mercado laboral, género y protección social: Reflexiones a partir de un estudio en hogares pobres urbanos en Bolivia y Ecuador." Pp. 141–175 in *La persistencia de la desigualdad: Género, trabajo y pobreza en América Latina,* ed. G. Herrera. Quito: FLACSO.

Benería, Lourdes, and Martha Roldán. 1987. *The Crossroads of Class and Gender: Industrial Homework, Subcontracting, and Household Dynamics in Mexico City.* Chicago: University of Chicago Press.

Bettie, Julie. 2002. *Women without Class: Girls, Race and Identity.* Berkeley: University of California Press.

Biggart, Nicole W. 1989. *Charismatic Capitalism: Direct Selling Organizations in America.* Chicago: University of Chicago Press.

Biggart, Nicole Woolsey, and Richard P. Castanias. 2001. "Collateralized Social Relations: The Social in Economic Calculation." *American Journal of Economics and Sociology* 60 (2): 471–500.

Binford, Leigh. 2005. "Migrant Remittances and (Under)Development in Mexico." *Critique of Anthropology* 23: 305–336.

Blum, Virginia L. 2005. *Flesh Wounds: The Culture of Cosmetic Surgery.* Berkeley: University of California Press.

BONIL. 2008. "¡Feliz Cumpleaños #1 . . . !" Cartoon. *El Universo* (Guayaquil, Ecuador), January 8, 2008.

Bordo, Susan. 2000. *The Male Body: A New Look at Men in Public and in Private.* New York: Farrar, Strauss and Giroux.

Bourdieu, Pierre. 2007 [1984]. *Distinction: A Social Critique of the Judgment of Taste.* Trans. R. Nice. Cambridge, MA: Harvard University Press.

Brodie, Stewart, and John Stanworth. 1998. "Independent Contractors in Direct Selling: Self-Employed but Missing from Official Records." *International Small Business Journal* 16: 95–101.

Brodie, Stewart, John Stanworth, and Thomas R. Wotruba. 2002. "Direct Sales Franchises in the UK: A Self-Employment Grey Area." *International Small Business Journal* 20: 53–76.

Burbano de Lara, Felipe. 2008. "Deinstitutionalized Democracy." Pp. 271–276 in *The Ecuador Reader: History, Culture, Politics*, ed. C. de la Torre and S. Striffler. Durham, NC: Duke University Press.

Butler, Judith. 1993. *Bodies That Matter: On the Discursive Limits of "Sex."* New York: Routledge.

Cahn, Peter S. 2006. "Building Down and Dreaming Up: Finding Faith in a Mexican Multilevel Marketer." *American Ethnologist* 33: 126–142.

———. 2007. "Ventas directas en Morelia, Michoacán." *Alteridades* 17 (33): 55–63.

———. 2009. "Using and Sharing: Direct Selling in the Borderlands" Pp. 317–352 in *Land of Necessity: Consumer Culture in the United States–Mexico Borderlands*, ed. A. McCrossen. Durham, NC: Duke University Press.

Candelario, Ginetta E. B. 2007. *Black behind the Ears: Dominican Racial Identity from Museums to Beauty Shops.* Durham, NC: Duke University Press.

Caplovitz, David. 1963. *The Poor Pay More: Consumer Practices of Low-Income Families.* New York: Free Press.

Casanova, Erynn Masi. 2003. "Women's Magazines in Ecuador: Re-reading 'la Chica Cosmo.'" *Studies in Latin American Popular Culture* 22: 89–102.

———. 2004. "No Ugly Women: Concepts of Race and Beauty among Adolescent Women in Ecuador." *Gender & Society* 18 (3): 287–308.

———. 2007. "Spanish Language and Latino Ethnicity in Children's Television Programs." *Latino Studies* 5 (4): 455–477.

Cerbino, Mauro, Cinthia Chiriboga, and Carlos Tutivén. 2000. *Culturas juveniles: Cuerpo, música, sociabilidad, y género.* Quito: Convenio Andrés Bello/Abya-Yala.

Chant, Sylvia. 1991. *Women and Survival in Mexican Cities: Perspectives on Gender, Labour Markets and Low Income Households.* Manchester, UK: Manchester University Press.

Chossudovsky, Michel. 2003. *The Globalization of Poverty and the New World Order.* Montreal: Global Research.

Cohen, Colleen Ballerino, Richard Wilk, and Beverly Stoeltje, eds. 1995. *Beauty Queens on the Global Stage: Gender, Contests, and Power*. New York: Routledge.

Cohen, Lizabeth. 2003. *A Consumers' Republic: The Politics of Mass Consumption in Postwar America*. New York: Vintage Books.

CONAMU. 2004. "Questionnaire to Governments on Implementation of the Beijing Platform for Action (1995) and the Outcome of the Twenty-Third Special Session of the General Assembly (2000)." CONAMU (Consejo Nacional de Mujeres), Quito, Ecuador.

Correa, Karen, and Pamela Velasco. 2007. "Las 500 mayores empresas del Ecuador." *Vistazo*, no. 961, September 6, 2007, pp. 53–128.

Crain, Mary M. 1996. "Negotiating Identities in Quito's Cultural Borderlands: Native Women's Performances for the Ecuadorean Tourist Market." Pp. 125–137 in *Cross-Cultural Consumption: Global Markets, Local Realities*, ed. D. Howes. London: Routledge.

Dávila, Arlene. 2001. *Latinos, Inc.: The Marketing and Making of a People*. Berkeley: University of California Press.

Dreby, Joanna. 2006. "Honor and Virtue: Mexican Parenting in the Transnational Context." *Gender & Society* 20: 32–59.

Duarte, Isis. 1989. "Household Workers in the Dominican Republic: A Question for the Feminist Movement." Pp. 197–220 in *Muchachas No More: Household Workers in Latin America and the Caribbean*, ed. E. M. Chaney and M. G. Castro. Philadelphia: Temple University Press.

Duneier, Mitchell. 1999. *Sidewalk*. New York: Farrar, Straus and Giroux.

Dwyer, Daisy, and Judith Bruce, ed. 1988. *A Home Divided: Women and Income in the Third World*. Stanford, CA: Stanford University Press.

Ecuavisa. 2007. "A partir de 2008 el salario mínimo vital será de 200 dólares, acordó el gobierno esta mañana." December 27, 2007. http://www.ecuavisa.com/Desktop.aspx?Id=958&e=1193.

El Comercio (Quito). 2003. "USD 217 millones se venden en cosméticos." December 11.

Elson, Diane. 1999. "Labor Markets as Gendered Institutions: Equality, Efficiency and Empowerment Issues." *World Development* 27 (3): 611–627.

El Universo. 2008a. "Canasta Básica se eleva a $503, revela el INEC." June 6, 2008. http://www.eluniverso.com/.

———. 2008b. "Régimen analiza cambios en el ICE al perfume local." February 3, 2008. http://www.eluniverso.com/.

———. 2008c. "Vendedoras de perfumes se quejan." January 26, 2008. http://www.eluniverso.com/.

———. 2009. "El desempleo en Guayaquil repuntó al 14% en marzo." April 15, 2009. http://www.eluniverso.com/.

England, Paula. 2005. "Emerging Theories of Care Work." *Annual Review of Sociology* 31: 381–399.

Escobar, María Teresa. 2006a. "El ejército de Yanbal." *América Economía*, August 2006.

———. 2006b. "El hombre de las mil mujeres." *América Economía*, September 2006, pp. 24–28.

Esteva, Gustavo, and Madhu Suri Prakash. 1998. *Grassroots Post-Modernism: Remaking the Soil of Cultures*. London: Zed Press.

Fapohunda, Eleanor R. 1988. "The Nonpooling Household: A Challenge to Theory." Pp. 143–154 in *A Home Divided: Women and Income in the Third World*, ed. D. Dwyer and J. Bruce. Stanford, CA: Stanford University Press.

Fernández-Kelly, María Patricia. 1983. *For We Are Sold, I and My People: Women and Industry in Mexico's Frontier*. Albany: State University of New York Press.

Floro, María, and John Messier. 2006. "Tendencias y patrones de crédito entre hogares urbanos pobres en Ecuador." Pp. 225–249 in *La persistencia de la desigualdad: Género, trabajo y pobreza en América Latina*, ed. G. Herrera. Quito: FLACSO.

Folbre, Nancy. 1994. *Who Pays for the Kids? Gender and the Structures of Constraint*. New York: Routledge.

Freeman, Carla. 1997. "Reinventing Higglering in Transnational Zones: Barbadian Women Juggle the Triple Shift." Pp. 68–95 in *Daughters of Caliban: Caribbean Women in the Twentieth Century*, ed. C. L. Springfield. Bloomington: Indiana University Press.

———. 2000. *High Tech and High Heels in the Global Economy: Women, Work, and Pink-Collar Identities in the Caribbean*. Durham, NC: Duke University Press.

Friedan, Betty. 1963. *The Feminine Mystique*. New York: Dell.

Friedemann-Sánchez, Greta. 2006. *Assembling Flowers and Cultivating Homes: Labor and Gender in Colombia*. Lanham, MD: Lexington Books.

Gestión. 2007. "Cifras." December 2007, p. 82.

Goetschel, Ana María. 1999. *Mujeres e imaginarios: Quito en los inicios de la modernidad*. Quito: Abya-Yala Ediciones.

Goldenberg, Mirian. 2007. "Introdução." Pp. 9–13 in *O corpo como capital: Estudos sobre gênero, sexualidade e moda na cultura brasileira*, ed. Mirian Goldenberg. São Paulo: Estação das Letras e Cores.

Hale, Charles R. 2006. *Más que un Indio = More Than an Indian: Racial Ambivalence and Neoliberal Multiculturalism in Guatemala*. Santa Fe, NM: School of American Research.

Halpern, Adam, and France Winddance Twine. 2000. "Antiracist Activism in Ecuador: Black-Indian Community Alliances." *Race and Class* 42: 19–31.

Herrera, Gioconda, ed. 2006a. *La persistencia de la desigualdad: Género, trabajo y pobreza en América Latina*. Quito: FLACSO.

———. 2006b. "Precarización del trabajo, crisis de reproducción social y migración femenina: Ecuatorianas en España y Estados Unidos." Pp. 199–223 in *La persistencia de la desigualdad: Género, trabajo y pobreza en América Latina*, ed. G. Herrera. Quito: FLACSO.

Herrera, Gioconda, María Cristina Carrillo, and Alicia Torres, eds. 2005. *La migración ecuatoriana: Transnacionalismo, redes, e identidades*. Quito: FLACSO.

Hochschild, Arlie Russell. 1983. *The Managed Heart: Commercialization of Human Feeling*. Berkeley: University of California Press.

———. 2003 [1989]. *The Second Shift*. New York: Penguin Books.

Hondagneu-Sotelo, Pierette, and Ernestine Ávila. 1997. "'I'm Here but I'm There': The Meanings of Latina Transnational Motherhood." *Gender & Society* 11:548–571.

Hopkins, Barbara E. 2007. "Western Cosmetics in the Gendered Development of Consumer Culture in China." *Feminist Economics* 13 (3–4): 287–306.

Hoy (Quito). 2005. "Colombian Yanbal Launches New Perfume in Ecuador." Accessed through LexisNexis.

Instituto Nacional de Estadística y Censos (INEC). 2007. *Encuesta del Sistema de Información Social (ESIS)*. CD-ROM. Guayaquil: INEC.

———. N.d. Website. http://www.inec.gov.ec/.

International Labor Organization (ILO). 2002. *Women and Men in the Informal Economy: A Statistical Picture*. Geneva: International Labor Organization.

Jokisch, Brad. 2007. "Ecuador: Diversity in Migration." http://www.migrationinformation.org/USfocus/display.cfm?ID=575.

Jokisch, Brad D., and David Kyle. 2008. "Ecuadorian International Migration." Pp. 350–358 in *The Ecuador Reader: History, Culture, Politics*, ed. C. de la Torre and S. Striffler. Durham, NC: Duke University Press.

Jokisch, Brad, and Jason Pribilsky. 2002. "The Panic to Leave: Geographic Dimensions of Recent Ecuadorian Emigration." *International Migration* 40 (3): 75–101.

Jolly, Richard. 1987. "Women's Needs and Adjustment Policies in Developing Countries." Address to the Women's Development Group of the OECD, Paris.

Kyle, David. 2003. *Transnational Peasants: Migrations, Networks, and Ethnicity in Andean Ecuador*. Baltimore: Johns Hopkins University Press.

Lan, Pei-Chia. 2002. "Networking Capitalism: Network Construction and Control Effects in Direct Selling." *Sociological Quarterly* 43: 165–184.

Lind, Amy. 2005. *Gendered Paradoxes: Women's Movements, State Restructuring, and Global Development in Ecuador*. University Park: Pennsylvania State University Press.

Loscocco, Karyn A. 1997. "Work-Family Linkages among Self-Employed Women and Men." *Journal of Vocational Behavior* 30 (2): 204–226.

Luciano, Lynne. 2002. *Looking Good: Male Body Image in Modern America*. New York: Hill and Wang.

Lutz, Catherine A., and Jane L. Collins. 1993. *Reading National Geographic*. Chicago: University of Chicago Press.

Mahmood, Saba. 2005. *Politics of Piety: The Islamic Revival and the Feminist Subject*. Princeton, NJ: Princeton University Press.

Martin, Philip. 1991. "Labor Migration: Theory and Reality." Pp. 27–42 in *The Unsettled Relationship: Labor Migration and Economic Development*, ed. D. Papademetriou and P. Martin. Westport, CT: Greenwood Press.

Medved, Caryn E. 2009. "Constructing Breadwinning-Mother Identities: Moral, Personal, and Political Positioning." *Women's Studies Quarterly* 37 (3–4): 140–156.

Meisch, Lynn A. 2002. *Andean Entrepreneurs: Otavalo Merchants and Musicians in the Global Arena*. Austin: University of Texas Press.

Miller, Daniel. 1997. *Capitalism: An Ethnographic Approach*. Oxford: Berg Publishers.

Mills, C. Wright. 2000 [1959]. *The Sociological Imagination*. New York: Oxford University Press.

Moghadam, Valentine M. 2005. *Globalizing Women: Transnational Feminist Networks*. Baltimore: Johns Hopkins University Press.

Mohanty, Chandra Talpade. 2003. *Feminism without Borders: Decolonizing Theory, Practicing Solidarity*. Durham, NC: Duke University Press.

Mose Brown, Tamara, and Erynn Masi de Casanova. 2009. "Mothers in the Field: How

Motherhood Shapes Fieldwork and Researcher-Subject Relations." *Women's Studies Quarterly* 37 (3–4): 42–57.

Moser, Caroline. 1989. "The Impact of Recession and Structural Adjustment Policies at the Micro-level: Low-Income Women and Their Households in Guayaquil, Ecuador." In *Invisible Adjustment*, vol. 2. Santiago, Chile: UNICEF Americas and the Caribbean Regional Office.

———. 1993. "Adjustment from Below: Low-Income Women, Time and the Triple Role in Guayaquil, Ecuador." Pp. 173–196 in *Viva: Women and Popular Protest in Latin America*, ed. S. A. Radcliffe and S. Westwood. London: Routledge.

———. 1997. *Household Responses to Poverty and Vulnerability: Confronting Crisis in Cisne Dos, Guayaquil, Ecuador*. Washington, DC: World Bank.

Mummert, Gail. 1992. "Rural Mexican Women's Struggle for Family Livelihood: Daughters, Wives, and Unmarried Women in Salaried Work." Paper prepared for the conference/workshop "Learning from Latin America: Women's Struggles for Livelihood," Los Angeles, February 27-29.

Nencel, Lorraine. 2008. "'Que viva la Minifalda!' Secretaries, Miniskirts and Daily Practices of Sexuality in the Public Sector in Lima." *Gender, Work and Organization* 17 (1): 69–90.

O'Dougherty, Maureen. 2002. *Consumption Intensified: The Politics of Middle-Class Daily Life in Brazil*. Durham, NC: Duke University Press.

Peiss, Kathy. 1998. *Hope in a Jar: The Making of America's Beauty Culture*. New York: Owl Books.

Pequeño Bueno, Andrea. 2007. *Imágenes en disputa: Representaciones de mujeres indígenas ecuatorianas*. Quito: Ediciones Abya-Yala/FLACSO Ecuador.

Pérez-Alemán, Paola. 1992. "Economic Crisis and Women in Nicaragua." Pp. 239–258 in *Unequal Burden: Economic Crises, Persistent Poverty, and Women's Work*, ed. L. Benería and S. Feldman. Boulder, CO: Westview Press.

Piller, Ingrid. 2002. "Passing for a Native Speaker: Identity and Success in Second Language Learning." *Journal of Sociolinguistics* 6 (2): 179–206.

Pitkin, Kathryn, and Ritha Bedoya. 1997. "Women's Multiple Roles in Economic Crisis: Constraints and Adaptation." *Latin American Perspectives* 24 (4): 34–49.

Pitts-Taylor, Victoria. 2007. *Surgery Junkies: Wellness and Pathology in Cosmetic Culture*. New Brunswick, NJ: Rutgers University Press.

Portes, Alejandro, Manuel Castells, and Lauren A. Benton, eds. 2004. *The Informal Economy*. Baltimore: Johns Hopkins University Press.

Poster, Winifred, and Zakia Salime. 2002. "The Limits of Microcredit: Transnational Feminism and USAID Activities in the United States and Morocco." Pp. 189–219 in *Women's Activism and Globalization: Linking Local Struggles and Transnational Politics*, ed. N. A. Naples and M. Desai. New York: Routledge.

Prieto, Mercedes, ed. 2005. *Entre la crisis y las oportunidades: Mujeres ecuatorianas, 1990–2005*. Quito: FLACSO.

Radcliffe, Sarah H. 2008. "Women's Movements in Twentieth Century Ecuador." Pp. 284–296 in *The Ecuador Reader: History, Culture, Politics*, ed. C. de la Torre and S. Striffler. Durham, NC: Duke University Press.

Radcliffe, Sarah, and Sallie Westwood. 1996. *Remaking the Nation: Place, Identity, and Politics in Latin America*. New York: Routledge.

Rahier, Jean Muteba. 1998. "Blackness, the Racial/Spatial Order, Migrations, and Miss Ecuador 1995–96." *American Anthropologist* 100 (2): 421–430.

Reich, Jennifer A. 2003. "Pregnant with Possibility: Reflections on Embodiment, Access, and Inclusion in Field Research," *Qualitative Sociology* 26 (3): 351–367.

Richtel, Matt. 2008. "Even at Megastores, Hagglers Find No Price Is Set in Stone." *New York Times*, March 23.

Rodríguez, Lilia. 1994. "Barrio Women: Between the Urban and the Feminist Movement." *Latin American Perspectives* 21 (3): 32–48.

Roldán, Martha. 1988. "Renegotiating the Marital Contract: Intrahousehold Patterns of Money Allocation and Women's Subordination among Domestic Outworkers in Mexico City." Pp. 229–247 in *A Home Divided: Women and Income in the Third World*, ed. Daisy Dwyer and Judith Bruce. Palo Alto, CA: Stanford University Press.

Root, Regina A., ed. 2005. *The Latin American Fashion Reader*. Oxford: Berg Publishers.

Rothstein, Frances Abrahamer. 1995. "Gender and Multiple Income Strategies in Rural Mexico: A Twenty-Year Perspective." Pp. 167–193 in *Women in the Latin American Development Process*, ed. C. E. Bose and E. Acosta-Belén. Philadelphia: Temple University Press.

Safa, Helen I. 1995. *The Myth of the Male Breadwinner: Women and Industrialization in the Caribbean*. Boulder, CO: Westview Press.

Salzinger, Leslie. 2003. *Genders in Production: Making Workers in Mexico's Global Factories*. Berkeley: University of California Press.

Santa Cruz, Adriana, and Viviana Erazo. 1980. *Compropolitan: El orden transnacional y su modelo femenino*. Mexico City: Editorial Nueva Imagen.

Seligmann, Linda J. 2004. *Peruvian Street Lives: Culture, Power, and Economy among Market Women of Cuzco*. Champaign: University of Illinois Press.

Sklair, Leslie. 2000. *The Transnational Capitalist Class*. Oxford: Wiley-Blackwell.

Smith, Dorothy E. 1989. *The Everyday World as Problematic: A Feminist Sociology*. Boston: Northeastern University Press.

Standing, Guy. 1999. *Global Labour Flexibility: Seeking Distributive Justice*. New York: St. Martin's Press.

Sutton, Barbara. 2010. *Bodies in Crisis: Culture, Violence, and Women's Resistance in Neoliberal Argentina*. New Brunswick, NJ: Rutgers University Press.

Tabb, William K. 2001. *The Amoral Elephant: Globalization and the Struggle for Social Justice in the Twenty-First Century*. New York: Monthly Review Press.

Taylor, Rex. 1978. "Marilyn's Friends and Rita's Customers: A Study of Party-Selling as Play and as Work." *Sociological Review* 26: 573–594.

Tugend, Alina. 2008. "For Champions of Haggling, No Price Tag Is Sacred," *New York Times*, January 19, 2008.

Twine, France Winddance. 1997. *Racism in a Racial Democracy: The Maintenance of White Supremacy in Brazil*. New Brunswick, NJ: Rutgers University Press.

United Nations Development Program (UNDP). 2008. *Human Development Report: 2007/2008*. http://hdr.undp.org/en/reports/global/hdr2007-2008/.

United Nations Division for the Advancement of Women (UNDAW). 1995. *Beijing Declaration and Platform for Action: The Fourth World Conference on Women*. http://www.un.org/womenwatch/daw/beijing/beijingdeclaration.html.

Vincent, Susan. 2003. "Preserving Domesticity: Reading Tupperware in Women's Changing Domestic, Social and Economic Roles." *Canadian Review of Sociology and Anthropology* 40: 171–196.

Vistazo. 2008. "Las mejores empresas para trabajar." January 4, 2008, pp. 32–40.

Ward, Kathryn, ed. 1990. *Women Workers and Global Restructuring.* Ithaca, NY: ILR Press.

Weismantel, Mary J. 2008. "Cities of Women." Pp. 359–370 in *The Ecuador Reader: History, Culture, Politics,* ed. C. de la Torre and S. Striffler. Durham, NC: Duke University Press.

Weiss, Wendy. 1997. "Debt and Devaluation: The Burden on Ecuador's Popular Class." *Latin American Perspectives* 24 (4): 9–33.

Whitten, Norman E. 1981. *Cultural Transformations and Ethnicity in Modern Ecuador.* Champaign: University of Illinois Press.

Whitten, Norman E., and Diego Quiroga. 1998. "'To Rescue National Dignity': Blackness as a Quality of Nationalist Creativity in Ecuador." Pp. 75–99 in *Blackness in Latin America and the Caribbean,* vol. 1, ed. N. E. Whitten and A. Torres. Bloomington: University of Indiana Press.

Williams, Christine L. 1992. "The Glass Escalator: Hidden Advantages for Men in the 'Female' Professions." *Social Problems* 39 (3): 253–267.

———. 1995. *Still a Man's World: Men Who Do "Women's Work."* Berkeley: University of California Press.

Wilson, Ara. 1999. "The Empire of Direct Sales and the Making of Thai Entrepreneurs." *Critique of Anthropology* 19: 401–422.

———. 2004. *The Intimate Economies of Bangkok: Tomboys, Tycoons, and Avon Ladies in the Global City.* Berkeley: University of California Press.

Wilson, Tamar Diana. 1998. "Approaches to Understanding the Position of Women Workers in the Informal Sector." *Latin American Perspectives* 25 (2): 105–119.

Wolkowitz, Carol. 2006. *Bodies at Work.* London: Sage.

The World Factbook. "Ecuador." 2008. Washington, DC: U.S. Central Intelligence Agency. https://www.cia.gov/library/publications/the-world-factbook/geos/ec.html.

Yanbal. N.d. *A triunfar con Yanbal.* Video.